Essential French Vocabulary

Teach® Yourself

Essential French Vocabulary

Noël Saint-Thomas

Series editor
Rosi McNab

For UK order enquiries: please contact Bookpoint Ltd,
130 Milton Park, Abingdon, Oxon OX14 4SB.
Telephone: +44 (0) 1235 827720. *Fax:* +44 (0) 1235 400454.
Lines are open 09.00–17.00, Monday to Saturday, with a 24-hour
message answering service. Details about our titles and how to
order are available at www.teachyourself.com

For USA order enquiries: please contact McGraw-Hill Customer
Services, PO Box 545, Blacklick, OH 43004-0545, USA.
Telephone: 1-800-722-4726. *Fax:* 1-614-755-5645.

For Canada order enquiries: please contact McGraw-Hill
Ryerson Ltd, 300 Water St, Whitby, Ontario L1N 9B6, Canada.
Telephone: 905 430 5000. *Fax:* 905 430 5020.

Long renowned as the authoritative source for self-guided
learning – with more than 50 million copies sold worldwide –
the *Teach Yourself* series includes over 500 titles in the fields of
languages, crafts, hobbies, business, computing and education.

British Library Cataloguing in Publication Data: a catalogue record
for this title is available from the British Library.

Library of Congress Catalog Card Number: on file.

First published in UK 2003 as Teach Yourself French Vocabulary
by Hodder Education, part of Hachette UK, 338 Euston Road,
London, NW1 3BH.

First published in US 2003 by The McGraw-Hill Companies, Inc.

This edition published 2010.

Typeset by MPS Limited, A Macmillan Company.

Printed in Great Britain for Hodder Education, a division of
Hodder Headline, 338 Euston Road, London, NW1 3BH,
by Cox & Wyman Ltd, Reading, Berkshire.

Impression number 10 9 8 7 6 5 4 3 2 1
Year 2014 2013 2012 2011 2010

Contents

Credits

Front cover: © Oxford Illustrators

Back cover and pack: © Jakub Semeniuk/iStockphoto.com, © Royalty-Free/Corbis, © agencyby/iStockphoto.com, © Andy Cook/iStockphoto.com, © Christopher Ewing/iStockphoto.com, © zebicho – Fotolia.com, © Geoffrey Holman/iStockphoto.com, © Photodisc/Getty Images, © James C. Pruitt/iStockphoto.com, © Mohamed Saber – Fotolia.com.

Meet the author

I am French – well, I hold a French passport. I have been immersed in languages ever since I was born – in Paris, to a mother who speaks four languages fluently, as did her own mother, in a truly European family. I decided at the age of 15 to take my A levels in Germany, making good use of my extensive family in Eastern and Central Europe. As recurring injuries put an end to my first career (as a ballet dancer), I went to university as a mature student to study English and German literature, civilization and linguistics, ending up in Glasgow as a language assistant during my final year. I fell in love with this rough but gentle city that had just emerged from the 1980s crisis, whose inhabitants are so friendly, and where everything is possible for anyone with an entrepreneurial spirit. I have been based there for over 15 years, teaching French as a foreign language, French grammar and civilization, translating, copywriting, facilitating communication and liaising for local and international organizations. My work is more than a way of making a living; it is a way of life. Knowing several languages helps me to understand, and shuttle between, different cultures. It allows me to think, and innovate, at a far higher level and within a much wider scope than I would have been able to do knowing only one language, one culture, one way of apprehending, and rendering, reality. But, even living in Scotland most of the time, I always keep a substantial place – both in my heart and in my diary! – for France.

I hope I will succeed in transferring to you some of my knowledge of, as well as my passion for, the particularly beautiful French language.

Welcome to **Essential French Vocabulary!**

Noël Saint-Thomas

Only got a minute?

For someone in a rush *(Pour quelqu'un de très pressé !)*

Why French vocabulary? Below are some of the reasons why learning French vocabulary makes sense.

From an English-speaker's perspective, it is a godsend: **50 per cent of English vocabulary comes from the French!**

The vocabulary used by any society, or community, is in essence the reflection of its culture: thus, learning the vocabulary of another language is like **opening a window onto another culture**, another world altogether with different colours, different tastes, different – and exciting! – practices;

Together with English, French is the **official legal language** of the European Union and, together with English, the **official working language** of the United Nations.

If you are considering taking up **ballet**, the entire ballet terminology is French!

If you are interested in *fashion* and *couture* – see? **couture** is a French word you know already!; in *cooking* and *cuisine* – see? **cuisine** is yet another word you know!; in make-up, beauty care, **perfume** and perfume-making; in diplomacy, which is another French word that you know, written *diplomacy* in English… and **la diplomatie** in French!; in *law*… and all things **risqué** – (a French word!) – it is definitely **a great idea!**

This short book, quite simple but not simplistic, will open that window for you – with lists of vocabulary organized in themed sections; a toolbox to help you put the vocabulary you learn into articulated sentences – a little like a frame on which one puts the decoration and final touches; numerous so-called 'author insights' to link the vocabulary that you are learning, or re-discovering, to the culture it reflects and describes; a self-assessment quiz at the end of each section; and a free audio download from the website with tips and guidance on spelling, pronunciation, accent and melody.

5 Only got five minutes?

For someone with just a little time *(Pour quelqu'un d'un peu moins pressé).*

Why French vocabulary? Below are some of the reasons, all valid, why learning French vocabulary makes sense.

From an English-speaker's perspective, it is a godsend: **50 per cent of English vocabulary comes from the French!**

From 1066, when William the Conqueror, Duke of Normandy (**Guillaume le Conquérant, duc de Normandie**) became King of England after his defeat over Harold at Hastings, until the death of Henri VI in 1471, French, both as a language and a culture, had a strong presence in England.

The former, William I, brought with him his court, soldiers, learned scholars and advisers, who offered a combination of Norman, Flemish, Provençal, Italian, Breton, Spanish, French and Latin influences in etiquette as well as spoken and written language.

The latter, Henri VI, was the last in a line of monarchs, starting with Henri II in 1154, who had established the tradition, so to speak, of marrying French-speaking princesses – Eléonor, or Aliénor; Isabelle; Marguerite; Catherine.

The vocabulary used by any society or community is in essence the reflection of its culture: thus, learning the vocabulary of another language is like **opening a window onto another culture**, another world altogether with different colours, different tastes, different – and exciting! – customs.

On the one hand, grammar and syntax – the technical terms for the structure and rules governing the language and the use of its vocabulary – are an indication of the way in which a society or community perceives the world, understands it and, consequently, depicts and renders it; how it 'thinks' and organizes reality.

On the other hand, lexis – the technical term for the body, or corpus, of vocabulary – gives an indication of the culture, of the 'folklore' of a society or community.

French, together with English, is the **official legal language** of the **European Union**: the European Union – currently 27 member States – operates in 23 official languages. When it comes to legal matters, official debates are conducted in both English and French, or in either one or the other.

Possible reasons for this are that French, it is claimed, is the language most suitable for **law** and legal matters. Until the 14th century, law in England was in French and Latin. It was not until the 16th century that a law manual in English was published in England.

Together with English, French is the **official working language** of the **United Nations**, partly due to a well-established preference for French as a diplomatic language, partly because the United Nations today includes more than 190 nations, many of which are French-speaking.

La Francophonie – French-speaking countries – may be described as a group, or network, of countries of which French is the official language, or one of the official languages, or one of the languages used generally. These countries share some elements of culture; certain values as well as social and political fundamental principles. There are 60 such countries today, and just over 170 million people who speak French, whether as their mother tongue, or as one of their official languages.

If you are considering taking up **ballet**, the entire ballet terminology is French!

Thus: **pirouette, cabriole, entrechat, saut de chat, pas de basque, révérence, port de bras, piqué, et cetera et cetera**… and also: **battu** – which means *beaten* – to refer to the beating of one leg by the other in certain jumps; **fouetté** – which means *whipped* – to refer to a whipping movement by the lower part of the leg; **plié** – which means *folded* – to refer to the folding of the leg, at the ankle, the knee and the hip, very much like the folding measure tape one uses in DIY – **un mètre pliant.**

Incidentally, these terms are also used in cooking – **en cuisine: des œufs battus en neige** – *beaten,* or *whisked eggwhites*; **de la crème fouettée** – *whipped cream*; **plier la pâte sept fois,** when making a puff pastry dough, would be *fold the dough seven times.*

If you are interested in *fashion* and *couture* and all things related to the world of fashion and couture, accessories, make-up, perfumes, beauty-care… much of the vocabulary used comes from, or is, French: **guipure, gros pois, crêpe Georgette, à façon, tourné, haute couture** – (and **hot couture!**) – **couturier, atelier, bouillonné, dévoré, satin, bustier, décolleté, eau de toilette et de parfum, rouge, poudré, pour femme et pour homme…**

If you are interested in *cooking* and *cuisine* – see? **cuisine** is yet another word you know! – you'll discover that quite a number of words, and the techniques they refer to, come from the French.

When at the end of the 14th century England decided to impose English as the official language, rather than French and Latin, it retained a number of French words where the English did not have any that were readily available. Thus, in things related to meals – their preparation as well as consumption – one finds quite a high number of French words: **hors d'œuvre, petits fours, soufflé, casserole, ramequin, pièce de résistance, entrée, à la carte, champagne, amuse-gueule, déglacer, réserver, canapés, vol-au-vent**, etc.

If you are attracted by a certain **je ne sais quoi**, and all things **risqué** – in modern French **osé – flirt, négligé, bidet, dessous**… learning French vocabulary is definitely a great idea!

This short book – quite simple, yet not simplistic – will open that window for you with lists of vocabulary organized in themed sections; a toolbox to help you to put the vocabulary you learn into articulated sentences; a number of 'author's insights' to link the vocabulary that you are learning, or re-discovering, to the culture it reflects and carries; a self-assessment quiz at the end of each section; and a free audio download from the website with tips and guidance on spelling, pronunciation, accent and melody.

10 Only got ten minutes?

For someone with time on their hands *(Pour quelqu'un de pas pressé du tout).*

Why French vocabulary? The following are some of the reasons, all valid, why learning French vocabulary makes sense.

Learning French vocabulary, from the perspective of an English speaker, is a godsend: 50 per cent of English vocabulary comes from, or is, French. A number of areas and techniques use French words on a regular, daily basis – and some have done so for a number of centuries.

From 1066, when William the Conqueror, Duke of Normandy (**Guillaume le Conquérant, duc de Normandie**) became King of England after his victory over Harold at Hastings, until the death of Henri VI in 1471, French, both as a language and a culture, had a strong presence in England.

The former, William I, brought with him his court, soldiers, learned scholars and advisers who offered a combination of Norman, Flemish, Provençal, Italian, Breton, Spanish, French and Latin influences in etiquette as well as spoken and written language.

The latter, Henri VI, was the last of the line of British monarchs, starting with Henri II in 1154, who had established the tradition, so to speak, of marrying French-speaking princesses –Eléonor, or Aliénor; Isabelle; Marguerite; Catherine.

For the greater part of three centuries, three main languages were used in Britain: Latin, French and English – Latin and 'educated' French were the languages of knowledge and power; while English and 'vernacular' French were the languages of everyday life which developed independently from the written form.

The 100 Years War (1337–1453), Black Death and the emergence of the middle class – a phenomenon of which Chaucer would be the perfect example – put an end to 'French domination'. Eventually, English imposed itself as the national language and in 1362 English was adopted as the official language of debates in Parliament.

This process of emancipation involves the borrowing, by the English language, of all the French words that it needs – in techniques and contexts such as heraldry, law, diplomacy and international relations, fashion and couture, beauty care and perfume, cooking and baking, ballet, maritime trade, home economics ...

Heraldry

To this day, the motto of the Most Honourable Order of the Garter, funded in 1342 by Edward III, is still **'Honni soit qui mal y pense'** (*Shame upon him who thinks evil upon it*) – a reference to the garter of the Countess of Salisbury, the mistress of Edward III, which had become loose and fallen while the Countess and the King were at a dance in... Calais.

Similarly, **'Dieu et mon droit'**, used for the first time in 1198 by Richard I, remains to this day the motto inscribed on the coat of arms which the Sovereigns of the United Kingdom of Great Britain and Northern Ireland use when representing their Kingdom abroad.

Law

Until the 16th century, and the publication for the first time of a law manual in English, law in England was in French – a codified system with rigidly set phrases contained in numerous manuals, all called **la court du baron**.

It is not rare to hear, as did those lawyers of the 18th century who came to regret the disappearance of French as the language of law **de rigueur**, that French has specific features that make it the ideal language of the law.

International Relations
French is, together with English, the official legal language of the European Union; The European Union – today 27 member States – operates in all official languages spoken and used in the European Union, 23 in total. When it comes to legal matters, however, official debates are conducted in both English and French, or in the one or the other.

Together with English, French is the official working language of the United Nations.

This may be due to the fact that for centuries, French has been the language of international relations and diplomacy. It may also be explained by the fact that the United Nations include today over 190 nations, a very high number of which are French-speaking.

French-speaking countries as a group are known as **La Francophonie** – a body of nations that may be described as a network of countries where French is used, whether it is the official language, or one of the official languages, and/or it is one of the habitual languages used by their inhabitants. There are 60 such countries today across all five continents, including Belgium, Switzerland, Luxembourg, Monaco, Haiti, Cambodia, Togo, Gabon, Niger, Madagascar, Morocco, Tunisia, Canada and the USA to cite a few. According to the High Council for the Francophonie, there are some 115 million people whose mother tongue is French, and some 60 million who speak it alongside one or more other languages.

Cuisine: la, dans la, faire la, nouvelle et haute
Among the subject areas in which English borrowed commonly used French words, or where the English did not have any word readily available, is cooking, **cuisine**, and generally things related to meals – their preparation as well as their consumption – savoury as well as sweet. Thus: **les hors d'œuvre, le menu, l'entrée, le soufflé, le bavarois, le chef, un apéritif, des amuse-gueule, des canapés, des petits fours, à la carte, un vol-au-vent, des entremets, la pièce**

de résistance, déglacer, réserver, le champagne, le café au lait, le maître d'[hôtel], gâteau etc.

You may remember Walter Scott's *Ivanhoe*, where live animals, known under their English names, take on French names when brought to the table as dishes!

It must be noted that one of the key reasons for French cuisine being so good is that it comes from a country blessed by both climate and geography: ingredients are abundant, infinitely varied, readily available, whether from the pastures, the forests, the mountains or the seas – no fewer than five of the latter! (**mer du Nord, mer de la Manche, mer d'Iroise, océan Atlantique, mer de la Méditerranée**). Naturally, passion, effort, time and a tradition that puts great emphasis on a sensorial apprehension of the world, come into play. Still, I would argue that the availability of such a wealth, excellence and diversity of ingredients is key.

Ballet

Almost the entirety of ballet terminology is French, including: **pirouette, cabriole, entrechat, saut de chat, pas de basque, révérence, porte de bras, piqué**… as well as **battu** – which means *beaten* – and refers to the beating of one leg by the other in certain jumps; **fouetté** – which means *whipped* – and refers to a whipping movement by the lower part of the leg; **plié** – which means *folded* – and refers to the folding of the leg, at the ankle, the knee and the hip, very much like the folding measure tape one uses in DIY – **un mètre pliant.**

… Incidentally, these terms are also used in cooking – **en cuisine**: *beaten egg whites* would be **des œufs battus en neige**; *whipped cream* would be **de la crème fouettée**; *fold the dough seven times* – when making puff pastry – would be **plier la pâte sept fois.**

Couture: haute, prêt-à-porter, pour femme et pour homme

Couture – la couture means *sewing*, and **coudre** *to sew* – lives and breathes in French. This is by no means to say that French things and trends and ateliers and couturiers are the sole, nor necessarily the best ones, in the world. But this is a tradition, very much like cooking, which has developed and gathered strength over many centuries; which has developed and refined its techniques, finer points and nuances, be it in relation to fabrics and the making of fabrics: cut, cutting and assembly; the treatment of a given genre, or the **détournement** – literally, the *hijacking* – of a garment to use it in a different context, as a 'newcomer' among old acquaintances.

Consequently, in fashion, couture, sewing, fabrics, accessories, shows, models and all things relating to, and revolving around garments, and garment-making as an art – perfumes, fragrances, make-up, beauty-care, etc. – French words are many and still very much in use today. Thus: **guipure**, **gros pois**, **crêpe Georgette**, **crêpe de Chine**, **à façon**, **tourné**, **bouillonné**, **haute couture**, **grand couturier**, **atelier**, **dévoré**, **tulle**, **satin**, **décolleté**, **sautoir**, **cravate**, **eau de toilette et de parfum**, **rouge**, **poudre**, **blanc**, **papier-mâché**, etc.

Port d'entrée

Finally, vocabulary is a fabulous port of entry – **port d'entrée fabuleux** – into another culture. Lexicologists, namely those linguists who specialize in the study of the 'lexis' – the technical term used to refer to vocabulary– generally agree on the fact that while grammar and syntax – which are the technical terms used to refer to the structure and the rules governing it and the use of the lexis, or vocabulary – give an indication of how a society, or community, perceives the world, how it understands it and, consequently, how it depicts and renders it; how it 'thinks', and organizes reality; the vocabulary used by any society, or community, is in essence the reflection of its culture, of its 'folklore': thus, learning the vocabulary of another language is like opening a window onto another culture, onto another world altogether – with different colours, different tastes, different – and exciting! – practices.

Learning another language also leads to discovering, or becoming better acquainted, with one's own. English is a Germanic language: as such, its structure is closer to German, as well as languages spoken in Scandinavian countries such as Swedish and Danish. Consequently, one may start to understand better its propensity to pragmatism and all things practical, which, one may argue, are a common denominator in Germanic cultures.

On the other hand, its lexis, or body of vocabulary, comes from a mixture of influences, but 50 per cent is French, or French-sourced. Drawing further from the observation above, one may reach the conclusion that French vocabulary would, logically, 'open a window' onto... English, as well as French, culture.

It must be borne in mind that this book has been compiled and written from a 'French-from-France' perspective, with reference to Britain – not, for example, from a 'French-from-Québec' perspective, with reference to North America.

Still, the **Académie française** created in 1635 by Richelieu, 'to strengthen the unity of a Kingdom based on political direction, and give it a tongue and a style that both symbolize and cement it', has remained to this day a very active and vigilant institution over the French language, both in its oral and written forms. The institution issues regular bulletins and directives on spelling, sentence structure, usage, appropriateness, etc.

One last word: one must bear in mind also that life is not organized in air-tight compartments, nor is the world. Consequently, although some 50 per cent of English vocabulary comes from the French, it is not to say that these words were acquired once and for all, say, in the 11th, or the 14th century, and have remained immobile since. Many, perhaps most, have shuttled: between the two countries, or the two linguistic communities – the English-speaking community and the French-speaking community; between meanings; between applications, disciplines, discourse registers, status. And, last but not least, people.

This short book – quite simple, yet not simplistic – will open that window for you – with lists of vocabulary, organized in themed sections; a toolbox to help you put the vocabulary you learn into articulated sentences – a little like a frame on which one puts the decoration and final touches; numerous – but not too many, I hope! – so-called 'author insights' to link the vocabulary that you are learning, or re-discovering, to the culture it reflects and describes; a self-assessment quiz at the end of each section; and a free audio download from the website with tips and guidance on spelling, pronunciation, accent and melody.

Introduction

There have been many studies carried out into the way we learn vocabulary. The Swiss, who are generally acknowledged as experts in multi-language learning, are also leaders in the understanding of the processes of language acquisition and some of their findings may be of interest to people wanting to broaden their vocabulary.

> **Studies have shown that the most successful way [of learning vocabulary] is when the student is able to relate the new word to a concept and to integrate it into a conceptual system.**
>
> (Wokusch, 1997)

Put simply, this means that the most successful way of learning vocabulary is to put the new language into a context.

When a child first learns a language they are learning the concepts as well as the language at the same time. If you give a child an ice cream and say 'ice cream' they are learning the word and the concept at the same time, associating the word and the object. An adult has the advantage of knowing the concept already – well, at least in most cases. An ice cream already conjures up other words: cold, vanilla, strawberry, like, don't like, size, price, etc.

It is for this reason that the vocabulary in this book has been organized by context, rather than, as in a dictionary, for example, in alphabetical order. The words proposed are those words which, from the author's perspective, are most likely to be useful or of interest to the learner and, as far as possible, examples have been given with a real context, providing the learner with a model, or even a readily useable phrase.

One of the most useful tips in learning a new language is to look for ways of remembering a word: find a 'hook' to hang your new word or phrase on.

How this book works

This book is more than just a list of words – it is a key to open the door to better communication. It is designed to give you the confidence you need to communicate better in French by increasing your knowledge of up-to-date vocabulary and at the same time showing you how to use the new words you are learning.

The first part of the book includes some useful learning tips, rules on pronunciation and short cuts to look out for when learning new words. The toolbox provides you with the tools you need to speak a language. It includes basic information about the structure of the language and useful tips, including how to address people, how to ask questions, how to talk about what you have done and what you are going to do, various useful and idiomatic expressions. This part of the book is designed to be used for general reference.

The main part of the book is divided into topic areas: personal matters, family, work, education, etc. The selected words are the ones which our research has shown are the ones which are likely to be the most useful or most relevant to the learner of today. The words have been carefully arranged, grouped with other related words, nouns, verbs, adjectives etc. and useful expressions with up-to-date notes about language fashions where relevant, so that the new language can be used immediately.

This book uses the French convention (in French text) of preceding punctuation marks such as question marks or semi-colon with a space. See Toolbox – Accents and punctuation for more information.

Make learning a list of words more interesting

Remember that words don't 'hang' in the air, empty, meaningless. Words express the world in which we live: this is why, when one learns a language, one opens a window into a whole new world, a world in which other people, those who speak the new language, live. Hence, one sure way of remembering words is to relate them to the objects, or concepts, which they express, and to link them to the situations in which they will appear.

- First, decide which list you are going to look at today. To increase your chances of memorizing them, choose words that correspond to your present mood or state of mind. Language is intrinsically dependent on emotions, affectivity, moods.
- See how many words you know already: either tick them off, or use them as 'locomotives' for others, linking a known word to one that you have decided to learn.
- Choose which new words you want to learn. However, don't try to learn too many at once! A Japanese study has shown that one must learn and forget words seven times on average before knowing them.
- Count them so you know how many you are going to try to learn.
- Say them aloud, sing them, or 'rap' them if you are musically inclined. Tune/word association works wonders for the memorization process.

Remembering new words

- Copy a list of the most important words onto A4 paper with a broad felt tip and stick it on the wall so that you can study it when, for example, washing up, ironing, shaving, or even putting on make-up.
- Remember: words express reality, they are not 'empty'! Bring them to life! For example, visualize in your mind the green-lit exit sign used in public places, and replace the word exit with **sortie**, or emergency exit with **sortie de secours**.
- One great way to associate words with the objects they represent (for objects that are tangible) is to affix post-it stickers on these objects, bearing the name, in French, of the

object. Your house may end up looking like an auctioneer's warehouse, filled with objects labelled in French!

- Play out – rehearse, in other words – a situation that you are going to experience: going to buy a newspaper, for example, or asking the concierge to keep a key for a friend who will arrive when you're at work. When I changed school, and country, and started going to school in Germany, I would rehearse all sorts of situations – how I would say 'hello' in the school playground, or at the youth centre, or the gymnastics club, how I would answer possible questions that would be put to me, etc. Not for the classroom, when I first had to write out everything – and almost learn by heart – but for social occasions and interaction; it worked!
- Copy lists in French and English in two columns, in a notebook. First, say each word aloud, then cover up one column, and try to remember each word in the other column.
- In your list, mark the difficult words: ask someone else to test you on the ones you have marked.
- Pick a few words you find difficult to remember: write each one down with the letters jumbled up; leave them for a while, then later try to unscramble each one.
- See if you can split the word into bits, some of which you know already: **super marché, hyper marché**.
- Look for words related to English words, remembering that some 50 per cent of English vocabulary comes from the French. Go for it! You have a 50 per cent chance of being right! Also, as French originates in great part from Latin, this latter influence is felt in both French and English: **maternel** (*maternal*), **sporadique** (*sporadic*), **diffamation** (*defamation*), **ponton** (*pontoon*), etc. However, you need to be aware that the original word may not have retained an identical meaning throughout the centuries on both sides of the Channel. For example, *to seduce* has taken on a strong, physical meaning in modern English, whereas in French, **séduire** corresponds to the English *to charm*.
- Look for words related to ones you know already: **jupe** (*skirt*), **jupon** (*underskirt*); **un magasin** (*a shop*), **un magasin de chaussures** (*a shoe shop*).

- The following prefixes added to the beginning of a word cause it to have the opposite or negative meaning:

dis- **joindre** (*to join, to contact, connect*), **disjoindre** (*to disjoin*) [...following the previous advice above: **disjoindre... disjoncteur** – literally, 'disjoiner'– is the *circuit-breaker*]
mal- **aisé** (*easy to do*), **malaisé** (*difficult, awkward*)
im- (with b) **battable** (*beatable*), **imbattable** (*unbeatable*)
im- (*with p*) **partial** (*biaised*), **impartial** (*impartial*)
in- **discutable** (*disputable*), **indiscutable** (*undisputable*)
il- **légal** (*legal*, *lawful*), **illégal** (*illegal*, *unlawful*)

You will have observed that the prefix **in-** in French changes into **im-** before a **p** and a **b**; the pronunciation, however, does not change!

Spelling tips

These don't always work but may help!

- Words with a vowel followed by an **-st** combination in English will often have a vowel with a circumflex followed by a **t**: *forest* – **forêt**; *mast* – **mât**; *August* – **août**; *honest* – **honnête**.
- Often, a French word imported into English will have 'dropped' all accents, whereas the same French word will have retained them. Do not forget them, otherwise the word is unpronounceable! For example, *desuetude* – **la désuétude**; *independence* – **l'indépendance**; *revolution* – **révolution**; *desert* – **le désert**.
- Words which begin with **con-**, **dis-**, **im-**, **in-**, **re-**, **sub-** in French usually begin in the same way in English; words beginning with **des-** in French also begin with **dis-** in English.

- Many words have similar endings in French and in English:
  - **-able** and **-ible** in French usually have the same ending in English, but are sometimes interchangeable, for example, **faisable** (*feasible*)
  - **-ité** in French is usually *-ity* in English: **la sérénité** (*serenity*)
  - **-ude** in French is often *-(i)(n)ty* in English: **l'incertitude** (*uncertainty*)
  - **-isme** in French is usually *-ism* in English: **le romantisme** (*romanticism*)
  - **-tion** in French is usually *-tion* in English: **la révolution** (*revolution*)

- Note that words derived from a noun, e.g. *impression – impressionism*, will double, in French, the final consonant of the original word in most cases: **une impression – l'impressionnisme; la raison – raisonnable; le pardon – pardonner.**

In the same manner, words that are built around an original noun will double the first consonant of the original word: **la troupe – s'attrouper; le crédit – accréditer; le cumul – accumuler.**

Short cuts: looking for patterns

Certain patterns reveal some important facts about the type of word:

- most nouns in French ending in **-ot** and **-eau** are masculine,

  le pot, le bateau, le ciseau à bois

- most words in French ending in -ie are feminine:

  la folie, l'incurie, la mélodie

- most words ending in **-ier**, **-et**, and **-ien** are masculine:

  le luthier, le volet, le soutien

- words ending in **-ssion, -tion, -ité** and **-tude** are feminine:

  la récession, l'invitation, l'immensité, la certitude

Other patterns can be seen in French which are similar to those in English. For example:

- words ending in **-ment** (adverbs) are similar to English words ending in *-ly*, such as **promptement** (*promptly*); **finalement** (*finally*). As you can see, in both French and English the adverbs are based on adjectives, in this case **prompt** (*prompt*), **final** (*final*) with the endings **-ment** and *-ly* added.

The alphabet

Here is the English alphabet with the approximate French pronunciation of each letter – useful if you need to spell your name or any other words out loud. The international convention – adopted by the NATO countries – is used in French too… with a French pronounciation, naturally! Note **comme**, and not **pour**, to link the letter to the noun starting with that letter. In the right-hand column, the corresponding French convention.

Thus, to spell out **Antoine**, you may say :

a n t o i n e, *or*

a **comme alpha,** ***n*** **comme novembre,** ***t*** **comme tango,** ***o*** **comme oscar,** ***i*** **comme india,** ***n*** **comme november,** ***e*** **comme echo,** ***or***

alpha – November – tango – Oscar – India – November – echo, ***or***

a **comme Anatole,** ***n*** **comme Nicolas,** ***t*** **comme Thérèse,** ***o*** **comme Oscar,** ***i*** **comme Irma,** ***n*** **comme Nicolas,** ***e*** **comme Eugène,** ***or***

Anatole – Nicolas – Thérèse – Oscar – Irma – Nicolas – Eugène.

A **ah**… comme alpha
B **bé**… comme bravo
C **cé**… comme Charlie
D **dé**… comme delta
E **eux**… comme echo
F **eff**… comme foxtrot
G **j'ai**… comme golf
H **ahsh**… comme hotel
I **ee**… comme India
J **j'y**… comme Juliette
K **kah**… comme kilo
L **elle**… comme Lima
M **emm**… comme Mike
N **enne**… comme November
O **oh**… comme Oscar
P **pé**… comme papa
Q **ku**… comme Québec
R **erre**… comme Roméo
S **ess**… comme sierra
T **té**… comme tango
U **u**… (as in **du**) comme uniforme
V **vé**… comme Victor
W **doubleu vé**… comme whisky
X **eeks**… comme x-ray
Y **ee grec**… comme yankee
Z **zed**… comme zoulou

A **ah**… comme Anatole
B **bé**… comme Berte
C **cé**… comme Célestin
D **dé**… comme Désiré
E **eux**… comme Eugène
F **eff**… comme François
G **j'ai**… comme Gaston
H **ahsh**… comme Henri
I **ee**… comme Irma
J **j'y**… comme Joseph
K **kah**… comme Kléber
L **elle**… comme Louis
M **emm**… comme Marcel
N **enne**… comme Nicolas
O **oh**… comme Oscar
P **pé**… comme Pierre
Q **ku**… comme Quintal
R **erre**… comme Raoul
S **ess**… comme Suzanne
T **té**… comme Thérèse
U **u**… (as in **du**) comme Ursule
V **vé**… comme Victor
W **doubleu vé**… comme William
X **eeks**… comme Xavier
Y **ee grec**… comme Yvonne
Z **zed**… comme Zoé

You may hear a number of letters that you are not familiar with, such as:

ê **e accent circonflexe**, as in **le carême**
è **e accent grave**, as in **le barème**
é **e accent aigu**, as in **la fidélité**
ç **c cédille**, as in **le reçu**
î **i accent circonflexe**, as in **la crème fraîche**, or in **une île** [and remember (see 'spelling tips'): the **accent circonflexe** in French often corresponds to an *s* in English, as here: **île** – *isle*, or *island*]

ô **o accent circonflexe**, as in **la côte de bœuf** – *a bone-in ribeye steak* (French cut)
û **u accent circonflex, as in la flûte traversière**
ù **u accent grave, as in où**
â **a accent circonflexe**, as in **l'appât**
à **a accent grave, as in là-bas**
œ **o e collés**, also spelt **e dans l'o**, as in **bœuf**, or **cœur**

Here are some other words and phrases you may need when spelling things out:

capital m	**m majuscule**
small c	**c minuscule**
in one word	**en un seul mot**
in two words	**en deux mots**
next word	**plus loin**
apostrophe	**apostrophe**
'at' symbol (@)	**arobase**
hyphen	**trait d'union**
dot (.)	**point**
dash	**tiret**
underscore	**underscore** or **tiret du 8** [the underscore on the French PC keyboard is under the 8]
on the web	**sur Internet**
website	**site Internet**
www.	**w w w point** or **trois w point**
forward slash	**slash** or **oblique**

Pronunciation

If you wish to speak French with a good accent, the following tips will be useful.

- In French, the same vowel sound may be written in different ways. The sound **o** may be written: **eau, au, aud, aut, ault, eaux, aux, ô, ot**, etc. The sound **é** may be written: **é, er, et** (when used to mean *and*), ée, ées, és. The sound è may be written: è, e before a double consonant + e -(ette, -esse), **ai, ais, ait, et** (at the end of a word, as in *bonnet*).

- Final consonants are not pronounced. For example, in **un croissant**, and **deux croissants** neither the **t**, nor the s in the plural, are pronounced.
- **H** is never pronounced.
- G followed by **e** or **i** is soft, as in the English *J*: **le genre, la girolle; g** followed by **a** or **o** is hard, as in the English *grant*: **le gâteau, la gondole; g** followed by **u** is hard: **le guet-apens, la guimauve.**
- The same principles apply to **c: c + e = se, c +** i **= si: le centime, la citrouille;** c **+ a =** ka, **c + o = ko: le camion, la convalescence;** c + u + e **= ke, c + u + i = kui: la cueillette, la cuiller.** The presence of the cedilla – **ç** – makes the **c** soft: **le garçon.**

Stress and melody

Unlike English, where words are stressed individually and on different syllables depending on the words, in French one cannot speak strictly of word stress. At most, every syllable in a word is stressed – or unstressed, for that matter – equally. Rather, the stress bears on the whole sentence: the last syllable of the last word bears the stress. For example, if you say 'Pierrot', the second – and last – syllable of the word is stressed. If you say 'Pierrot est là', 'là' is the stressed word.

In French, the voice rises towards a comma, but falls towards the end of a statement. It rises towards the end of a question asking for a 'yes' or 'no' answer, and descends in a question starting with an interrogation conjunction, such as 'when', 'where', etc.

- to hear these, and other words, pronounced by a native French speaker, a number of learning tips, and an amusing anecdote to illustrate my point above on 'melody v. lack of stress', go to www.teachyourself.com to download a free 25-minute audio.

A useful method of developing one's pronunciation is to listen to French as often as possible, on the radio, at the cinema, on television, or in the street.

- Every time you go to France or another French-speaking country, take a small portable cassette player, or a dictaphone, and some blank cassettes. Try recording local 'ambiances', or people speaking ... though you ought to ask their permission first!
- In some parts of the UK and the US, especially in the south, you can pick up French radio stations: get into the habit of choosing a French-speaking station when you drive, or when you are cooking, or tidying up your study, etc. The brain absorbs background music and words without you necessarily having to concentrate on the actual meaning. That 'unconscious absorption' nourishes your memory with other linguistic melodies and stress patterns.
- If you have French-speaking friends, ask them to make recordings for you (tapes, CDs, iPods, etc.), perhaps sending you messages with their family news, or giving their views on topics of interest to you.
- If you have satellite or cable TV, see if you can also include a French-speaking, or several, channel(s). TV5 is the TV-Channel of the French-speaking world – **la chaîne de la francophonie**, from Europe to North-America, Australia and Polynesia, Africa and the Mediterranean.
- And if you have Internet access, try to find French radio broadcasts via the Internet. Most radio stations nowadays have a website. It will allow you to acquaint yourself with different accents, not only those from France, but also from Quebec, Belgium, Africa, North-Africa, the Caribbean, etc.
- Using the recordings you have made, or downloaded, or those sent by friends, you may want to do a fun exercise: repeat what you hear, imitating the sounds, a little as if you were rehearsing for a play!
- When speaking with French people, ask them to correct your pronunciation when possible (and if practical).

- If you live in the UK, you may also wish to go and have lunch in Lille, Paris, Brussels, Cherbourg or Le Havre, via the Channel Tunnel, hopping on the high-speed train – the Eurostar – or boarding one of the ferries that cross the Channel, over to Normandy.
- Finally: learning French in Geneva – in French, Genève – Switzerland, is quite nice, as people speak rather slowly, giving you the opportunity to follow exactly what is being said, and participate in conversations already at an early stage!

Toolbox

Nouns

Singular vs. plural

The plural of most nouns is formed by the addition of a final s, which you do not pronounce as it is there for grammatical reasons only. It may influence the pronunciation in cases when the plural noun is followed by an adjective starting with a vowel:

un commentaire attendu	**des commentaires attendus** (pronounce: **zatendu**)

There are some exceptions, naturally, but these will be indicated in any good dictionary:

un chou	**des choux –** *as in:* **les choux de Bruxelles,** *Brussels sprouts*
un canal	**des canaux**
un feu	**des feux –** *as in:* **les feux de croisement,** *dipped beam*

Some nouns – most of which are feminine – are always plural:

les arrhes	*deposit*
les fiançailles	*engagement*
les funérailles	*(grand) funeral*

Some nouns change both spelling and pronunciation in the plural:

un œil	**des yeux**

Gender

French has two genders – the masculine and the feminine.

There is no definite rule in relation to gender – in other words, one cannot say about any noun 'this noun is feminine because ...', 'this noun is masculine because ...'.

Still, some broad indications may be of help:

- The 'reality rule': nouns that refer to an element of reality that is feminine or masculine are equally, in most cases, feminine or masculine in their lexical gender.

  Thus all nouns that designate a status that may be acquired solely by a boy/a man/a male animal are masculine:

a cousin (male)	**un cousin**
an uncle	**un oncle**
a father	**un père**
a bull	**un taureau**

  All nouns that designate a status that may be acquired solely by a girl/a woman/a female creature are feminine:

a cousin (female)	**une cousine**
an aunt	**une tante**
a mother	**une mère**
a mermaid	**une sirène**

- Nouns referring to an occupation: if the occupation is held by a male person, the noun will be masculine:
  un instituteur, un avocat, un boulanger

  If the occupation is held by a female person, the noun will be feminine:
  une institutrice, une avocate, une boulangère

- The 'euphony rule': this refers to the way the language sounds and flows. The ending of a word will be characterized as 'sounding masculine', or 'sounding feminine'. Anyone with a musical ear will hear it spontaneously, anyone who does not think that he/she has a musical ear will soon be able to hear it. Thus:

- Nouns that sound feminine: nouns ending in **-ette, -elle, -enne, -ière, -esse, -ine, -oire, -trice, -ance, -ade,** are usually feminine. The following nouns, one argues, sound feminine. They 'have a spring in their gait', so to speak:

une fermette	*a small farm, a croft*
une hirondelle	*a swallow… as in:* **une hirondelle ne fait pas le printemps!**
la maîtresse	*the primary school teacher or the mistress*
une ambassade	*embassy*

- Nouns that sound masculine: nouns ending in **-eur, -et, -ent, -emps, -ier, -in, -oir, -eau,** are usually masculine. They do not 'bounce' as do the feminine nouns, one may argue:

un ingénieur	*engineer*
un cabinet	*cupboard (see the English 'cabinet maker')/a partnership, a firm (legal firm –* **un cabinet juridique***; accounting firm –* **un cabinet comptable, un cabinet d'audit***)*
un parent	*parent, or relative*
un bavoir	*bib*
un bandeau	*banner, or hairband*

- All nouns in **-ssion, -tion, -sion,** are feminine.
  la révolution (*think French Revolution, 1789!*), **la chanson, la raison**

- Some nouns can be feminine or masculine, depending on their meaning:

le vase *vase* — **la vase** *sludge*
le moule *mould* — **la moule** *mussel*
le somme *snooze* — **la somme** *sum*

- If you are not sure of the gender of a noun, just use the one or the other – it will not, except possibly in very rare cases, impair communication. And if you have chosen the wrong one, your interlocutor will most likely let you know.

Articles/determiners

	the	*a*
masculine singular	**le**	**un**
feminine singular	**la**	**une**
plural	**les**	**des**

le parfum	*perfume, fragrance*	**un beffroi**	*belfry*
la déchirure	*tear (in a fabric, or figuratively, in a relationship)*	**une araignée**	*spider*
les années 1970	*the 1970s*	**des invités**	*guests*

	this
masculine singular	**ce/cet**
feminine singular	**cette**
plural	**ces**

ce train, cet « intercités »	*this train, this intercity (train)*
ce train-là	*that train*
ce train-ci ou ce train-là ?	*this train or that train?*

cette voiture	*this coach (or car, in an automobile context)*
cette voiture-là	*that coach*
cette voiture-ci ou cette voiture-là ?	*this coach or that coach?*
ces arabesques, ces arabesques-ci, ces arabesques-là	*these arabesques*

	my	*your*	*his/her**	*our*	*your*	*their*
masculine singular	**mon**	**ton**	**son**	**notre**	**votre**	**leur**
feminine singular	**ma**	**ta**	**sa**	**notre**	**votre**	**leur**
plural	**mes**	**tes**	**ses**	**nos**	**vos**	**leurs**

his/her* in French remains the same, as the possessive pronoun **ma/mon agrees with the noun possessed, not with the possessor:

son carton d'invitation; sa carte de débarquement – *his,* or *her, invitation card; his* or *her, landing card*

mon stylo-plume	**ton problème**	**son secret**	**notre Père, qui êtes aux cieux...**	**votre lâcheté**	**leur endroit préféré**
my fountain pen	*your problem*	*his* or *her, secret*	*our Father in heaven...*	*your cowardice*	*their favourite place*
ma carte de crédit	**ta recette**	**sa délicatesse**	**notre ancienne maison**	**votre appareil photo**	**leur indécision**
my credit card	*your recipe*	*his* or *her, delicateness – or thoughtfulness*	*our former house*	*your camera*	*their indecisiveness*

Note: le and **la** become **l'** when used in front of most nouns which begin with a vowel or silent **h**:

l'incertitude	*uncertainty*	**l'expulsion**	*eviction, or expulsion*
l'horloge	*clock*	**l'holocauste**	*holocaust*
But, e.g. **la honte**	*shame*	**le hooligan**	*hooligan*

Verbs – infinitives and present tense

The infinitive is the 'name of the verb'. It is the part of the verb you find when you look one up in the dictionary. In English it is always preceded by *to* (*to go/to eat*). In French, it usually ends in **-er**, **-ir**, or **-re**.

In French, the ending of the verb changes according to the subject. Thus, *I eat*: *I* is the subject, *eat* is the verb form that goes with *I*; **Je mange**: **je** is the subject, and **mange** the verb form that goes with **je** – it is different from **manger**, the infinitive.

Pronouns

singular		*plural*	
I	**je**	*we*	**nous**
you	**tu**	*you*	**vous**
he/she/one	**il/elle/on**	*they*	**ils/elles**

Remember: **vous** is the pronoun to use to address someone formally as well as to address a group of people.

aller *to go*

je vais	**nous allons**
tu vas	**vous allez**
il/elle/on va	**ils/elles vont**

être *to be*

je suis	**nous sommes**
tu es	**vous êtes**
il/elle/on est	**ils/elles sont**

avoir *to have*

j'ai	**nous avons**
tu as	**vous avez**
il/elle/on a	**ils/elles ont**

faire *to do, to make*

je fais	**nous faisons**
tu fais	**vous faites**
il/elle/on fait	**ils/elles font**

venir *to come*

je viens	**nous venons**
tu viens	**vous venez**
il/elle/on vient	**ils/elles vont**

Here are 25 of the most commonly-used verbs:

to answer	**répondre, je réponds**
to arrive	**arriver, j'arrive**
to ask	**demander, je demande**
to be able to, can	**pouvoir, je peux**
to bring	**apporter, j'apporte**
to call	**appeler, j'appelle**
to cancel	**annuler, j'annule**
to find	**trouver, je trouve**
to forget	**oublier, j'oublie**
to go in, enter	**entrer, j'entre**
to go out	**sortir, je sors**
to have to, must	**devoir, je dois** (*also*: **falloir, il faut que je)**
to know	**savoir, je sais**
to leave	**quitter, je quitte**
to look for	**chercher, je cherche**
to need	**avoir besoin de, j'ai besoin de**
to put	**mettre, je mets**
to regret	**regretter, je regrette**
to remember	**se rappeler, je me rappelle**

to reserve	**réserver, je réserve**
to see	**voir, je vois**
to send	**envoyer, j'envoie**
to take	**prendre, je prends**
to want	**vouloir, je veux**
to write	**écrire, j'écris**

For a table of irregular verbs see **Toolbox – Some irregular verbs.**

Talking about the past

In French, the tenses that are most used to talk about the past are the perfect, the imperfect and the pluperfect. The past historic is confined to written French and used nowadays exclusively in the third persons singular and plural.

The perfect tense – consisting of an auxiliary verb, **être** or **avoir**, and a past participle – is used to talk about something that happened in the past at a specific time, i.e. a segment of time that can be identified.

The imperfect tense, on the other hand, cannot be circumscribed in time – it serves the purpose of giving information, describing, 'setting the scene' and, in a specific use, of telling of something that used to be or used to happen.

The pluperfect is used to establish a chronology of events, exactly as in English.

They finally went on the cruise about which they had spoken to us numerous times.

Ils sont finalement partis faire la croisière dont ils nous avaient parlé de nombreuses fois.

The perfect tense *le passé composé*

avoir or être + past participle

e.g. with **avoir**	**Elle a déjà appelé quatre fois**	*She has rung four times already*
with **être**	**Vous êtes rentrées tard ?**	*Did you come home late?*

Verbs with **avoir**

The majority of French verbs take **avoir**. Here are some of the most common ones:

to answer répondre

J'ai déjà répondu que je n'irais pas. — *I have already replied that I would not go.*

to ask demander

Nous avons demandé l'addition. — *We have asked for the bill.*

to attend or to witness assister à

J'ai assisté à une scène terrible dans le métro ce matin en venant travailler. — *I witnessed a horrible scene in the underground on my way to work this morning.*

to buy acheter

Nous avons acheté trois douzaines d'huîtres comme entrée pour le dîner. — *We have bought three dozen oysters as a starter for dinner.*

to complete remplir

Avez-vous rempli votre carte de débarquement ? — *Have you filled in your landing card?*

to do/make faire

J'ai fait le maximum légal mais est-ce bien suffisant ? — *I have done the maximum in law, but will it be enough?*

to drink boire

Et comme toujours quand nous sommes invités chez eux, nous avons trop bu.

As always when we are invited to their house, we drank too much.

to eat manger

Il a mangé de bon appétit, pour la première fois depuis longtemps.

He ate with real appetite, for the first time for ages.

to hear entendre

Je crois que je l'ai entendu dire qu'il ne viendrait pas.

I think that I heard him say that he would not come.

to listen écouter

Je t'ai écoutée : maintenant, c'est à moi de parler.

I have listened to you – now it's my turn to speak.

to read lire

Ils ont lu et relu les aventures des trois mousquetaires.

They have read and re-read the adventures of the three musketeers.

to say dire

Je lui ai dit de passer prendre l'apéritif avec nous.

I told him to pop in and have drinks before dinner with us.

to sleep dormir

On a dormi dans mon lit !

Someone has slept in my bed!

to take prendre

J'ai pris le dernier métro.

I took the last metro.

to talk parler

Ils ont parlé de tout et de rien, comme s'il ne s'était rien passé.

They talked about this and that, as if nothing had ever happened.

to think penser

Elle a pensé à annuler la réservation, ne t'inquiète pas. *She has thought about cancelling your booking, don't worry.*

to write écrire

ils ont écrit au Père Noël. *They have written a letter to Santa Claus.*

Verbs with **être**

Not many verbs take **être**; those that do are called 'perfective verbs', as they express both a process and a result (with the exception of **aller** *to go*). The action expressed by a verb that takes **être** cannot be undertaken indefinitely. For example, **monter – je suis monté(e) le voir.** *I went up to see him.* One cannot possibly go up and up and up and up, etc. To go up expresses the action of moving up, the result being at a higher level in space.

to go aller

Nous sommes allés passer les derniers jours de l'été en Provence. *We spent the remaining days of the summer in Provence.*

to arrive arriver

Elle est arrivée sans problème, j'espère ? *I hope she arrived safely, did she?*

to leave partir

Vous êtes partis sans dire « au revoir » ! *You left without saying 'goodbye'!*

to go up monter

Nous ne sommes jamais montés sur la tour Eiffel. *We never went up the Eiffel tower.*

to go down descendre

Il est descendu chercher du vin à la cave. *He went down to the cellar to fetch some wine.*

to come venir

Ils sont venus nous voir cet été pour la première fois. *They came to visit this summer for the first time.*

to enter entrer

Il est entré au séminaire en janvier dernier. *He joined the seminary last January.*

to exit/go out sortir

Nous sommes sortis prendre l'air. *We went out for a breath of fresh air.*

In addition, the reflexive verbs take **être**. A reflexive verb also uses the personal pronoun and may mean 'oneself' – **Je me suis douché(e):** *I showered* – or it may refer to a mutual action – **Nous nous sommes parlés au téléphone.** *We spoke on the telephone.*

to enjoy oneself s'amuser

Je me suis bien amusé(e), pour une fois ! *For once, I truly enjoyed myself!*

to wake up se réveiller

Elle s'est réveillée à peine deux heures après la fin de l'opération. *She woke up barely two hours after the operation ended.*

to get up se lever

Tu t'es encore levé du mauvais pied, je vois ? *You got out of bed on the wrong side, I see?*

to fall asleep s'endormir

Je me suis endormie à peine le train parti. *I fell asleep as soon as the train departed.*

to sit down s'asseoir

Elle s'est assise, prête à s'évanouir. *She sat down, close to fainting. (note:* **s'évanouir** *– to faint – is also a reflexive verb)* *to get rid of* se débarrasser

Ils se sont débarassés de tout ce qui encombrait le grenier pour en faire une chambre d'amis. *They got rid of everything that cluttered the attic so as to be able to turn it into a guest room.*

to have/show an interest in s'intéresser à

Ils se sont particulièrement intéressés au témoignage du seul témoin à charge. *They were particularly interested in the testimony of the only witness for the prosecution.*

to expect s'attendre à

Elle s'est toujours attendue au pire, avec lui. *With him, she has always expected the worst to happen.*

to expand on/to lie down s'étendre

Il s'est étendu sur le sujet à tel point que ça en est devenu gênant pour tout le monde. *He expanded on the subject so much that it became embarrassing for everyone.*

or

Elle s'est étendue une heure après le déjeuner. *She lay down for an hour after lunch.*

to get on/to agree s'entendre

Vous vous êtes toujours bien entendus, non ? *You have always got on well, haven't you?*

or

Ils se sont entendus sur des mesures de contention climatiques relativement audacieuses. *They have agreed on rather bold climate containment measures.*

The imperfect tense *l'imparfait*

The conjugation of the imperfect tense is as follows:

aimer *to love*	
j'aimais	**nous aimions**
tu aimais	**vous aimiez**
il/elle aimait	**ils/elles aimaient**

I was	**j'étais**
I had	**j'avais**
I had to	**je devais**
I could	**je pouvais**
It was raining	**il pleuvait**
It was hot/cold	**il faisait chaud/froid**
I was drinking	**je buvais**
I was talking	**je parlais**
I was eating	**je mangeais**
I was working/I would work	**je travaillais**
I was going/I would go	**j'allais**
I was living	**j'habitais** *or* **je vivais**
I was thinking/I would think	**je pensais**
I was reading/I would read	**je lisais**
I was spending/I would spend	**je passais** *or* **je dépensais**

Talking about the future

As in English, there are, in French, two tenses to express the future: the future (**le futur**) and the near future (**le futur proche**).
The future tense expresses events/actions that will most probably take place and the near future expresses events/actions that are about to take place and/or intentions. Plus, as always in French, a number of exceptions to the rule! But, as with most exceptions, those tend to derive from usage – you will encounter them as you develop your knowledge and fluency.

The future: infinitive + ending

aimer *to love*	
j'aimerai	**nous aimerons**
tu aimeras	**vous aimerez**
il/elle aimera	**ils/elles aimeront**

I will definitely be there.	**J'y serai sans faute.**
I will call (you) when I arrive.	**Je vous appellerai en arrivant.**
Will you be all right?	**Ça ira ?**
Shall we go by the market and get a rabbit?	**On passera au marché prendre un lapin ?**
I will go tomorrow.	**J'irai demain.**
Will you pick me up?	**Vous viendrez me chercher ?**
Will you have lunch with us?	**Vous déjeunerez avec nous ?**

The near future: going to + infinitive = *aller* + infinitive

partir *to leave*	
je vais partir	**nous allons partir**
tu vas partir	**vous allez partir**
il/elle va partir	**ils/elles vont partir**

We will leave as soon as the fog clears.	**Nous allons partir dès que le brouillard sera levé.**
I will confirm our bookings in a mo'.	**Je vais confirmer nos réservations tout-à-l'heure.**
Are you going to take the 9 o'clock train?	**Tu vas prendre le train de neuf heures ?**
They are going to sail around the world.	**Ils vont faire le tour du monde à la voile** *or* **en bateau.**
We are going to use general anaesthesia for his operation, to be on the safe side.	**Nous allons l'opérer sous anesthésie générale, c'est plus prudent.**

The conditional

The conditional is formed using the infinitive and adding the endings of the imperfect tense:

aimer *to love*	
j'aimerais	**nous aimerions**
tu aimerais	**vous aimeriez**
il/elle aimerait	**ils/elles aimeraient**

The conditional:

- replaces the future tense after the past tense:
  I know that you will make it. (present + future) =
  I knew that you would make it. (past tense + conditional)
  Je sais que tu y arriveras. (future) = **je savais que tu y arriverais.** (conditional)
- is used to express politeness: *I would like* rather than *I want.*
- is used to express a hypothetical reality subject to a condition:
  If I were a witch, I would make you disappear. Now!
  Si j'étais une sorcière, je te ferais disparaître … et hop!

to like: I would like	**j'aimerais,** *or* **j'aimerais bien**
to prefer: I would prefer	**je préfèrerais**
to appreciate: I would appreciate	**j'apprécierais**
to be able to: I would be able to …	**je pourrais**
to go: I would go	**j'irais**
to have: I would have	**j'aurais**
to be: I would be	**je serais**
to do: I would do	**je ferais**
to take: I would take	**je prendrais**

The subjunctive

This is not a tense, but a mood: in effect, it does not express time. The mood in charge of expressing time (**Chronos**) is the indicative mood with all its tenses (see above: present, perfect, imperfect, future).

The subjunctive is used after a number of conjunctions (set usage), after **il faut que** and after a certain number of verbs expressing opinions (i.e. the self/one's subjective opinions/feelings, hence its name: the subjunctive). It is further used in relative clauses that qualify one's desired/wished expectation.

The subjunctive is formed by using the root of the third person plural – *they* – in the present tense and adding the present tense ending for the three persons singular and the third person plural:

prendre *to take* **ils prennent → prenn + e, -es, -e, -ent**

The first two persons plural – *we, you* – are formed using the root of the first person plural in the present tense and adding the endings of the imperfect tense.

prendre *to take* **nous prenions → pren + -ions, + -iez**

prendre *to take*	
que je prenne	**que nous prenions**
que tu prennes	**que vous preniez**
qu'il/qu'elle prenne	**qu'ils/qu'elles prennent**

The conjugation of the subjunctive is given with **que** as it rarely functions on its own – it must follow a conjunction or a verb.

Another form of the subjunctive is the 'past subjunctive', formed using **être** or **avoir** – as for the perfect tense – in the subjunctive and adding the past participle:

- with être: **Ils craignaient que leur voisin ne se soit suicidé.** *They feared that their neighbour had committed suicide.*
- with **avoir**: **J'aimerais que vous ayez fini de tout préparer avant l'arrivée des premiers invités.** *I would like you to have finished all preparations before the first guests arrive.*

être *to be*

que je sois	**que nous soyions**
que tu sois	**que vous soyiez**
qu'il ou qu'elle soit	**qu'ils ou qu'elles soient**

avoir *to have*

que j'aie	**que nous ayions**
que tu aies	**que vous ayiez**
qu'il ou qu'elle ait	**qu'ils ou qu'elles aient**

The main conjunctions followed by the subjunctive are as follows:

Insight

Après que does not take the subjunctive – even though you will often hear it used, for mimetic reasons, probably.

bien que/quoique	*although*
avant que	*before*
jusqu'à ce que	*until*
afin que/pour que/de sorte que	*so that*
à moins que	*unless*
pourvu que	*hopefully*
en supposant que	*supposing that*
il faut que	*it is necessary to*

Insight

In normal usage, **il faut que** is the equivalent of *I have to*. *I have to go* = **Il faut que j'y aille** or *I have to be there for 12 noon latest* = **Il faut que j'y sois à midi au plus tard**, etc. You may perfectly well use **je dois** to say *I have to*. The difference lies in the slight moral nuance. For example, **Je dois passer voir madame Genêt à l'hôpital**. *I have to go and see Mrs Genêt in hospital*. (Sub-text: she is a colleague, a nice one, and although we may not be friends, I feel *I have* to go and see her.)

- after verbs expressing opinions, desires, expectations:

exiger que	*to demand that*
craindre que	*to fear that*
ordonner que	*to order that*
désirer que	*to desire that*
vouloir que	*to want that*
penser que	*to think that*
douter que	*to doubt that*
souhaiter que	*to wish that*
aimer que	*to like that*

- in a relative clause that qualifies one's expectation:

I was looking for a hat that would go with this coat.	**Je cherchais un chapeau qui aille avec ce manteau.**

Insight

Note the use of the past, just like in English: *I was looking* – **je cherchais**, for refinement/additional politeness. You may for example use it on the telephone: **Je cherchais à joindre M. Ledrouet** – *I was trying to contact Mr Ledrouet*.

Negative expressions

How to say you don't do/like/remember, etc. something

ne ... pas

I don't like ...	**Je n'aime pas ...**
I don't drink.	**Je ne bois pas.**
He cannot take any time off.	**Il ne peut pas se libérer.**
We cannot see the sea!	**On ne voit pas la mer !**
I don't smoke.	**Je ne fume pas.**
Q: Have you got any change?	**As-tu de la monnaie ?**
A: No I haven't.	**Non, je n'en ai pas.**
Q: Haven't you been to see your doctor?	**Tu n'es pas allé(e) voir ton médecin ?**
A: No, I couldn't get an appointment.	**Non, je n'ai pas réussi à avoir de rendez-vous.**
Didn't you go to the bank?	**Tu n'es pas passé(e) à la banque ?**
No, I never had the time.	**Non, je n'ai pas eu le temps.**
Didn't you say that you would speak to him?	**Tu n'avais pas dit que tu lui parlerais ?**
Yes, I did. I got cold feet.	**Si, c'est ce que j'avais dit ; mais je me suis dégonflé(e).**

Note: One uses **si** instead of **oui** to answer a negative question affirmatively.

Insight

Se dégonfler is colloquial when used to mean 'to get cold feet'; literally, *to deflate*. You would use it otherwise in its proper context, for a bicycle tyre: **Mon pneu se dégonfle,** or **s'est dégonflé.**

ne ... rien

I cannot see anything.	**Je ne vois rien.**
I am not having anything, thank you.	**Merci, je ne prends rien.**

ne ... personne

I don't know anyone.	**Je ne connais personne.**
I haven't seen anyone.	**Je n'ai vu personne.**
No one ever goes to that island.	**Personne ne va jamais sur cette île-là.**
Q: Do you have a reservation?	**Vous avez réservé ?**
A: No; no-one answered the phone.	**Non, personne ne répondait.**

ne ... jamais

I have never been to Paris.	**Je ne suis jamais allé(e) à Paris.**
He has never eaten snails.	**Il n'a jamais mangé d'escargots.**
I never have any dessert.	**Je ne prends jamais de dessert.**

ne ... aucun

She doesn't have any common sense.	**Elle n'a aucun sens pratique.**
They don't have any friends.	**Ils n'ont aucun ami.**

ne ... plus

We don't go out any more.	**Nous ne sortons plus**
Q: Didn't you get the cinema tickets?	**Tu n'as pas pris les tickets (de cinéma) ?**
A: No, there weren't any left for the 9.00 pm show.	**Non, il n'en restait plus pour la séance de 21 heures.**

Don't ...!

No entry	**Entrée interdite**
No exit	**Sortie interdite**
No admission	**Accès interdit**
No smoking	**Interdit de fumer**
No dogs	**Chiens non admis**
Don't do it!	**Ne fais/faites pas ça !**
Don't eat it!	**Ne mange/mangez pas ça !**
Don't open the window.	**N'ouvre/n'ouvrez pas la fenêtre.**
Don't cross the road.	**Ne traverse/traversez pas la rue.**
... is not allowed/permitted.	**Il est interdit de...**
Kissing on the platform is not permitted.	**Il est interdit de s'embrasser sur le quai.**

Insight

The last example is a humorous reference – **un clin d'œil**, in French – to the introduction of 'no-kissing areas' at Warrington Bank Quay railway station, in Cheshire, England, early in 2009. I am not sure that it would go down well in France!

Non-drinking water	**Eau non potable**
Do not lean out of the window	**Ne pas se pencher par la fenêtre**
Do not try to get off once the train is moving	**Ne pas descendre du train en marche**
Private – No trespassing	**Propriété privée – Défense d'entrer**

Interrogative – asking questions

Questions that will trigger a 'no' or a 'yes' answer

There are three possible ways to formulate a question in French:

1 The most formal method is to invert the verb and subject.

Serez-vous chez vous en début d'après-midi ? *Will you be at home early this afternoon?*

2 The structure est-ce que, which indicates a question.

Est-ce que vous serez chez vous en début d'après-midi ?

3 The most informal method is to use the affirmative sentence, and raise one's voice at the end to make it sound like a question.

Vous serez chez vous en début d'après-midi ?

Questions asking for information

Questions that ask for specific information are introduced by one of the following question words:

Who?	**Qui ?**	*How?*	**Comment ?**
When?	**Quand ?**	*How much?*	**Combien ?**

Where?	**Où ?**	*How many?*	**Combien ?**
Why?	**Pourquoi ?**	*How long?*	**Combien de temps ?**
What?	**Que/qu' ?**		

Adjectives

Remember that adjectives in French agree with the noun, both in terms of its gender and number.

- The mark of the feminine is a final e: **vert + e = verte** *green*

  un thé vert *a green tea*
  une plante verte *a green plant*

- If the adjective has already got an **e** in the masculine, it remains the same: **alerte** *fit*

  un homme alerte *a fit man*
  une femme alerte *a fit woman*

- The mark of the plural is a final s: **argenté + s = argentés** *silvery*

  Un renard argenté *a silver fox*
  Des renards argentés *silver foxes*

- If the noun is both feminine and plural, the adjective takes both an **e** and an **s**:

  un conflit évident *an obvious conflict*
  des disputes évidentes *obvious arguments*

Generally adjectives tend to be placed after the noun. If they are placed before the noun, there is a reason for this, whether stylistic, poetic, or, in the case of some adjectives such as **beau, grand, long, petit,** and **vieux,** because this order is a set usage.

Some adjectives to describe people

tall/big	**grand**	*short*	**petit**
thin	**mince**	*fat*	**gros/gras**

happy	**heureux**	*unhappy*	**malheureux**
shy	**timide**	*loud*	**bruyant**
quiet	**réservé**	*outgoing*	**ouvert**
relaxed/laid back	**détendu**	*stressed*	**stressé**
considerate	**attentionné**	*cavalier*	**cavalier**
self-centred	**égocentrique**	*lazy*	**paresseux**

Insight

To a self-centred adolescent, you may want to say: **Arrête de te regarder le nombril !** Literally: *Stop gazing at your navel!*

active	**actif**	*ugly*	**laid (***pronounced:* **lè)**
good-looking	**beau/séduisant**	*ordinary*	**ordinaire**
outstanding	**extraordinaire**	*scruffy*	**négligé/pas soigné**
smart	**chic/élégant**	*unpleasant*	**désagréable,** *or* **déplaisant**
well brought up	**bien élevé**	*rude*	**grossier**
polite	**poli**		

Some adjectives to describe things

old	**vieux**	*new*	**neuf** *(bought)* **nouveau** *(novelty)*
good	**bon/bien**	*bad*	**mauvais/mal**
cheap	**bon marché**	*expensive*	**cher**
fast	**rapide**	*slow*	**lent**
damaged	**abîmé/ endommagé**	*in good condition*	**en bon état**
flimsy	**branlant**	*solid*	**solide**
rough	**rêche**	*smooth*	**doux**
shiny	**brillant**	*matt*	**mat**

The comparative and the superlative

The comparative

more ... than	**plus ... que**
less ... than	**moins ... que**
as ... as	**aussi ... que**
more interesting than	**plus intéressant* que** *(in both the intellectual and financial sense)*

less interesting than	**moins intéressant que**
as interesting as	**aussi intéressant que**
bigger than	**plus grand/gros que**
worse than	**pire que**
better than	**meilleur/mieux que**

***intéressant** should agree with the noun

The superlative

the most ...	**le plus ...***
the most interesting	**le plus intéressant**
the biggest	**le plus grand/gros**
the worst	**le pire**
the best	**le meilleur/le mieux**

*The adjective used should agree with the noun.

Colours and sizes

Colours

black	**noir**	*grey*	**gris**
blue	**bleu**	*orange*	**orange**
blue-grey	**bleu-gris**	*pink*	**rose**
pale blue	**bleu pâle**	*salmon pink*	**saumon**
light blue	**bleu ciel**	*fuchsia*	**fuchsia**
dark blue	**bleu foncé**	*purple*	**violet**
navy blue	**bleu marine**	*mauve*	**mauve**
royal blue	**bleu roi**	*red*	**rouge**
sapphire	**bleu saphir**	*bright red*	**rouge vig**
turquoise	**bleu turquoise**	*scarlet*	**écarlate**
brown	**brun**	*burgundy*	**bordeau**
dark brown	**marron**	*white*	**blanc**
green	**vert**	*off white*	**blanccassé**
pale green	**vert pâle**	*ivory*	**ivoire**
dark green	**vert foncé**	*cream*	**crème**
olive green	**vert olive**	*yellow*	**jaune**

leaf green	**vert tendre**	*buttercup yellow*	**jaune d'or**
bottle green	**vert bouteille**	*beige*	**beige**
khaki	**khaki**		

Sizes

tiny	**minuscule**	*huge*	**immense**
very small	**tout petit**	*wide*	**large**
small	**petit**	*narrow*	**étroit**
medium	**de taille moyenne**	*long*	**long**
large	**grand**	*short*	**court**
very large	**très grand**		

Adverbs

An adverb – as its name suggests – adds something to the verb:
to run (verb) + *quickly* (adverb) = *to run quickly*

Some adverbs exist 'in their own right', so to speak:

fast	**vite**	*very*	**très**
too much	**trop**	*well*	**bien**

The other adverbs are formed using the adjective and adding the ending **-ment** or **-ement** (except if the adjective ends in **-ant** or **-ent**, where the final **-nt** is replaced with **-mment**).

quickly	**rapidement**
slowly	**lentement**
immediately	**immédiatement**
completely	**complètement**
suddenly	**soudainement**
noisily	**bruyamment**
painfully	**douloureusement**
happily	**heureusement**
appropriately	**correctement**

economically	**économiquement**
relevantly	**pertinemment**
technically	**techniquement**
sadly	**tristement/malheureusement**
very	**très**
a little	**un peu**
more	**plus**
most	**la plupart de**
less	**moins**
rarely	**rarement**
occasionally	**occasionnellement**
frequently	**fréquemment**
sometimes	**parfois**
from time to time	**de temps en temps** *(or* **ponctuellement** *in legal documents, for example)*
often	**souvent**
very often	**très souvent**
soon	**bientôt**
later	**plus tard**
afterwards	**après**
already	**déjà**
then	**à cette époque-là, à ce moment-là**
previously	**précédemment**
earlier	**plus tôt**

Numbers, days, dates and the time

Cardinal numbers

0 zéro	13 treize	32 trente-deux
1 un	14 quatorze	40 quarante
2 deux	15 quinze	50 cinquante
3 trois	16 seize	60 soixante
4 quatre	17 dix-sept	70 soixante-dix
5 cinq	18 dix-huit	80 quatre-vingts
6 six	19 dix-neuf	90 quatre-vingt-dix

7 sept
8 huit
9 neuf
10 dix
11 onze
12 douze
300 trois cents
500 cinq cents
1 000 mille
2 000 deux mille
2 100 deux-mille-cent

20 vingt
21 vingt-et-un
22 vingt-deux
23 vingt-trois
30 trente
31 trente-et-un
5 000 cinq mille
10 000 dix mille
1 000 000 un million
1 000 000 000 un milliard

100 cent
101 cent-un
102 cent-deux
111 cent-onze
112 cent-douze
200 deux-cents

Insight

The convention for numbers in French is different from that in English: thus, where you find a comma in English, e.g. 1,000, you will find a space in French, as above.
In decimals, where you find a full stop in English, e.g. *4.50 GBP*, you will find a comma in French: **4,50 livres sterling.**

Ordinal numbers

first	**premier/première**
second	**deuxième/second**
third	**troisième**
fourth	**quatrième**
fifth	**cinquième**
tenth	**dixième**
21st	**vingt-et-unième**
half	**demi**
quarter	**quart**
… and also: last	**dernier/dernière**

Insight

Note: *The first three* – **les trois premiers**, or **les trois premières**
The last five – **les cinq derniers**, or **les cinq dernières.**

Dates

century	**un siècle**
the 1970s	**les années 1970**
the 20th century	**le XXᵉ siècle**
the 21st century	**le XXIᵉ siècle**
millennium	**un millénaire**
the third millennium	**le troisième millénaire**
the year 2000	**l'an 2000**
next year	**l'année prochaine**
the following year	**l'année suivante**
last year	**l'année passée/dernière**
the previous year	**l'année précédente**
the year before last	**il y a deux ans**
the year after next	**dans deux ans**

Days and months

Insight

As France is essentially a Catholic country, you may also come across **Lundi de Pâques**, *Easter Monday* and **Vendredi Saint**, *Good Friday*. And since Islam is the second largest religion, you may come across **l'aïd** (pronounced *ah – eed*) at the end of *Ramadan*.

Monday	**lundi**	*Friday*	**vendredi**
Tuesday	**mardi**	*Saturday*	**samedi**
Wednesday	**mercredi**	*Sunday*	**dimanche**
Thursday	**jeudi**		

January	**janvier**	*July*	**juillet**
February	**février**	*August*	**août**
March	**mars**	*September*	**septembre**
April	**avril**	*October*	**octobre**
May	**mai**	*November*	**novembre**
June	**juin**	*December*	**décembre**

Note that days and months do not take a capital in French (except at the start of a sentence – and except for the 'special days', as noted above in the Insight box).

Expressions of time

day	**le jour**	*month*	**le mois**
week	**la semaine**	*year*	**l'an/l'année**

If you are referring to the duration of a day, i.e. to all the hours that constitute it, then **la journée** will be used rather than **le jour**:

Have a good day!	**Bonne journée !**
yesterday	**hier**
the day before yesterday	**avant-hier**
today	**aujourd'hui**
tomorrow	**demain**
the day after tomorrow	**après-demain**
morning	**le matin***
afternoon	**l'après-midi**
evening	**le soir**
night	**la nuit**
this afternoon	**cet après-midi** *or* **cette après-midi** *(both the masculine and the feminine can be used)*
tonight	**ce soir**
tomorrow afternoon	**demain après-midi**
yesterday morning	**hier matin**

*As with **le jour** above, **le matin** will be replaced by **la matinée** if you are referring to the specific hours that make up the morning:

J'ai passé la matinée au téléphone	*I have been on the phone all morning*

The seasons

spring	**le printemps**	*autumn, or fall*	**l'automne**
summer	**l'été**	*winter*	**l'hiver**

spring-like	**printanier**	*autumnal*	**automnal**
summery	**estival**	*wintry*	**hivernal**

Time

second	**une seconde**
micro-second	**une micro-seconde**
nano-second	**une nano-seconde**
minute	**une minute**

Insight

If someone is rushing you and you have already answered that yes, you are coming in a moment, you may, this time, say: **Minute!**, stressing both syllables in exasperation: **miiiii-nuuuuuute !**

hour	**une heure**
half hour	**une demi-heure**
quarter of an hour	**un quart d'heure**
midnight	**minuit**
midday	**midi**
clock	**la pendule**
grandfather's clock	**l'horloge** *(Note: both* **la pendule** *and* **l'horloge** *may refer to the clock in a public place – railway station, town hall, airport, etc.)*
watch	**la montre**
alarm clock	**le réveil**

Telling the time

Il est ...	**neuf heures**	*It is ...*	*nine o'clock*
	neuf heures dix		*ten past nine*
	neuf heures et quart		*quarter past nine*
	neuf heures et demie		*half past nine*
	dix heures moins vingt		*twenty to ten*
	dix heures moins le quart		*a quarter to ten*
	dix heures moins cinq		*five to ten*

Insight

In French, the 24-hour clock is used increasingly in personal matters, e.g. **On déjeune ensemble à 13 heures, ça te va ?** *Is 1pm for lunch okay for you?* In professional/business/transport/international dealings, the 24-hour clock is always used; the ante and post meridiem (am and pm) convention does not exist in French.

Quantity and quality

weight	**le poids**
height	**la hauteur**
length	**la longueur**
size	**la taille**
shoe size	**la pointure**

Weights and measures

kilo	**un kilo**
half a kilo	**un demi-kilo**
a pound	**une livre**
a litre	**un litre**
a metre	**un mètre**
a centimetre	**un centimètre**
an inch	**un pouce**
a foot	**un pied**
a kilometre	**un kilomètre**
a pair	**une paire**
a dozen	**une douzaine**
half a dozen	**une demi-douzaine**
bottle	**une bouteille**
jar	**un flacon**
tin	**une boîte de conserve**
box	**une boîte**
pot	**un pot**
package	**un paquet/un emballage**
lots of	**beaucoup de**

little of	**peu de**
more of	**plus de**
approximately one hundred	**une centaine de ...**
approximately ten	**une dizaine de ...**

Exclamations, giving orders and being polite

Help!	**Au secours !/A l'aide !**
Fire!	**Au feu !**
Watch out!	**Attention !**
Cheers!	**Chin ! A votre santé !**
Wait!	**Attendez !**
Stop!	**Stop !** *or* **Arrêtez !**
Listen!	**Écoutez !**
Look!	**Regardez !**
Be careful!	**Soyez prudent !/Faites attention !**

Giving orders

These examples are between people who know each other well – using the **tu** form.

Pass me a knife.	**Donne-moi un couteau.**
Fetch a glass.	**Va chercher un verre.**
Take the chocolates with you, if you wish.	**Emporte les chocolats, si tu veux.**
Please bring me my bag.	**Apporte-moi mon sac, s'il-te-plaît.**
Excuse me.	**Excusez-moi.**
Pardon.	**Pardon.** *(This is mostly used when one bumps into someone else.)*
I'm sorry.	**Je suis désolé(e).**
I didn't mean it.	**Je ne l'ai pas fait exprès.**
I do apologize.	**Pardonnez-moi.**
You're welcome.	**Je vous en prie.**

Insight

Adding **veux-tu** at the end of the sentence is not as formal as **s'il-te-plaît**, but softens an order that may sound a little abrupt on its own. For example, **Donne-moi un couteau, veux-tu ? Va chercher un verre, veux-tu ?**

Accents and punctuation

Accents

When an accent appears, the name of the letter will be given first, followed by the accent.

ê = e accent circonflexe	**ë = e tréma**
é = e accent aigu	**è = e accent grave**
à = a accent grave	**â = a accent circonflexe**
ô = o accent circonflexe	**î = i accent circonflexe**
û = u accent circonflexe	**ù = u accent grave**

and, although strictly speaking it is not an accent: **ç = c cédille**

Punctuation

full stop	**point**
semi-colon	**point-virgule**
comma	**virgule**
colon	**deux points**
ellipsis (dot-dot-dot)	**... points de suspension**
exclamation mark	**point d'exclamation**
question mark	**point d'interrogation**
quotation marks	**les guillemets**
open quote	**« ouvrez les guillemets**
close quote	**» fermez les guillemets**
in quotes	**entre guillemets**

Insight

French has only one kind of inverted commas, or quotes – the 'chevron' type above – whereas English has single and double ones.

in brackets	**entre parenthèses**
open bracket	**ouvrez la parenthèse**
close bracket	**fermez la parenthèse**
hyphen	**trait d'union**
dash	**tiret**

Insight

The 'spacing convention' in French word processing is different from that in English. Any double punctuation sign, semi-colon, exclamation or question mark will be preceded and followed by a space. Full stops and commas are not preceded by a space and are followed by a single space.

@	**arobase**
www.	**w - w - w – point** *or* **trois w – point**
small letter/lower case	**minuscule**
capital	**majuscule**
new sentence	**nouvelle phrase**
new paragraph	**nouveau paragraphe**

A paragraph, according to the formatting convention in French, starts with an indented line, called **alinéa**.

Vocabulary tips

With his victory in 1066 over Harold, William the Conqueror, Duke of Normandy – in French, **Guillaume le Conquérant, Duc de Normandie** – became King of England. He brought with him his court and learned scholars, who introduced the written word to England which, until then, had worked within an oral tradition.

As a result, it is said that 50 per cent of English vocabulary comes from the French – originally from Norman, and Old French. Over the centuries, further words have 'shuttled' between the two countries and languages. Consequently, the great news is that you may guess at a word, and have a 50 per cent chance of getting it right!

Many words ending in *-tion* and *-sion* are the same in French and in English. And in most cases they have retained a similar, or part of their original, meaning. And they are all feminine!

Here are some examples:

A	l'appropriation, l'attention, l'apparition
B	la béatification, la bénédiction
C	la capitulation, la correction, la contusion, la création
D	la détérioration, la dévolution, la délation
E	l'évaluation, l'équation, l'expulsion
F	la fiction, la falsification, la fornication
G	la gravitation, la graduation
H	l'hibernation, l'hallucination
I	l'inspection, l'irrigation, l'itération
L	la libération, la lubrication
M	la menstruation, la motivation, la masturbation
N	la nomination, la navigation, la négation
O	l'opération, l'oscillation, l'observation
P	la prévision, la participation, la passion
Q	la qualification, la question
R	la réhabilitation, la rénovation, la rééducation, la réservation
S	la saturation, la simplification, la suspension
T	la transition, la tribulation, la trépidation
U	l'utilisation, l'usurpation, l'union
V	la versification, la variation, la vision

The following are, in current, common usage, 'false friends' – **des faux-amis**. They may, in some instances, have the same meaning in specialist or technical fields [examples given in square brackets].

la confection	*ready-to-wear industry*
la déviation	*diversion in roadworks (note: from deviate)*
la formation	*education and training [geological formation]*
la fabrication	*manufacturing [the fabrication of evidence in criminal law]*

Words ending in *-ial* in English usually end in **-iel** in French:

potential	**potentiel**
essential	**essentiel**

But:

martial	**martial**
crucial	**crucial**

Nouns ending *-ity/-ty* in English – often, not always! – have an equivalent ending with **-ité/-té** in French:

royalty	**la royauté**
quality	**la qualité**
quantity	**la quantité**
novelty	**la nouveauté**
liberty	**la liberté**
fraternity	**la fraternité**
equality	**l'égalité** *etc.*

Nouns ending in *-ism* in English end in **-isme** in French:

amorphism	**un amorphisme**
classicism	**le classicisme**
euphemism	**un euphémisme**
positivism	**le positivisme**
romanticism	**le romantisme**

Some irregular verbs

être avoir aller faire

Past participle	être – été	avoir – eu	aller – allé	faire – fait
Present participle	étant	ayant	allant	faisant

Present tense

Être	*Avoir*	*Aller*	*Faire*
je suis	**j'ai**	**je vais**	**je fais**
tu es	**tu as**	**tu vas**	**tu fais**
il/elle est	**il/elle a**	**il/elle va**	**il/elle fait**
nous sommes	**nous avons**	**nous allons**	**nous faisons**
vous êtes	**vous avez**	**vous allez**	**vous faites**
ils/elles sont	**ils/elles ont**	**ils/elles vont**	**ils/elles font**

Imperfect tense

Être	*Avoir*	*Aller*	*Faire*
j'étais	**j'avais**	**j'allais**	**je faisais**
tu étais	**tu avais**	**tu allais**	**tu faisais**
il/elle était	**il/elle avait**	**il/elle allait**	**il/elle faisait**
nous étions	**nous avions**	**nous allions**	**nous faisions**
vous étiez	**vous aviez**	**vous alliez**	**vous faisiez**
ils/elles étaient	**ils/elles avaient**	**ils/elles allaient**	**ils/elles faisaient**

Perfect tense

Être	*Avoir*	*Aller*	*Faire*
j'ai été	**j'ai eu**	**je suis allé(e)**	**j'ai fait**
tu as été	**tu as eu**	**tu es allé(e)**	**tu as fait**
il/elle a été	**il/elle a eu**	**il/elle est allé(e)**	**il/elle a fait**
nous avons été	**nous avons eu**	**nous sommes allé(e)s**	**nous avons fait**
vous avez été	**vous avez eu**	**vous êtes allé(e)(s)**	**vous avez fait**
ils/elles ont été	**ils/elles ont eu**	**ils/elles sont allé(e)(s)**	**ils/elles ont fait**

Future tense

Être	*Avoir*	*Aller*	*Faire*
je serai	**j'aurai**	**j'irai**	**je ferai**
tu seras	**tu auras**	**tu iras**	**tu feras**
il/elle sera	**il/elle aura**	**il/elle ira**	**il/elle fera**
nous serons	**nous aurons**	**nous irons**	**nous ferons**
vous serez	**vous aurez**	**vous irez**	**vous ferez**
ils/elles seront	**ils/elles auront**	**ils/elles iront**	**ils/elles feront**

The conditional

Être	*Avoir*	*Aller*	*Faire*
je serais	**j'aurais**	**j'irais**	**je ferais**
tu serais	**tu aurais**	**tu irais**	**tu ferais**
il/elle serait	**il/elle aurait**	**il/elle irait**	**il/elle ferait**
nous serions	**nous aurions**	**nous irions**	**nous ferions**
vous seriez	**vous auriez**	**vous iriez**	**vous feriez**
ils/elles seraient	**ils/elles auraient**	**ils/elles iraient**	**ils/elles feraient**

The subjunctive

Être	*Avoir*	*Aller*	*Faire*
que je sois	**que j'aie**	**que j'aille**	**que je fasse**
que tu sois	**que tu aies**	**que tu ailles**	**que tu fasses**
qu'il/qu'elle soit	**qu'il/qu'elle ait**	**qu'il/qu'elle aille**	**qu'il/qu'elle fasse**
que nous soyions	**que nous ayions**	**que nous allions**	**que nous fassions**
que vous soyiez	**que vous ayiez**	**que vous alliez**	**que vous fassiez**
qu'ils/qu'elles soient	**qu'ils/qu'elles aient**	**qu'ils/qu'elles aillent**	**qu'ils/qu'elles fassent**

The past subjunctive

Être	*Avoir*	*Aller*	*Faire*
que j'aie été	**que j'aie eu**	**que je sois allé(e)**	**que j'aie fait**
que tu aies été	**que tu aies eu**	**que tu sois allé(e)**	**que tu aies fait**
qu'il/qu'elle ait été	**qu'il/qu'elle ait eu**	**qu'il/qu'elle soit allé(e)**	**qu'il/qu'elle ait fait**
que nous ayions été	**que nous ayions eu**	**que nous soyions allé(e)s**	**que nous ayions fait**
que vous ayiez été	**que vous ayiez eu**	**que vous soyiez allé(es)**	**que vous ayiez fait**
qu'ils/qu'elles aient été	**qu'ils/qu'elles aient eu**	**qu'ils/qu'elles soient allé(e)s**	**qu'ils/qu'elles aient fait**

pouvoir devoir falloir

Note: falloir is a 'defective' verb – some persons are missing as they have fallen from use.

Past participle	**pouvoir – pu**	**devoir – dû**	**falloir – fallu**
Present participle	**pouvant**	**devant**	**fallant**

Present tense

pouvoir	*devoir*	*falloir*
je peux	**je dois**	
tu peux	**tu dois**	
il/elle peut	**il/elle doit**	**il faut**
nous pouvons	**nous devons**	
vous pouvez	**vous devez**	
ils/elles peuvent	**ils/elles doivent**	

Imperfect tense

pouvoir	*devoir*	**falloir**
je pouvais	**je devais**	
tu pouvais	**tu devais**	
il/elle pouvait	**il/elle devait**	**il fallait**
nous pouvions	**nous devions**	
vous pouviez	**vous deviez**	
ils/elles pouvaient	**ils/elles devaient**	

Perfect tense

pouvoir	*devoir*	*falloir*
j'ai pu	**j'ai dû**	
tu as pu	**tu as dû**	
il/elle a pu	**il/elle a dû**	**il a fallu**
nous avons pu	**nous avons dû**	
vous avez pu	**vous avez dû**	
ils/elles ont pu	**ils/elles ont dû**	

Future tense

pouvoir	*devoir*	*falloir*
je pourrai	**je devrai**	
tu pourras	**tu devras**	
il/elle pourra	**il/elle devra**	**il faudra**
nous pourrons	**nous devrons**	
vous pourrez	**vous devrez**	
ils/elles pourront	**ils/elles devront**	

The conditional

pouvoir	*devoir*	*falloir*
je pourrais	**je devrais**	
tu pourrais	**tu devrais**	
il/elle pourrait	**il/elle devrait**	**il faudrait**
nous pourrions	**nous devrions**	
vous pourriez	**vous devriez**	
ils/elles pourraient	**ils/elles devraient**	

The subjunctive

pouvoir	*devoir*	*falloir*
que je puisse	**que je doive**	
que tu puisses	**que tu doives**	
qu'il/qu'elle puisse	**qu'il/qu'elle doive**	**qu'il faille**
que nous puissions	**que nous devions**	
que vous puissiez	**que vous deviez**	
qu'ils/qu'elles puissent	**qu'ils/qu'elles doivent**	

The past subjunctive

pouvoir	*devoir*	*falloir*
que j'aie pu	**que j'aie dû**	
que tu aies pu	**que tu aies dû**	
qu'il/qu'elle ait pu	**qu'il/qu'elle ait dû**	**qu'il ait fallu**
que nous ayions pu	**que nous ayions dû**	
que vous ayiez pu	**que vous ayiez dû**	
qu'ils/qu'elles aient pu	**qu'ils/qu'elles aient dû**	

1

Personal matters

1.1 Titles, greetings and making arrangements

Core vocabulary

Titles

Mr	**monsieur**
Mrs	**madame**
Ms	**mademoiselle**
Miss	**mademoiselle**

Insight

Ladies first! A letter in French will start with **Madame, Monsieur**, to translate as both *Dear Sir/Madam* and *Dear Sirs*.

Greetings

hello/hi	**salut***
good morning	**bonjour**
good afternoon	**bonjour**
good evening	**bonsoir**
good night	**bonne nuit**
goodbye	**au revoir**

Insight

*If you consider yourself to be an adult, as opposed to an adolescent, it is best not to use this except with old friends or colleagues with whom you get on well.

Other greetings

See you later.	**À plus tard.** *(or any of the following three, depending on what you mean exactly)*
See you soon.	**À bientôt.**
See you shortly.	**À tout-à-l'heure.**
See you in a bit.	**À tout-de-suite.**
How are you?	**Comment allez-vous ?** *(formal)*
Very well, thank you.	**Très bien, merci.** *(formal)*
Have a nice/good day!	**Bonne journée !**
Have a good weekend.	**Bon week-end !**
Enjoy the evening.	**Bonne soirée !**
Enjoy your holiday.	**Bonnes vacances !**

Useful phrases

Introductions

May I introduce myself? I am Henry Field.	**Permettez-moi de me présenter : Henry Field.**
This is my wife/husband partner (personal) assisant partner (professional)	**Voici ma femme/mon mari ma compagne/mon compagnon mon assistant(e)/ mon associé(e)/...**
Do you know Mr ...?	**Vous connaissez sûrement Monsieur ...**
I am Mrs ...	**Je suis Madame ...**
And you are Mr ...?	**Et vous êtes Monsieur ... ?**
Pleased to meet you.	**Enchanté(e)**
May I sit here?	**Cette place est libre ?** *or* **Ce siège est occupé ?** *(lit. 'is this seat free/taken?')*
Are you alone?	**Vous êtes venu(e) seul(e) ?**

Useful verbs

to introduce	*présenter*
to introduce oneself	*se présenter*
to allow	*permettre*
allow me to ...	*permettez-moi de ...*

Extras

- **À plus!** the trendy, shortened version of **à plus tard** (*see you later*). Very informal, hence: handle with care!
- In the south of France, which shares borders with Spain and Italy, you may hear **adieu** rather than **au revoir**, which derives from the Spanish **adiós**.

Making arrangements *prendre rendez-vous*

bar	**le bar**
night club	**une boîte de nuit**

Insight

Although rather informal, the expression **une boîte** has almost completely replaced **la discothèque**. To say *We went to a club last night*, you might say **On est allé (danser) dans une boîte**, or **On est sorti en boîte.**

restaurant	**le restaurant**
theatre	**le théâtre**
cinema	**le cinéma**
dance	**une soirée dansante/un bal**
drink	**un verre**
pre-dinner drinks	**l'apéritif**
meal	**un repas**
show	**un spectacle**
play	**une pièce de théâtre**
musical	**un music-hall**
comedy	**une comédie**
concert	**un concert**
May I invite you to a drink?	**Je vous offre un verre ?**
What shall we do this evening?	**Qu'est-ce qu'on fait ce soir ?**
What would you like to do?	**Qu'est-ce que vous avez envie de faire ?**
Where would you like to go?	**Où aimeriez-vous aller ?**
When shall we meet?	**On se retrouve à quelle heure ?**
Should we meet for drinks before dinner?	**On se retrouve pour l'apéritif ?**

I will pick you up.	**Je passerai vous prendre** *or* **vous chercher.**
to arrange a meeting	**se donner rendez-vous**
to book a table	**réserver une table**
to go to the cinema	**aller au cinéma**
to go to the theatre	**aller au théâtre**
to go out	**sortir**
to go to a night club	**aller en boîte**
to watch a video/a DVD	**regarder une cassette (vidéo)/ un DVD**
I enjoyed it very much.	**Ça m'a beaucoup plu.**
I had a lovely time.	**J'ai passé un moment/une soirée/ une journée délicieux(-se).**
We must do it again sometime.	**On refera ça.**
I will see you tomorrow.	**À demain !**
I would like to see you again.	**J'aimerais beaucoup vous revoir.**

Polite phrases ***expressions de politesse***

Thank you very much.	**Merci beaucoup** *or* **Merci infiniment** *or* **Merci mille fois.**
Excuse me.	**Excusez-moi.**
Pardon?	**Pardon ?**
I don't understand.	**Je ne comprends pas.**
I did not quite understand.	**Je n'ai pas bien compris.**
Can you speak more slowly?	**Est-ce que vous pourriez parler un peu plus lentement ?**
I apologize.	**Pardonnez-moi** *or* **Je suis désolé(e),** *or* **excusez-moi.**
I'm sorry.	**Je suis désolé(e).**
I beg your pardon?	**Pardon ?**
I didn't mean it.	**Je suis désolé(e), je ne l'ai pas fait exprès.**
Forgive me.	**Pardonnez-moi.**
Sorry, it was my fault.	**Je suis désolé(e), c'est de ma faute** *or* **C'est entièrement de ma faute.**

Insight

Je suis désolé(e) ! can be used, as the French say, **à toutes les sauces** (literally: 'in every sauce'). Use it to extend your apologies at the start of the sentence to try and attract at once the sympathy of your interlocutor(s). Thus : **Je suis désolé(e), je ne parle pas très bien français.** Or **Je suis désolé(e), je ne vous avais pas vu(e)** ; or **Je suis vraiment désolé(e), mon avion avait deux heures de retard** , etc.

It is your fault.	**C'est de votre faute.**
With pleasure.	**Avec plaisir.**
It was a pleasure.	**Ce fut un plaisir.**

Insight

Note the use of the past historic tense **fut**, which emphasizes the formality.

Amusez-vous bien !	**Have a good time!**
Bon voyage !	**Have a safe journey!**
Bonne chance !	**Good luck!**

Insight

The literal translation of 'good luck' is **bonne chance.** However, it is considered to bring bad luck if you actually say it! To wish someone good luck in French, you say **Merde !**

All the best	**Bonne continuation** *or* **Mille bonnes choses** *(the latter for someone you know well, someone close)*
Happy birthday	**Joyeux anniversaire**
Merry Christmas	**Joyeux Noël**
Congratulations	**Félicitations**
Happy New Year	**Bonne année**

1.2 Where are you from?

Core vocabulary

Where do you come from?	**D'où venez-vous ?**

Insight

venir de + noun means to come from a place: **Je viens de Paris**, *I come from Paris* or **Je viens du Sénégal**, *I come from Senegal.*

Incidentally, the phrase 'I see where you are coming from' in French would be **Je vois ce que vous voulez dire.**

Which nationality are you?	**De quelle nationalité êtes-vous ?**
Which language do you speak?	**Quelle langue parlez-vous ?**

European Union Member States (2003)	*Pays membres de l'Union européenne (2003)*	*Nationality*	*Language spoken*
Greece	La Grèce	grec/grecque	grec
Portugal	Le Portugal	portugais/-se	portugais
Spain	L'Espagne	espagnol/-e	espagnol
Italy	L'italie	italien/-ne	italien
France	La France	français/-e	français
Luxembourg	Le Luxembourg	luxembourgeois/-e	le patois luxembourgeois
Ireland	L'Irlande	irlandais/-e	anglais/gaëlique
United Kingdom	Le Royaume Uni	britannique	anglais/ gaëlique (Écosse)/gallois (Pays de Galles)
Belgium	La Belgique	belge	français/ flamand
Netherlands	Les Pays-bas	néerlandais/-e	néerlandais

European Union Member States (2003)	*Pays membres de l'Union européenne (2003)*	*Nationality*	*Language spoken*
Germany	L'Allemagne	allemand/-e	allemand
Denmark	Le Danemark	danois/-e	danois
Austria	L'Autriche	autrichien/-ne	allemand
Sweden	La Suède	suédois/-e	suédois
Finland	La Finlande	finlandais/-e	finnois

European Union as Since 1st May 2004	*Pays de L'Union européenne le 1er mai 2004*		
Estonia	L'Estonie	estonien/-ne	estonien
Latvia	La Lettonie	letton/-ne	letton
Lithuania	La Litaunie	lithuanien/-ne	lithuanien
Poland	La Pologne	polonais/-e	polonais
Czech Republic	La République tchèque	tchèque	tchèque
Slovak Republic	La République slovaque	slovaque	slovaque
Hungary	La Hongrie	hongrois/-e	hongrois
Slovenia	La Slovénie	slovène	slovène
Malta	Malte	maltais/-e	maltais/anglais
Cyprus	Chypre	chypriote	grec/turc
Since 14th and 15th December 2006			
Bulgaria	La Bulgarie	bulgare	bulgare
Romania	La Roumanie	roumain/-e	roumain

Other European Union candidates	*Autres pays candidats à l'Union européenne*		
Turkey	**La Turquie**	turc/turque	turc

(Contd)

a national	**un ressortissant**
passport control point	**le point de contrôle des passeports**
all EU nationals	**ressortissants de l'Union européene**
non-EU nationals	**non-ressortissants de l'Union européenne**

Some European regions	*Quelques régions d'Europe*	*Nationality*	*Language*
Northern Ireland	L'irlande du Nord	irlandais/-e du Nord	anglais
Scotland	L'Écosse	écossais/-e	gaélic écossais
Wales	Le Pays de Galles	gallois/-e	gallois
England	L'Angleterre	anglais/-e	anglais
Channel Islands	Les Îles anglo-normandes	anglais, français, jersiais, guernesiais	
Catalonia	La Catalogne	catalan/e	catalan
Wallonie	La Wallonie	wallon/-ne	wallon
Brittany	La Bretagne	breton/-ne	breton
Alsace	L'Alsace	alsacien/-ne	alsacien
Galicia	La Galice	galicien	galicien
Bavaria	La Bavière	bavarois/e	bavarois
Sicily	La Sicile	sicilien/-ne	sicilien

Middle East	*Le Moyen-Orient*	*Nationality*	*Language*
Israel	Israël	israélien/-ne	arabe/hébreu
Palestine	La Palestine	palestinien/-ne	arabe
Lebanon	Le Liban	libanais/-e	arabe
Jordan	La Jordanie	jordanien/-ne	arabe

Maghreb (petit) et	*Afrique de l'Ouest*	*Nationality*	*Language*
Tunisia	Tunisie	tunisien/-ne	arabe, français
Algeria	Algérie	algérien/-ne	arabe, français, berbère
Morocco	Maroc	marocain/-ne	arabe, français, berbère
Senegal	Sénégal	sénégalais/e	français, langues régionales
Ivory Coast	Côte d'Ivoire	ivoirien/-ne	français, langues régionales
Mali	Mali	malien/-ne	français, langues régionales
Guinea	Guinée	guinéen/-ne	français, langues régionales
Gabon	Gabon	gabonais/e	français, langues régionales

Americas	*Les Amériques*	*Nationality*	*Language*
USA	Les États-Unis	américain/-e	anglais
Lousiana	La Louisiane	louisiannais	louisiannais, cadien, anglais
Canada	Le Canada	canadien/-ne	anglais/français
Quebec	Le Québec	québécois/e	québécois, anglais
Mexico	Le Mexique	mexicain/-e	espagnol
Brasil	Le Brésil	brésilien/-e	portugais
Argentina	L'Argentine	argentin/-e	espagnol
Chile	Le Chili	chilien/-ne	espagnol
Bolivia	La Bolivie	bolivien/-ne	espagnol

South-East Pacific	*Region Pacifique Est*	*Nationality*	*Language*
Australia	L'Australie	australien/-ne	anglais
New Zealand	La Nouvelle Zélande	nouveau zélandais/-e	anglais
Thailand	La Thaïlande	thaïlandais/-e	thaï
Vietnam	Le Viêtnam	vietnamien/-ne	vietnamien
Cambodia	Le Cambodge	cambodgien/-ne	cambodgien

Far East	*L'Extrême-Orient*	*Nationality*	*Language*
Japan	Le Japon	japonais/-e	japonais
China	La Chine	chinois/-e	mandarin
India	L'Inde	indien/-ne	hindi
Pakistan	Le Pakistan	pakistanais/-e	urdû
Hong Kong	Hong-Kong	chinois/-e de Hong-Kong	chinois de Hong-Kong

Useful phrases

Do you speak English?	**Parlez-vous anglais ?**
Where were you born?	**Où êtes-vous né(e) ?**
I was born in …	**Je suis né(e) à** + *city;* **au** + *masculine country;* **en** + *feminine country*
I live …	**Je vis** *or* **j'habite …**
in the north/south/east/west	**dans le nord/le sud/l'est/l'ouest**
in the centre	**dans le centre**
near the sea	**au bord de la mer** *or* **près de la mer**
on the coast	**sur la côte**
in the mountains	**dans la montagne**
in the city	**en ville**
in a village	**dans un village**
in the suburbs	**dans la banlieue de** + *city*
in the country	**à la campagne**

Useful verbs

to live	**vivre/habiter**
to speak	**parler**
to be born	**être né(e)**
to come from	**venir de**

1.3 What do you look like?

Core vocabulary

What do you look like? **À quoi ressemblez-vous ? Comment êtes-vous ?**

What does he/she look like? **À quoi ressemble-t-il/-elle ? Il/elle est comment ?**

Use the following table to help you to build up what you need to describe yourself and someone you know well:

I am	**Je suis**	*quite*	**assez**	*tall*	**grand(e)**
Are you ...?	**Êtes-vous ...?**	*very*	**très**	*small*	**petit(e)**
He/she is	**Il/Elle est**	*rather*	**plutôt**	*average (sized)*	**de taille moyenne**
				slim	**mince**
				comfortable	**enrobé(e)**
				skinny	**maigre/ maigrichon(ne)**
I have	**J'ai**	*long hair*		**les cheveux longs**	
She has	**Elle a**	*short hair*		**les cheveux courts**	
He has	**Il a**	*medium-length hair*		**les cheveux aux épaules**	
		blue eyes		**les yeux bleus**	
		brown eyes		**les yeux bruns**	
		green eyes		**les yeux verts**	
		a small nose		**un petit nez**	
I am ... tall	**Je mesure ...**	*1 metre 75*		**un mètre 75**	

attractive **séduisant(e)**
unattractive **pas particulièrement séduisant(e), quelconque**
fit **sportif/sportive, en grande forme** *(lit. in great shape)*

unfit	**pas sportif/sportive du tout** *or* **pour deux sous**
good looking	**beau/belle;** *also for a girl:* **jolie**
ugly	**laid(e), moche**
neat	**soigné(e)**
untidy	**pas soigné(e), négligé(e)**
smart	**élégant(e), bien habillé(e)**
scruffy	**débraillé(e)**
ordinary	**quelconque**
different	**original**

Size ***la silhouette***

tall	**grand(e)**
short	**petit(e)**
underweight	**maigre, maigrichon(ne)**
slim	**mince**
overweight	**gros(se)**
well built	**bien bâti(e), bien fait**
weak	**fluet(te)**
frail	**frêle**
obese	**obèse**

More about me ***deux ou trois autres choses à propos de moi …***

I am …	**je suis …**
right-handed	**droitier/droitière**
left-handed	**gaucher/gauchère**
short-sighted	**myope**
long-sighted	**astigmate**
I am sight-impaired	**Je vois mal** *or* **j'ai une très mauvaise vue**
I am hearing-impaired	**J'entends mal**
I use a hearing aid	**Je porte un appareil auditif**
I wear glasses	**Je porte des lunettes**
I am allergic to …	**Je suis allergique à …**
I am asthmatic	**J'ai de l'asthme**
I am agoraphobic	**Je suis agoraphobe**
… claustrophobic	**… claustrophobe**

Useful phrases

How much do you weigh?.	**Combien pesez-vous ?**
I weigh 90 kg.	**Je pèse 90 kilos.**
How tall are you?	**Combien mesurez-vous ?**
I am 1.89 m.	**Je mesure 1 mètre 89.**

Useful verbs

to look like someone	**ressembler à quelqu'un**
to put on weight	**grossir** *or* **prendre du poids**
to lose weight	**maigrir** *or* **perdre du poids**
to get fit	**refaire du sport** *or* **se refaire une santé**

Extras

être bien en chair	*plump, well-padded (positive comment)*
être de bonne composition	*to be a happy person*
costaud(e)	*sturdy*
d'un certain âge	*of a certain age*
avoir un petit quelque chose de ...	*to look, somehow, ...*
elle a un petit quelque chose d'Edith Piaf.	*she looks like Edith Piaf, somehow.*

(what comes after **'quelque chose de'** can be very varied.)

les ados	*teenagers (used in teenagers' magazines, or by parents/education personnel)*
le/la môme	*kid (informal)*
les filles	*girls (informal, colloquial)*
les nanas	*girls (very informal)*
les types	*guys (informal, colloquial)*
les mecs	*guys (very informal)*

1.4 What sort of person are you?

Core vocabulary

Character and feelings ***la personalité, les sentiments***

lone	**solitaire**
shy	**timide**
talkative	**sociable**
happy	**heureux/heureuse**
unhappy	**malheureux/malheureuse**
friendly	**aimable, agréable**
unfriendly	**pas très aimable, désagréable**
funny	**drôle**
humourless	**elle/il n'a pas d'humour**

He/she is… can be translated as **Il est/Elle est …**, but also as **C'est quelqu'un de …:**

She is very funny	**Elle est très drôle** *or* **C'est quelqu'un de très drôle**
accommodating	**accommodant**
unaccommodating	**pas très accommodant**
He/She is hard-working	**Il/Elle travaille beaucoup** *(lit. he/she works a lot)*
lazy	**paresseux/paresseuse**
interesting	**intéressant(e)**
boring	**ennuyeux/ennuyeuse** *or* **rasoir** *(informal)*
nice	**sympa** *(short for* **sympathique***)*
nasty	**mauvais(e)**
quiet	**discret/discrète**
loud	**bruyant(e)**
strong	**fort(e)**
weak	**faible**
unbearable	**insupportable**
easy-going	**facile à vivre, pas compliqué, cool** *(informal)*

difficult to get on with	**pas commode**
peculiar	**particulier/particulière**
clever	**fin(e), intelligent(e)**
capable	**capable**
useless	**n'avoir aucun sens de ...**, *or* **n'avoir aucun sens pratique** *or* **n'être d'aucune aide**
to be confident	**avoir confiance en soi**
nervous	**nerveux/nerveuse**
generous	**généreux/généreuse**
mean	**radin(e), pingre**
helpful	**serviable**
unhelpful	**pas serviable, d'aucune aide**
odd	**bizarre, étrange**
normal	**normal, passe-partout**
polite	**poli(e)**
courteous	**courtois(e)**
rude	**grossier/grossière ; mal embouché(e)** *(very informal)*
practical	**avoir l'esprit pratique, avoir le sens pratique**
unpractical	**ne pas avoir l'esprit pratique, n'avoir aucun sens pratique**
reliable	**fiable, sur qui on peut compter** *as in:* **c'est quelqu'un sur qui on peut compter**
unreliable	**pas fiable, sur qui on ne peut pas compter**
relaxed	**décontracté(e)**
uptight	**coincé(e)**
sensitive	**sensible**
unfeeling	**insensible**
serious	**sérieux/sérieuse**
frivolous	**frivole**
sincere	**sincère**
insincere	**pas sincère**
strong willed	**déterminé(e)**

weak	**faible, influençable**
well-behaved	**bien élevé(e)**
badly behaved	**mal élevé(e)**
with it	**dans le coup, au courant**
out-of-date	**dépassé(e)**

The five senses

sight	**la vue**	*to see*	**voir**
hearing	**l'ouïe**	*to hear*	**entendre**
taste	**le goût**	*to taste*	**goûter**
smell	**l'odorat**	*to smell*	**sentir**
touch	**le toucher**	*to touch*	**toucher**

Useful phrases

He/She has ...	**Il/Elle a ...**
a sense of humour	**le sens de l'humour, de l'humour**
plenty of will power	**une grande volonté**
a weakness for	**un petit faible pour**, *or* **une certaine faiblesse pour**
a good imagination	**de l'imagination**
a kind heart	**un bon cœur**

Useful verbs

to get bored	**s'ennuyer**
to be interested in something	**s'intéresser à, être intéressé(e) par (quelque chose m'intéresse)**
to be worried about something	**s'inquiéter**

Insight

The following are so-called 'false friends' – **de faux amis** : **sensible** – *sensitive*; **raisonnable** – *sensible*; **sympathique** – *nice, pleasant*; **compréhensif** – *sympathetic.*

1.5 My things

Core vocabulary

My things *mes trucs* (informal)

my bag	**mon sac**
my handbag	**mon sac à main**
my briefcase	**ma serviette**, *or* **mon cartable**
my cheque book	**mon carnet de chèques**
my credit card	**ma carte de crédit**
my bank card	**ma carte bancaire**
my diary	**mon agenda**
my driving licence	**mon permis de conduire**
my glasses/sunglasses/ reading glasses	**mes lunettes/mes lunettes de soleil/mes lunettes pour lire**
my keys	**mes clefs**
my notebook	**mon carnet**
my passport	**mon passeport**
my ID card	**ma carte d'identité**
my pen/my fountain pen	**mon stylo/mon stylo-plume**
my purse	**mon sac à main**
my wallet	**mon porte-monnaie/mon portefeuille**
my watch	**ma montre**

On my desk/on my working table *sur mon bureau/sur mon plan de travail*

my computer	**mon ordinateur** *or* **mon micro**
my hard drive	**mon disque dur**
my mobile	**mon portable**
my mouse	**ma souris**
my laptop	**mon ordinateur portable**
my USB storage device/ pen drive/flash drive	**ma clé USB**
my organizer	**mon organisateur**
my phone	**mon téléphone**

my mobile phone	**mon portable**
my printer	**mon imprimante**
my scanner	**mon scanner**

Insight

As IT has been developed mostly in English, computing equipment, software and applications are usually – not always – called by their original, English name... with a French accent; e.g. *my iPhone* will be **mon iPhone** – pronounced 'mon-nee-foan'.

At home *chez moi*

my DVD player	**mon lecteur DVD** *(pronounced* **dévédé** *– see above Insight)*
my CD player	**mon lecteur de CD** *(pronounced* **cédé***)*
my discs	**mes disques**
my playstation	**ma playstation,** *or* **ma console (de jeux vidéo)**
my camera	**mon appareil-photo**
my video camera	**ma caméra**
my digital camera	**mon appareil-photo numérique**
my film	**ma pellicule**
my photos	**mes photos**

My friends *mes amis*

girl friends	**mes amies** *(very close)* **; mes copines** *(more informal and not as close – BUT:* **ma grande copine** *refers to a close, long-standing friend!)*
boy friends	**mes amis** *(very close)* ; **mes copains** *(more informal and not as close)* **mes potes** *(informal)*
girlfriend	**ma (petite) copine** *(adolescent and adult)* ; **ma petite amie** *(young adult)* ; **ma compagne** *or* **mon amie** *(adult in a long-standing relationship)*
boyfriend	**mon (petit) copain** *(adolescent)* ; **mon petit ami** *(young adult)* ; **mon compagnon** *or* **mon ami** *(adult in a long-standing relationship)*
best friend	**ma meilleure amie, mon meilleur ami**

Useful phrases

Have you got a ...?	**Avez-vous un/une ... ?**
I have lost my ...	**J'ai perdu mon/ma ...**
I can't find my ...	**Je ne retrouve plus mon/ma ...**
Have you seen my ...?	**Avez-vous vu mon/ma ... ?**

Useful verbs

to forget	**oublier**
to lose/mislay	**perdre, égarer**
to find	**trouver**
to find something that one had lost	**retrouver**

Extras – slang

my work	**mon boulot**
I go to work by tram	**Je vais au boulot en tramway**
I have got a hell of a lot of work at the moment!	**J'ai un boulot monstre en ce moment !**
my car	**ma bagnole**
I drive to work	**Je vais au boulot en bagnole**
depending on the context can be 'my PC', or 'my bike' (motor)	**ma bécane**
My PC froze	**J'ai planté ma bécane**
I had an accident with my motorbike	**Je me suis planté en bécane**

1.6 I think, I feel

Core vocabulary

liking; to like	**l'appréciation/l'affection ; apprécier/ bien aimer**
love; to love	**l'amour ; aimer**

preference; to prefer	**la préférence ; préférer**
dislike; to dislike	**l'aversion ; ne pas aimer**
hate; to hate	**la haine ; haïr/détester**
feeling; to feel	**le sentiment/la sensation ; ressentir**
worry; to worry	**l'inquiétude ; s'inquiéter**
encouragement; to encourage	**les encouragements ; encourager**
exaggeration; to exaggerate	**l'exagération ; exagérer**
joke; to joke	**la plaisanterie ; plaisanter**
lie; to lie	**le mensonge ; mentir**
promise; to promise	**la promesse ; promettre**
advice; to advise	**le conseil ; conseiller**
belief; to believe	**la croyance ; croire**
thought; to think	**la pensée ; penser**
reflection: to think about, to reflect on	**la réflexion ; réfléchir**
realization; to realize	**la réalisation** ; *but:* **s'apercevoir**

Useful verbs

Negative experiences	*Positive experiences*
to be disappointed	**être déçu(e)**
to be relieved	**être soulagé(e)**
to be depressed	**être déprimé(e)**
to be elated	**être ravi(e)**
to be stressed	**être stressé(e)**
to be relaxed	**être détendu(e)**
to be discouraged	**être découragé(e)**
to be encouraged	**être encouragé(e)**
to be embarrassed	**être gêné(e)**
to be at ease	**être à l'aise**
to be nervous	**être nerveux/nerveuse**
to be reassured	**être rassuré(e)**
to be sad	**être triste**
to be happy	**être content(e)/ heureux/heureuse**
to be frightened	**avoir peure**
to be ashamed	**être gêné(e)**

Negative experiences	*Positive experiences*
to be proud	**être fier/fière**
to be worried	**être inquiet(e)**

The following verbs are used with another verb:

to want to	**vouloir**
I want to go	**Je veux partir**
to be able to	**pouvoir/être capable de**
to be in a position to	**être en mesure de**
I can understand	**Je suis capable de comprendre/ Je peux comprendre**
to have to	**devoir/avoir à/il faut que +** *subjunctive*
I must leave	**Je dois partir/Il faut que je parte**
to be allowed to	**pouvoir**
I am allowed to go out	**Je peux sortir** *(Note: one of the many meanings of* **pouvoir = avoir le droit de***)*
I ought to	**Je devrais**
I should stay at home	**Je devrais rester à la maison**

1.7 Expressing an opinion

Core vocabulary

to believe	**croire**

'To believe' is followed by the subjunctive only when used in the negative form. For example, **Je crois qu'il est déjà arrivé** but **Je ne crois pas qu'il soit déjà arrivé.**

to consider	**considérer**
to think	**penser**
to agree	**être d'accord**
to argue	**penser**
to ask	**demander**

to question	**questionner**
to quote	**citer**
quote … unquote	**Je cite : …**
to request	**demander**
to suggest	**proposer/suggérer**
to wonder	**se demander**
still, I would like to say	**J'aimerais quand même dire …**
to consider	**estimer, considérer**
to compare	**comparer**
to discuss	**discuter de**
to dispute	**contester**
to conclude	**conclure**
to reach the conclusion	**arriver à la conclusion**
on the one hand	**d'un côté/d'une part**
on the other hand	**de l'autre/d'autre part**
firstly	**premièrement**
secondly	**deuxièmement**
thirdly	**troisièmement**
first	**d'abord**
then	**ensuite**
and then	**et ensuite** *or* **et puis**
finally	**enfin**
actually	**en fait**
basically	**en fait**
clearly	**de toute évidence** *or* **il est clair que**
consequently	**en conséquence** *or* **par conséquent** *or*… **et c'est comme ça que …**
essentially, mostly	**essentiellement, en grande partie**
fortunately	**heureusement**
unfortunately	**malheureusement**
generally	**en général, de manière générale**
honestly	**honnêtement**
mainly	**principalement**
normally	**d'habitude** *or* **normalement**
obviously	**de toute évidence** *or* **il est évident que**

particularly	**particulièrement, notamment**
principally	**principalement**
really/truly/genuinely	**véritablement**
usually	**habituellement** *or* **d'habitude** *or* **normalement**
in my opinion	**d'après moi …** *or* **à mon avis …***or* **à mon sens**

*(You may equally say '***Moi, je …***', stressing the '***moi***' before going onto your argument.)*

above all	**par-dessus tout**
although	**bien que**
as a result	**par conséquent**
as well as	**aussi bien que**
however	**cependant** *or* **toutefois** *or* **néanmoins**
in many respects	**à bien des égards**
in spite of	**malgré**
instead of	**au lieu de**
nevertheless	**pourtant**
otherwise	**sinon**
similarly	**de la même façon**
the reason is	**la raison est que …**
to tell the truth	**pour être tout-à-fait franc (franche)**
I wish I could agree	**J'aimerais pouvoir vous donner raison** *or* **j'aimerais pouvoir être d'accord avec vous**
I beg to differ	**Permettez-moi de ne pas être d'accord**
I maintain …	**Je persiste à penser que …**
for example	**par exemple** *or* **ainsi**
in brief	**en bref**
the advantages are	**l'avantage, c'est que**
the disadvantages	**l'inconvénient, c'est que**
there are pros and cons	**il y a du pour et du contre**
to conclude	**pour finir** *or* **en conclusion**

1.8 Don't panic!

Help!	**Au secours !**
Listen	**Écoute/Écoutez**
Do you understand?	**Vous comprenez ?** *or* **Tu comprends ?**
Do you speak English?	**Vous parlez anglais ?**
Can you say it more slowly?	**Est-ce que vous pourriez répéter plus lentement, s'il-vous-plaît ?**
I didn't catch what you said	**Je suis désolé(e), je n'ai pas compris ce que vous avez dit**
Please can you find someone who speaks English?	**Pourriez-vous penser à quelqu'un qui parle anglais ?**
Can you write it down for me please?	**Est-ce que vous pourriez me l'écrire ?**
How do you spell it?	**Comment est-ce que ça s'écrit ?**
Have you got the phone number for ...?	**Est-ce que vous avez le numéro de téléphone ... ?**
police	**de la police**
fire brigade	**des pompiers**
ambulance and ermergency services	**du SAMU – service d'aide médicale urgente**
doctor	**d'un médecin**
breakdown services	**d'un dépanneur**
What do I need to dial first?	**Est-ce qu'il y a un indicatif ?**
What is the area code for ...?	**Quel est l'indicatif de ... ?**
How do I get an outside line?	**Comment est-ce que je fais pour avoir une ligne extérieure ?**

TEST YOURSELF

À vous !

A mini stock-taking exercise on the unit you have just worked on

1 'Have a good time' in French is...
- **a** Enjoyiez-vous bien !
- **b** Ayez un bon temps !
- **c** Amusez-vous bien !

2 'May I introduce my partner Emily' (the person you are with in life, as opposed to professionally) is...
- **a** Puis-je introduire ma partenaire, Emily ?
- **b** Permettez-moi de vous présenter ma partenaire, Emily.
- **c** Permettez-moi de vous présenter ma compagne, Emily.

3 How could you say 'Do you speak English?' in French? *[note: several correct answers]*
- **a** Parlez-vous anglais ?
- **b** Excusez-moi : parlez-vous anglais ?
- **c** Parlez-moi anglais, ou ?
- **d** Est-ce que vous parlez anglais ?
- **e** Vous parlez anglais, peut-être ?

4 'Pleased to meet you' in French is...
- **a** Plaisamment surpris(e) de vous rencontrer !
- **b** Enchanté(e).
- **c** Avec plaisir !

5 'Happy birthday!' in French is...
- **a** Joyeux jour de naissance !
- **b** Heureux jour de Grâce !
- **c** Bon anniversaire !

6 The five senses in French are:
- **a** L'o...
- **b** La v...

c Le t.......
d Le g........
e L'o..........

7 The most common way to say 'I am sorry' in French is...
- **a** Je suis infiniment contrit(e).
- **b** Je suis désolé(e).
- **c** Je suis impardonnable.

8 'My mobile phone' in French is...
[note: several correct answers]
- **a** mon téléphone portable.
- **b** mon mobile.
- **c** mon portable.
- **d** mon mobile portable.
- **e** ma téléphonie portable.

9 'How do you spell it?' in French is...
[note: several correct answers]
- **a** Vous écrivez ça comment ?
- **b** Comment ça s'écrit ?
- **c** Comment ça s'épelle ?
- **d** Vous épellerez comment ?
- **e** Ça s'épelle comment ?

10 Please give three words ending in *–tion*, starting respectively with....
- **a** c
- **b** r
- **c** u

Answers: 1 c; 2 c; 3 a b d e; 4 b; 5 c; 6 l'ouïe; la vue; le toucher; le goûter; l'odorat; 7 b; 8 a b c; 9 a b c e; 10 starting with c: la création, la civilisation, la corruption, la citation etc.; starting with r: la réalisation, la rotation, la réception, la ratification, etc.; starting with u: l'union, l'usurpation, l'unification, l'utilisation, etc.

2

Family

2.1 My family

Core vocabulary

My family and relatives *les membres de ma famille*

my parents	**mes parents**		
my mother	**ma mère**	*my father*	**mon père**
my sister	**ma sœur**	*my brother*	**mon frère**
my half-sister	**ma demi-sœur**	*my half-brother*	**mon demi-frère**
my twin sister	**ma sœur jumelle**	*my twin brother*	**mon frère jumeau**
my grandparents	**mes grands-parents**		
my grandmother	**ma grand-mère**	*my grandfather*	**mon grand-père**
my aunt	**ma tante**	*my uncle*	**mon oncle**
my cousin (f)	**ma cousine**	*my cousin (m)*	**mon cousin**
my great-grand parents	**mes arrière-grands-parents**		
my godmother	**ma marraine**	*my godfather*	**mon parrain**
my wife	**ma femme, mon épouse**	*my husband*	**mon mari, mon époux**
my partner	**ma conjointe, ma compagne**	*my partner*	**mon conjoint, mon compagnon**
my girlfriend	**mon amie**	*my boyfriend*	**mon ami**
my mother-in-law	**ma belle-mère**	*my father-in-law*	**mon beau-père**
my sister-in-law	**ma belle-sœur**	*my brother-in-law*	**mon beau-frère**

my younger sister	**ma petite sœur**	*my younger brother*	**mon petit frère**
my older sister	**ma grande sœur, ma sœur aînée**	*my older brother*	**mon grand frère, mon frère aîné**
my granddaughter	**ma petite-fille**	*my grandson*	**mon petit-fils**
my grandchildren	**mes petits-enfants**		
my niece	**ma nièce**	*my nephew*	**mon neveu**
my goddaughter	**ma filleule**	*my godson*	**mon filleul**
a married couple	**un couple marié**		
a widow	**une veuve**	*a widower*	**un veuf**

Useful phrases

May I introduce my ...	**Permettez-moi de vous présenter ...**
Pleased to meet you	**Enchanté(e)**
I am sorry to hear about your separation/divorce/ bereavement	**J'ai été désolé(e)/peiné(e) d'apprendre que vous vous étiez séparés/que vous aviez divorcé/que vous aviez perdu votre .... mère/père/mari/femme ...**
I am going out with ...	**Je sors avec ...** *(informal)*
We are just good friends ...	**Nous sommes amis, c'est tout.**

Useful verbs

to go out with someone	**sortir avec quelqu'un**
to like someone	**bien aimer quelqu'un**
to flirt	**flirter**
to kiss	**embrasser**
to kiss one another hello/goodbye	**se faire la bise**
to kiss someone hello/goodbye	**faire la bise à quelqu'un** *or* **embrasser**

Insight

At school in France, you have to allow sufficient time in your morning routine to kiss everyone – classmates you get on well with, friends – before classes start. Depending on the region and/or on how close you are to people and/or your personal/family tradition, you may kiss people two, three or four times on the cheek: **faire la bise, deux bises, trois bises, quatre bises** !

As an adult, if you meet or are introduced informally to someone you don't know, the person may say: « **Allez, on s'embrasse** », or « **Allez, on se fait la bise !** » Be prepared. Note also that **se faire la bise** does not mean anything romantic, nor does it carry any hidden message that the person you are kissing is hinting at the fact that they like you specifically.

to get on with someone	**bien s'entendre avec quelqu'un**
to have a good time	**bien s'amuser**
to have sex with someone	**coucher avec quelqu'un**
to make love with/to someone	**faire l'amour avec/à quelqu'un**
to get married	**se marier**
to go into a civil partnership	**se pacser** *(Note: from* **PACS, pacte civil de solidarité***)*

Insight

France's civil partnership has been created for two adults: those who are not directly related; those of the same or opposite sex; those who wish to live together.

to get on one's nerves	**énerver quelqu'un**
to get on each other's nerves	**se taper sur les nerfs** *(very informal)*
to look after someone	**s'occuper de**
to quarrel	**se disputer**
to squabble	**se chamailler**
to separate	**se séparer**
to divorce	**divorcer**
to file for divorce	**demander le divorce**

Extras

Pet names ***les petits noms***

Pour quelqu'un qu'on aime :	*For a loved one:*
mon chou	*my cabbage*

mon chat	*my cat*
mon trésor	*my treasure*
ma biche	*my doe*
chéri(e)	*darling*
mon cœur, mon doux cœur	*sweetheart*
Pour un enfant :	***For a child:***
mon canard	*my duck*
mon bout d'chou	*my piece of cabbage*
mon p'tit chou	*my little cabbage*
ma puce	*my flea*
mon puceron	*my greenfly*
chouchou	*cabbage-cabbage (Note:* **le chouchou** *is the teacher's pet, or the boss's pet)*

2.2 Children

Core vocabulary

a baby	**un bébé**
an infant	**un bébé** *or* **un enfant en bas âge**
a toddler	**un tout-petit**
a child	**un enfant**
a boy	**un garçon**
a girl	**une fille**
a twin	**un jumeau, une jumelle**
twins	**les jumeaux, les jumelles**
a teenager	**un adolescent, un/une ado** *(informal)*
an adolescent	**un adolescent**
pregnancy	**la grossesse**
a miscarriage	**une fausse couche**
a delivery	**un accouchement**
birth	**la naissance**
a newborn baby	**un nouveau-né**

a premature baby	**un prématuré**
nanny	**la nourrice**
babysitter	**la/le babysitter**
midwife	**la sage-femme**
obstetrician	**le médecin-accoucheur, l'obstétricien (-ne)**
crèche	**la crèche**
playschool	**l'école maternelle**
baby's bottle	**le biberon**
teat	**la tétine**
dummy	**la suce**
bib	**le bavoir**
baby milk	**le lait pour bébé**
high chair	**une chaise haute, une chaise pour bébé**
nappy	**la couche**
travel cot	**un couffin**
cot	**un berceau**
lullaby	**une berceuse**
pram	**un landau**
pushchair	**une poussette**
toy	**un jouet**
colic	**la colique**
an only child	**un enfant unique**
an adopted child	**un enfant adopté**
an orphan	**un orphelin, une orpheline**
children's playground	**une aire de jeux (pour enfants)**
swing	**la balançoire**
slide	**le toboggan**
roundabout	**le manège**
climbing frame	**la cage à écureuils**

Useful verbs

to expect a baby	**attendre un bébé**
to miscarry	**faire une fausse couche**
to break one's waters	**perdre les eaux**
to give birth	**accoucher**

to give birth early	**accoucher en avance**
to breastfeed	**donner le sein, allaiter**
to burp	**roter**
to change a nappy	**changer une couche, changer +** *name of baby, or* **+ bébé**

Insight

In a moment of despair and slight post-natal depression after having had twins, for example, you may hear yourself saying: **« Je ne suis plus bonne qu'à changer des couches ! »**

to cry	**pleurer**
to feed	**donner à manger**
to give a bottle	**donner un biberon**
to rock	**bercer**
to teethe	**faire ses dents**
to look after	**s'occuper de**
to childmind	**garder (des enfants)**
to babysit	**faire du babysitting**

Useful phrases

I am pregnant	**Je suis enceinte** *or* **J'attends un enfant**
It's a boy/girl	**C'est un garçon/une fille**
sibling rivalry	**la rivalité entre frères et sœurs**
a spoilt child	**un enfant gâté**
I need ...	**Il me faudrait ...**
a cream for a sore bottom	**une crème pour des petites fesses irritées**
sun cream/shampoo for children	**du lait solaire/du shampoing pour enfants**
something for wind/teething	**quelque chose pour la colique/pour ses dents**

2.3 Anniversaries, marriage and death

Core vocabulary

birthday	**l'anniversaire**
engagement	**les fiançailles**
marriage	**le mariage**
anniversary	**l'anniversaire**
death	**la mort, le décès**
a wedding	**un mariage**
wedding ceremony	**la cérémonie du mariage**
church, temple, synagogue, mosque	**l'église, le temple, la synagogue, la mosquée**
wedding service	**la célébration du mariage**
town hall	**l'hôtel de ville** *(larger cities) or* **la mairie**
engagement ring	**la bague de fiançailles**
wedding invitation	**une invitation à un mariage**
wedding day	**le jour du mariage**
wedding dress	**la robe de mariée**
wedding ring	**l'alliance**
wedding certificate	**le certificat de mariage**
wedding cake	**le gâteau de mariage, la pièce montée**

Insight

Une pièce montée (literally: *a mounted up piece*) is also translated as *tiered cake*, but the classic 'pièce montée' does not have tiers – it is a cone-shaped and artistic assembly of **choux** (small hollow balls of dough, the same dough used for profiteroles), filled with **crème pâtissière**, stuck together with caramel, decorated with caramel threads – **cheveux d'ange** – and other delicacies, such as **dragées, violettes** and **baisers.**

bride	**la mariée**
bridegroom	**le marié**

bridesmaid	**la demoiselle d'honneur**
best man	**le témoin**
honeymoon	**la lune de miel**
married life	**la vie de couple**
heterosexual	**hétérosexuel**
homosexual	**homosexuel**
bisexual	**bi-sexuel** – *informal:* **bi** *pronounce 'bee'*
lesbian	**lesbienne**
gay	**homo** *or* **gay**
a funeral	**un enterrement**
corpse	**le cadavre**
coffin	**le cercueil**
cemetery	**le cimetière**
burial	**l'enterrement**
cremation	**la crémation** *or* **l'incinération**

Insight

Usually, the noun **crémation** is used, and the verb **incinérer**. You may want to say: **« Moi, je me ferai incinérer »**. Or, in your will: **« Je souhaite être enterré(e) près de Tante Dora. »**

grave	**la tombe**
vault	**le caveau**
death duties	**les droits de succession**
death certificate	**le certificat de décès**
will	**le testament**

Useful verbs

to get engaged	**se fiancer**
to get married	**se marier**
to die	**mourir**
to pass away	**décéder**
to be buried	**être enterré**
to be cremated	**être incinéré**
to be in mourning	**être en deuil**
to kill oneself	**se suicider**

Useful phrases

Congratulations!	**Félicitations !**
Happy birthday!	**Joyeux anniversaire !**
We would like to wish you every future happiness.	**Nous vous souhaitons tout le bonheur possible.**
We would like to send you our best wishes.	**Nous vous adressons nos vœux les meilleurs.**
We entered into a civil partnership last summer.	**Nous nous sommes pacsés l'été dernier.**
I would like to convey my condolences.	**Acceptez, je vous prie, mes plus sincères condoléances.**
I am very sorry to learn of your sad loss.	**J'ai été peiné(e) d'apprendre que votre (mère/père etc.) nous a quittés.**

TEST YOURSELF

À vous !

A mini stock-taking exercise on the unit you have just worked on

1 'To change nappies' in French is…
[*note: more than one answer possible*]
- **a** Changer les couches
- **b** Changer le bébé
- **c** Changer les couchés

2 'Honeymoon' in French is…
- **a** lune de miel
- **b** miel de lune
- **c** miel en lune

3 How could you say 'to have sex with someone' in French?
- **a** se sexuer avec quelqu'un
- **b** avoir sexe avec quelqu'un
- **c** coucher avec quelqu'un

4 'Congratulations' in French is…
- **a** Congratulations !
- **b** Félicitations !
- **c** Gratulations !

5 'My godson' in French is…
- **a** mon filleul
- **b** mon fils de Dieu
- **c** mon filleur

6 'To kiss someone hello, or goodbye' in French may be
[*note: more than one answer possible*]
- **a** s'embrasser
- **b** s'embrassouiller
- **c** se biser

d se faire la bise
e se faire des bisous

7 The professional person who assists the birth, in French, is... [*note: more than one answer possible*]
a le sage-homme
b la sage-femme
c l'accoucheur
d l'obstétricien

8 'The slide', in a children's play-area, in French is...
a la serpentine
b le toboggan
c le colimaçon

9 'We would like to send you our best wishes' in French may be... [*note: several correct answers*]
a Nous vous adressons nos vœux les meilleurs.
b Nous vous adressons nos vœux souhaités.
c Nous aimerions vous envoyer nos meilleurs.
d Nous voulons vous souhaiter nos vœux.
e Nous vous adressons nos meilleurs vœux.

10 Une pièce montée is ....
a a spare part for wedding ceremonies
b a piece of cake
c a high, cone-shape classic cake for weddings and similar festive occasions

Answers: 1 a b; 2 a; 3 c; 4 b; 5 a; 6 a d; 7 b c d; 8 b; 9 a e; 10 c

3

Work

3.1 Job titles

Core vocabulary

I am a ...	**Je suis ...**
I work as a...	**Je travaille comme ...**

Insight

In French, there is no article before the name of your occupation: **Je suis danseuse classique.** *I am a ballet dancer.* **Je travaille comme assistante maternelle.** *I work as a classroom assistant in a nursery school.* **Je suis comptable.** *I am an accountant.* (Note: **expert-comptable** = *chartered accountant*)

actor/actress	**l'acteur/l'actrice**
apprentice	**l'apprenti(e)** + *name of the trade*
architect	**l'architecte** *(m. and f.)*
bricklayer	**le maçon** *(m. and f.)*
businessman/woman	**l'homme/la femme d'affaires**
chef	**le cuisinier/la cuisinière**
civil servant	**le/la fonctionnaire**
dentist	**le/la dentiste**
director (film, theatre)	**le metteur en scène** *(m. and f.)*
doctor	**le médecin** *(m. and f.)*

driver (bus)	**le conducteur/la conductrice de bus**
driver (train)	**le mécanicien/la mécanicienne**
driver (taxi)	**le chauffeur de taxi** *(m. and f.)*
driver (lorry)	**le chauffeur de poids-lourd** *(m. and f.) or* **le camionneur** *or* **le routier**
electrician	**l'électricien/l'électricienne**
engineer	**l'ingénieur** *(m. and f.)*
farmer	**l'agriculteur/l'agricultrice**
financier	**le financier**

Insight

Un financier is also an oblong cake, made from almonds and beaten egg white, that you buy from a pâtisserie.

fireman	**le pompier** *(m. and f.)*
hairdresser	**le coiffeur/la coiffeuse**
journalist	**le/la journaliste**
lawyer	**le/la juriste** *or* **l'avocat/l'avocate**
lecturer	**le/la professeur**
professor	**le/la professeur**
mechanic	**le mécanicien/la mécanicienne**
musician	**le musicien/la musicienne**
nurse	**l'infirmier/l'infirmière**
plumber	**le plombier** *(m. and f.)*
policeman	**l'agent de police** *(m. and f.),* **l'officier de police**
postman	**le facteur/la factrice**
receptionist	**le/la réceptionniste**
researcher	**le chercheur/la chercheuse**
secretary	**le/la secrétaire**
shop assistant	**le vendeur/la vendeuse**
shopkeeper	**le gérant/la gérante d'un magasin/d'une boutique**
sole trader	**travailleur indépendant,** *or* **prestataire indépendant**
student	**l'étudiant(e)**
waiter/waitress	**le serveur/la serveuse**

undertaker	**l'entrepreneur/l'entrepreneuse de pompes funèbres**
unemployed person	**le chômeur/la chômeuse**
retired	**retraité(e)**
pensioner	**le retraité/-e**
the staff	**le personnel** *or* **les personnels**
chairman	**le président/la présidente**
chief executive	**le directeur/la directrice**
managing director	**le président-directeur général, le/la PDG**
director	**l'administrateur/l'administratrice**
company secretary	**le/la secrétaire**
departmental head	**le/la chef de département** *or* **le/la chef de service**

Insight

The head or manager of a company department is often called **responsable** or **chargé**, e.g. Head of PR: **Chargé des relations publiques (RP)**

auditor	**l'auditeur/l'auditrice** *or* **contrôleur financier** *(the feminine does not really work, here)*

Insight

Note: you may say **« Je suis contrôleur financier »** or **« Je fais de l'audit »**. While you would refer to 'the auditors' in English, the French will often, though not always, refer to the **« cabinet d'audit »**.

business consultant	**le consultant/la consultante** *or* **le conseiller/la conseillère**
personal assistant	**l'assistant personnel/l'assistante personnelle**
employer	**l'employeur/l'employeuse**
employee	**l'employé(e)**
sales representative	**le représentant/la représentante de commerce**
computer operator	**l'opérateur/l'opératrice informatique**
computer programmer	**l'informaticien/informaticienne**

cleaner	**l'homme/la femme de ménage** *(personal/ home)* ; **agent de surface,** *or* **agent d'entretien** *(company)*
trainee	**le/la stagiaire**

Insight

Stagiaire may refer to a paid, qualifying junior professional – e.g. trainee lawyer – as well as to an unpaid school pupil on a work experience placement.

Industries ***Secteurs***

agriculture	**l'agriculture**
banking	**la banque**
building trade, construction	**l'industrie du bâtiment/le BTP –** *pronounce* **bétépé** *– for* **bâtiments et travaux publics**
catering	**la restauration**
civil service	**la fonction publique**
commerce	**le commerce, les affaires**
fashion	**la mode**
finance	**la finance**
the hotel industry	**l'industrie hôtelière**
insurance	**les assurances**
ITC (information technology and communications)	**TIC (technologies de l'information et de la communication)**
leisure services	**l'industrie des loisirs**
manufacturing	**la fabrication**
medicine	**la médecine**
health services	**les services de santé**
the media	**les médias**
retail	**la vente**
service industry	**l'industrie des services**
show business	**le show business**
textile industry	**l'industrie textile**
tourism	**le tourisme**
transport	**les transports**
logistics	**la logistique**
wholesale	**la vente en gros**

Useful verbs

to work	**travailler** *or* **bosser** *(informal)*
to earn one's living	**gagner sa vie**
to earn a decent, a comfortable living	**bien gagner sa vie**
to be self-employed, to work for oneself	**être/travailler à son compte, être indépendant**
to be out of work	**être sans emploi**
to buy/to sell	**acheter/vendre**
to import/export	**importer/exporter**
to manage	**gérer, diriger**
to manufacture	**fabriquer**

Useful phrases

I would like to work in …	**J'aimerais travailler dans …**
I work in …	**Je travaille dans …**
I used to work in …	**Avant, je travaillais dans …**
This is my second career (already)	**J'en suis (déjà) à ma seconde carrière**

Extras

The following are all words derived from *employ*:

employment	**l'emploi, un emploi** *or* **embauche** *(f)* – *as in employment conditions* **conditions d'embauche**
unemployment	**le chômage**
employer	**l'employeur/l'employeuse**
employee	**l'employé(e)**
to employ	**employer**
employed	**employé(e)**
unemployed	**au chômage**
an unemployed person	**un chômeur/une chômeuse**
employable	**employable**
unemployable	**inemployable**
employability	**l'employabilité**

3.2 The work place

Core vocabulary

bank	**une banque**
building site	**un chantier**
factory	**une usine**
farm	**une ferme/une exploitation agricole**
garage	**un garage**
hospital	**un hôpital**
hotel	**un hôtel**
mine	**une mine**
nightclub	**une boîte de nuit**
nursery	**une crèche**
office	**un bureau**
post office	**un bureau de poste**
railway	**les chemins de fer**
recording studio	**un studio d'enregistrement**
restaurant, bar, café	**un restaurant/un bar/un café**
school	**une école**
service station	**une station-service**
shopping centre	**un centre commercial**
slaughter house	**un abattoir**
stock exchange	**la Bourse**
town hall	**une mairie**
workshop	**un atelier**

The company *la société*

headquarters	**le siège**
subsidiary	**la filiale**
firm	**le cabinet** *or* **l'agence**
factory	**l'usine**
branch	**l'agence** *or* **la succursale**

The premises *les locaux*

boardroom	**la salle du conseil**
canteen	**la cantine** *or* **le restaurant d'entreprise**

Insight

France being a country where eating – and eating well in good company – is a very important dimension of life, if you work for a French company, your employment contract will often provide for **« tickets restaurant »**, also called **« chèques repas »** or **« chèques déjeuner »**. These are vouchers of a certain value, negotiated under collective bargaining arrangements.

meeting room	**la salle de réunion**
reception	**la réception** *or* **l'accueil**
entrance	**l'entrée**
entrance hall	**le hall d'entrée**
exit	**la sortie**
security code	**le code de sécurité**
pass	**le passe**
staff ID card	**le badge**
I work in the ... department	**Je travaille dans le service ...**
accounts	**comptabilité**
advertising	**publicité**
administration	**administratif**
after-sales	**après-vente**
catering	**restauration**
distribution	**distribution**
export	**export**
import	**import**
facilities management	**maintenance**
information technology	**informatique**
insurance	**assurance**
legal	**juridique**
manufacturing	**fabrication**
production	**production**
marketing	**marketing**
personnel/human resources	**ressources humaines**

property	**immobilier**
purchasing	**des achats**
sales	**des ventes**
technical	**technique**

Useful verbs

to buy	**acheter**
to manage	**diriger** *or* **gérer**
to manufacture, to produce	**fabriquer, produire**
to research	**faire des recherches (sur)**
to sell	**vendre**
to study	**étudier**
to travel	**voyager** *or* **se déplacer**
to work	**travailller** *or* **bosser** *(informal)*

Useful phrases

Where do you work?	**Vous travaillez où ?**
Which department do you work in?	**Dans quel service travaillez-vous ?**
Our head office is based in …	**Notre siège est installé à …/en …**
Please sit down.	**Asseyez-vous, je vous en prie.**
Can I get you a coffee?	**Voulez-vous un café ?**
Would you like to meet …?	**Aimeriez-vous rencontrer** *or* **faire la connaissance de … ?**

3.3 Conditions of employment

Core vocabulary

working conditions	**les conditions de travail**
the working day	**la journée de travail**
the working week	**la semaine de travail**
holidays	**les vacances**
paid holidays	**les congés**

annual holiday	**les congés annuels**
national holidays	**les jours fériés**
pay	**la paie**
salary	**le salaire**
income	**le revenu**
tax return	**la déclaration d'impôts**
tax relief	**le dégrèvement d'impôt**
income tax	**l'impôt sur le revenu**
VAT	**la TVA, Taxe de Valeur Ajoutée**
applicant	**le candidat**
application	**la candidature**
application form	**le formulaire de candidature**
curriculum vitae, CV	**le curriculum vitae, le CV** *(pronounced cévé)*

Insight

CV, from the Latin curriculum vitae, 'course of life', or 'path of life', means the same in English and French; the difference is in the pronounciation as is the case for all Latin words and phrases directly imported into one's language: it can lead to amusing situations.

contract	**le contrat**
job interview	**un entretien d'embauche**
full-time job	**un travail à plein temps**
part-time job	**un travail à temps partiel**
office hours	**les heures de bureau**
overtime	**les heures supplémentaires**
flexitime	**le temps à la carte** *or* **le temps convenu**
coffee break	**la pause café**
lunch-time	**la pause déjeuner** *or* **l'heure du déjeuner**
meeting	**la réunion**
leave	**le congé**
unpaid leave	**le congé sans solde**
sick leave	**le congé-maladie**
sick note	**le certificat de maladie**
compassionate leave	**le congé pour raisons personnelles**
dismissal	**le licenciement**

redundancy	**le licenciement**
redundancy compensation payment	**une indemnité de licenciement**
union	**le syndicat**
union meeting	**la réunion syndicale**
strike	**la grève**
strikers	**les grévistes**
demands	**les revendications syndicales**
bankruptcy	**la faillite**
standard of living	**le niveau de vie**
unemployment rate	**le taux de chômage**
legal minimum wage	**le SMIC, Salaire minimal indexé sur la croissance**

Useful phrases

It is stressful	**C'est stressant**
stimulating	**stimulant**
motivating	**motivant**
exciting	**passionnant**
He/She is very …	**Il/Elle est très …**
efficient	**efficace**
organized	**organisé/e**
disorganized	**désorganisé/e** *or* **bordélique** *(very informal)*
lazy	**paresseux/paresseuse**
hard working	**travaille beaucoup**

Useful verbs

to be behind with one's work	**être en retard dans,** *or* **sur, mon boulot**
to be snowed under	**être sous l'eau** *(colloquial) – literally, 'under water'*
to catch up	**ratrapper**
to be ahead	**être en avance**
to have a deadline	**avoir un délai**
to respect the deadline	**respecter les délais, être dans les délais**

to be overworked	**être débordé** *or* **être charette** *(informal, used mostly by freelancers)*
to panic	**stresser**
to be stressed	**être stressé**

Extras

le gérant, la gérante	*shop/property manager*
gérer	*to manage*
la gestion	*management process, for any application/ discipline*
le/la gestionnaire	*manager*

3.4 Writing a business letter and using the phone

Core vocabulary

Ways to start the letter

Dear Sir	**Monsieur,** *or* **Cher monsieur,**
Dear Madam	**Madame,** *or* **Chère madame,**
Dear Mr. Smith	**Monsieur,**
Dear Mrs. Smith	**Madame,**
Dear Sir/Madam	**Madame, Monsieur,**
Dear Sirs	**Madame, Monsieur,**

Ways to end the letter

We/I look forward to hearing from you in the near future.

En espérant vous lire prochainement, + link to one of the following:

Please do not hesitate to contact us/me if you require any further information.

Nous nous tenons/Je me tiens à votre entière disposition pour toute information complémentaire.

Yours sincerely/Yours faithfully

Nous vous prions/Je vous prie d'agréer, Madame, Monsieur, l'assurance de mes sentiments distingués.

or

Nous vous prions/Je vous prie d'accepter, Madame, l'expression de mes sentiments distingués.

or

Nous vous prions/Je vous prie d'agréer, Monsieur, l'assurance de ma considération distinguée.

or

Nous vous prions/Je vous prie d'agréer, Madame, Monsieur, l'assurance de mes sentiments respectueux.

or

Recevez, Chère Madame, mes sentiments les plus dévoués. (Only used by a man to a woman.)

Using the telephone

telephone	**le téléphone**
phone jack	**la prise téléphone**
fax	**le fax** *or* **la télécopie**
answerphone	**le répondeur**
the tone	**le bip sonore**
receiver	**le combiné**
extension	**le poste**
mobile	**le téléphone portable**
battery	**la batterie**
voicemail	**la messagerie**
telephone number	**le numéro de téléphone**
directory	**l'annuaire**

directory inquiries — **les renseignements (téléphoniques)**
local call — **un appel local**
long distance call — **un appel longue distance**
international call — **un appel international**

Useful verbs

to phone — **téléphoner**
to call — **appeler**
to call back — **rappeler**
to divert a call — **transférer un appel**
to put someone through — **passer quelqu'un à quelqu'un**
to look up a number — **chercher un numéro de téléphone**
to put on hold — **faire patienter** *or* **mettre en attente**

Useful phrases

Could I speak to ...? — **Pourrais-je parler à ... ?**
Can I have extension ... please? — **J'aurais voulu le poste ..., s'il-vous-plaît.**
Can I have someone who deals with ...? — **J'aimerais parler à quelqu'un qui s'occupe de ..., s'il-vous-plaît.**
I would like to speak to ... the Head of Sales — **Je cherche à joindre .... le directeur des ventes**
I would have liked to speak to ... Mrs Delarue — **Je cherchais à joindre ... Madame Delarue**
Who is calling? — **C'est de la part de qui ?**
Can you tell me what it is about? — **C'est à quel sujet ?**
Who would you like to speak to? — **A qui aimeriez-vous/voulez-vous parler ?**
Speaking! [name yourself and add]: — **à l'appareil !**
Can you wait a moment? — **Je vous fais patienter un instant.** *or* **Patientez un instant, je vous prie.**
I am putting you through. — **Je vous le/la passe.**
The line is engaged/busy. — **La ligne est occupée.**
Do you want to hold? — **Voulez-vous patienter ?**
Would you like to leave a message? — **Désirez-vous laisser un message ?**

Can I take your name and number?	**Voulez-vous laisser vos coordonnées ?**
I haven't got a signal.	**Je n'ai pas de signal.**
My battery is running low.	**Je n'ai bientôt plus de batterie.**
Can you ring back?	**Pourriez-vous rappeler, s'il-vous-plaît ?**
Can you text me?	**Pourriez-vous m'envoyer un texto ?** *or* **un MSM**

3.5 Using the computer

Core vocabulary

computer	**l'ordinateur** *or* **le PC** *or* **le micro**
keyboard	**le clavier**
mouse	**la souris**
touch pad	**le touch pad** *(pronounced with a French accent!) or* **la souris au clavier**
microphone	**le micro**
speakers	**les enceintes (une enceinte)**
tower	**la tour**
home hub	**la box**
modem	**le modem**
router	**le routeur**
connector	**une connexion**
hard drive	**le disque dur**
a pen drive, a flash drive	**une clé USB**
drive	**un lecteur**
screen	**un écran**
digital screen	**un écran tactile**
monitor	**un écran**
screen saver	**un économiseur d'écran** *or* **un écran de veille**
laptop	**un ordinateur portable**
printer	**une imprimante**
cartridge	**une cartouche**

paper ream	**une rame de papier**
scanner	**un scanner**
email	**un email** *or* **un mèl** *or* **un courriel**
attachment	**une pièce jointe** – *abbreviated: 'pj'*

Insight

Pièce jointe – *attachment* – may be abbreviated as 'pj' when corresponding with French-speaking colleagues or friends by email, e.g.« **Comme convenu, veuillez trouver en pj le document à faire signer par l'ingénieur-conseil** » *Please find attached as agreed the document to be signed by the consultant engineer.*

world-wide-web/net	**l'Internet** *or* **le Web** *or* **la Toile**
login name	**un identifiant**
user name	**nom d'utilisateur**
code	**le code**
password	**le mot de passe**
backup	**une sauvegarde**
programme	**un programme**
software programme	**un logiciel**
hardware	**un matériel**

Useful verbs

switch on	**allumer**
type in	**saisir** *or* **informer**
log on	**se connecter**
log off	**se déconnecter**
save	**sauvegarder**
go on line	**se connecter**
send an email	**envoyer un mèl**
receive mail	**recevoir un mèl**
download, or upload a file	**télécharger un fichier**
attach a file	**joindre un fichier**
recharge the battery	**recharger la batterie** *or* **mettre la batterie à charger**

Useful phrases

Have you got a ...?	**Auriez-vous un/une ... ?**
Where can I plug my laptop in?	**Où est-ce que je peux brancher mon ordinateur portable ?**
My computer isn't working.	**Mon ordinateur ne marche pas.**
Is there any one who can help me?	**Est-ce que quelqu'un pourrait m'aider ?**
My computer froze	**Mon ordinateur a planté**

TEST YOURSELF

À vous !

A mini stock-taking exercise on the unit you have just worked on

1 How would you say 'Head of Human Resources' in French? [*note: more than one answer possible*]
   a Responsable des Ressources Humaines
   b Responsable des Ressources Humaines
   c Directeur des RH

2 'Undertaker' in French is…
   a le sous-traitant
   b le sous-preneur
   c l'entrepreneur

3 'Unemployed' in French is…
   a l'inemployé/e
   b le chômeur/la chômeuse
   c l'inemployable

4 How would you say in French 'I used to work in…'
   a J'ai eu l'habitude de travailler dans …
   b Avant, j'avais l'habitude de travailler dans …
   c Avant, je travaillais dans …

5 'Accounting department' in French is… [*note: more than one answer possible*]
   a le département comptable
   b le service de la comptabilité
   c la comptabilité
   d le service comptable

6 'Stock exchange' in French is…
   a l'échange des stocks
   b le stock échangé

c la Bourse
d la Bourse des stocks

7 'Yours sincerely/Yours faithfully' may be in French...
[*note: more than one answer possible*]
a Je vous prie d'agréer, Madame, Monsieur, l'expression de mes sentiments respectueux.
b Je vous prie d'agréer, Madame, Monsieur, l'expression de mes meilleurs sentiments.
c Nous vous prions d'agréer, Madame, Monsieur, l'expression de nos salutations distinguées.
d Recevez, Chère Madame, mes sentiments les plus dévoués.
e Je vous prie, Madame, Monsieur, des salutations respectueuses.

8 'I'll put you through to Mrs Hortefeux' *(on the telephone)* in French is...
a Je vous fais passer à Madame Hortefeux
b Je vous passe à travers Madame Hortefeux
c Je vous passe Madame Hortefeux

9 'A pen drive/flash drive' in French is...
a un lecteur pen
b une clé Flash
c une clé USB
d un lecteur USB

10 'An email' in French may be ...
[*note: more than one answer possible*]
a un email
b un courriel
c un mèl

Answers: 1 a b c; 2 c; 3 b; 4 c; 5 b c d; 6 c; 7 a b c d; 8 c; 9 c; 10 a b c

4

Education

4.1 Primary and secondary education

The different schools

Please note that the table below is not an exhaustive panorama of the French education system, but rather a view of the mainstream schooling path, followed by 70 per cent of young people in education. It is, in 95 per cent of cases, a publicly funded, secular, mixed system. Jules Ferry (1832–1893), a lawyer and politician, is the founder of the modern school system in France – based on three principles – compulsory (until the age of 16); free (non fee-paying); secular. This is why a number of schools are called after him, e.g. 'Groupe scolaire Jules Ferry'.

la crèche	3 months to 2 yrs	Not a school in the strict sense; rather a 'socialization' stage. Publicly funded, available throughout France.
la maternelle	from 2 to 5 yrs	Divides into three sections: **la petite section** or **section des petits, la moyenne section la section des moyens, la grande section la section des grands**

l'école primaire	from 6 to 10 yrs	Divided into 5 classes, **CP – cours préparatoire; CE1 – cours élémentaire 1ère année; CE2 – cours élémentaire 2ème année; CM1 – cours moyen 1ère année; CM2 – cours moyen 2ème année**. Teaching staff is equally composed of men and women, the formed called **l'instituteur**, the latter **l'institutrice.**

Insight

L'instituteur and **l'institutrice** are the formal designations but at the **maternelle**, or **l'école primaire**, children would usually call them **maîtresse** and **maître.** E.g. « **Maîtresse ! J'ai oublié mon cahier à la maison !** »

CES collège d'enseignement secondaire, usually referred to as 'le collége'	from 11 to 14 yrs At the end of four years, one takes the BEPC **(Brevet des Collèges)**	Divided into four years, known as **la sixième, la cinquième, la quatrième, la troisième**. Some collèges offer boarding facilities, known as **'l'internat'**. It tends to disappear at lycée stage, where adolescents may find a room in a family home.
le lycée … classique or technique	from 15 to 18 yrs At the end of the three years, one takes the **baccalauréat**	Usually favoured by those who intend to go to university or higher education afterwards.

(Contd)

	examination, consisting of 7 compulsory subjects plus a number of chosen subjects.	
le lycée ... d'enseignement professionnel	from 15 to 17 yrs At the end of three years, one may take a **CAP – certificat d'aptitude professionnelle** From 17 to 18/19 yrs: an additional 1 or 2 years towards a BEP **(Brevet d'enseigement Professionnel)**	Most of France's traditional trades are still taught this way, usually on a sandwich course or apprenticeship basis, for example, **pâtissier, boucher, boulanger, ébéniste, plombier, cuisinier, etc.**

Core vocabulary

At primary school *à l'école primaire*

headmaster/mistress	**le directeur/la directrice**
teacher	**le maître, la maîtresse, l'instituteur, l'institutrice**
teacher's pet	**le chouchou** – *as in* **le chouchou de la maîtresse**
pupil	**l'élève**
school nurse	**l'infirmière**
playground	**la cour de récréation**
covered playground	**le préau**
satchel	**le cartable**
pen case	**la trousse**
(school) canteen	**la cantine (scolaire)**
black/white board	**le tableau**
chalk	**la craie**
marker	**le marqueur**
break	**la récréation** (*usually referred to as* **la récré**)
bell	**la cloche** *or* **la sonnerie**
term	**le trimestre**

Insight

La semaine de quatre jours – The four-day week: Monday, Tuesday, Thursday, Friday – is currently the subject of much controversy in France's primary school system. Before, the school days were Monday, Tuesday, Thursday, Friday and Wednesday or Saturday morning. Since the rationalization of the 'semaine de quatre jours', in September 2009, education experts and psychologists indicate that it is being pushed through at the expense of the children, who have to spend four, heavy and very long days at school – among the longest in Europe.

holidays	**les vacances**
summer holidays	**les grandes vacances**
school bus service	**le ramassage scolaire**

Insight

Le ramassage scolaire means, literally, the 'school picking', from **ramasser** – *to pick, to harvest*; you may come across it in agriculture, e.g. **le ramassage des noix, le ramassage des pommes de terre.**

lesson	**la leçon**
homework	**les leçons**
reading	**la lecture**
reciting	**la récitation**
writing	**l'écriture**
arithmetic	**le calcul**
dictation	**la dictée**
colouring	**le coloriage**
cutting	**le découpage**
geography	**la géographie**
history	**l'histoire**
nature study/science	**l'observation, la leçon de choses, les sciences naturelles**
manual activities, crafts	**les activités manuelles**

At secondary school *à l'école secondaire*

headmaster	**le/proviseur la** *or* **madame le proviseur**
deputy head	**le censeur/madame le censeur**
secondary teacher	**le professeur**
pupil	**l'élève ; le collégien** *(attending the collège)* **le lycéen** *(attending the lycée)*
prefect	**le/la délégué(e) de classe**
school secretary	**le/la secrétaire**
school caretaker	**le/la concierge** *or* **l'intendant(e)**
class	**le cours**
break	**la récréation** *or* **la pause**
lunch-time	**l'heure du déjeuner** *or* **la pause de midi**
the bell	**la cloche** *or* **la sonnerie**
the end of lessons	**la fin des cours**
term	**le trimestre**
holidays	**les vacances**
summer holiday	**les grandes vacances**
timetable	**un emploi du temps**

Insight

A typical week in a secondary school in France would be distributed over four or five days. During the first four years: Monday, Tuesday, Thursday, Friday from 8 am to 12 noon and 2 pm to 5 pm, and either Wednesday or Saturday from 8 am to 12 noon. During the final three years: Monday, Tuesday, Thursday, Friday from 8 am to 12 noon and from 2 pm to 5 pm, and Wednesday and Saturday from 8 am to 12 noon, but in some cases all day Wednesday.

school period	**une heure de cours**
school subject	**la matière**
Art	**le dessin**
Biology	**la biologie** (**biolo** *in pupil slang)*
Chemistry	**la chimie**
Civics	**l'instruction civique**

English	**l'anglais**
French	**le français**
Geography	**la géographie**
German	**l'allemand**
History	**l'histoire**
Technical drawing (TD)	**le dessin industriel** *(dess'duss' in pupil slang)*
Information technology	**l'informatique**
Italian	**l'italien**
Maths	**les mathématiques** *(usually referred to as* **les maths***)*
Music	**la musique**
Philosophy	**la philosophie**
P.E.	**l'E.P. (éducation physique)**
Physics	**la physique**
Natural Science	**les sciences naturelles** *(sciences nat' in pupil slang)*
Life Sciences	**les sciences de la terre et de la vie** *(see* **biologie***)*
Russian	**le russe**
Spanish	**l'espagnol**
Technology	**la technologie**
building	**le bâtiment**
classroom	**la salle de classe**
corridor	**le couloir**
science lab	**le laboratoire scientifique** *(usually referred to as* **le labo***)*
gym	**le gymnase**
changing rooms	**les vestiaires**
lockers	**les casiers**
games pitch	**le terrain de sport**
music room	**la salle de musique**
library	**la bibliothèque**
computer room	**la salle d'informatique** *or* **la salle des ordinateurs**
toilets	**les toilettes**
assembly hall	**le hall**
desk	**le bureau**

black/white board	**le tableau**
projector	**le projecteur**
overhead-projector	**le rétroprojecteur**
computer	**l'ordinateur**
book	**le livre**
exercise book	**le cahier**
pen	**le crayon**
pencil	**le crayon à papier**
biro	**le stylo-bille**
fountain pen	**le stylo-plume**
felt-tip pen	**le stylo-feutre** (*short:* **le feutre**)
homework	**les devoirs**
written assignment (at home)	**le devoir à la maison**
written test	**le devoir sur table** *(longer – 3–4 hours) or* **l'interrogation écrite,** *usually referred to as* **l'interro écrite** *(short – ½ or 1 hour)*
oral test	**une colle**
eraser	**la gomme**
calculator	**la calculette**
ruler	**la règle**
report	**le rapport**
school report	**le carnet scolaire** *or* **le carnet de notes**
school bag	**le sac de classe**
sports kit	**le sac de gym/de sport** *or* **les affaires de gym/de sport**

Useful verbs

to recite	**réciter**
to read	**lire**
to speak/to talk	**parler**
to listen	**écouter**
to discuss	**discuter**
to write	**écrire**
to copy	**copier**

to take notes	**prendre des notes**
to be quiet	**se calmer**
to learn by heart	**apprendre par cœur**
to do one's homework	**faire ses devoirs** *(secondary school)* ; **apprendre sa/ses leçon(s)** *(primary school)*
to get a good/bad mark	**avoir une bonne/mauvaise note**
to sit an exam	**passer un examen**
to pass an exam	**réussir un examen**
to fail an exam	**échouer à un examen**
to re-sit	**repasser**

4.2 Further and higher education

Insight

School is compulsory up to 16. After that, you may go to university (usually at 18), enrol as an apprentice for training in a trade, go to specialist schools in areas such as fashion design, architecture, art, music, or start as a junior with an employer.

France also has an élite further education system called **Les Grandes écoles**, originally founded by Napoleon I, essentially for engineering, but also for politics, chemistry, public administration, social sciences...

Core vocabulary

college/technical college	**IUT, un Institut universitaire de technologie**
university	**l'université**
faculty	**la faculté**
lecture	**le cours magistral (CM)**
seminar/tutorial	**les TD, les travaux dirigés**
professor/lecturer	**le/la professeur** *(usually referred to as* **le/la prof***)*
student	**l'étudiant(e)**

research student	**le thésard (*from* la thèse, thesis)**
graduate	**un(e) jeune diplômé(e)**
undergraduate	**un(e) étudiant(e) de premier *ou* second cycle**
apprentice	**l'apprenti(e)**
trainee	**le stagiaire**
examination	**l'examen**
curriculum	**le curriculum**
level	**le niveau**
mark	**les notes**
grade	**l'année**
research	**la recherche**
paper (research paper)	**un papier**
a report	**un rapport**
a training/work experience report	**un rapport de stage**
essay	**une dissertation**
dissertation	**un mémoire**
thesis	**une thèse**

Insight

The recent LMD (Licence, Master, Doctorate) Reform in the European Union aims at harmonizing and streamlining the higher education courses of all Member States of the European Union, encouraging student mobility within the EU and further afield, facilitating cross-border and cross-discipline higher studies and qualifications. It is based on a semester and credit approach and does away with endless PhD-level research which, in some countries, could take up to 10 years!

Useful verbs

to present a paper	**présenter un papier**
to do a sandwich course	**suivre une formation en alternance**
to study part-time	**faire des études à mi-temps**
to attend an evening class	**prendre/suivre des cours du soir**
to do work experience	**faire un stage**
to correct	**corriger**

to explain	**expliquer**
to learn	**apprendre**
to qualify	**passer (avec succès) un examen de qualification professionnelle**
to register/enrol	**s'inscrire**
to study	**faire des études**
to teach	**enseigner**
to translate	**traduire**
to understand	**comprendre**
to do research	**faire des recherches, faire une recherche**

Les faux amis *False friends*

passer un examen	*to sit an exam*
réussir un examen	*to pass an exam*
le/la candidat/e	*applicant*
le concours	*competition exam*
la scolarité	*schooling*
un stage	*work experience, or professional/vocational training*
un cours	*a class*
des cours	*a course*

TEST YOURSELF

À vous !

A mini stock-taking exercise on the unit you have just worked on

1 In a school context, how would you say 'primary school teacher' in French…
[*note: more than one answer possible*]

- **a** la maîtresse
- **b** le maître
- **c** l'instituteur
- **d** l'institutrice

2 'School bus service' in French is…

- **a** le service scolaire
- **b** le service de bus de l'école
- **c** le ramassage scolaire

3 The subject 'biology' in French may be…
[*note: more than one answer possible*]

- **a** la biologie
- **b** la science naturelle
- **c** les sciences naturelles

4 How would you say in French 'Miss! I left my notebook at home!'?

- **a** Mademoiselle ! J'ai oublié mon livre de notes chez moi !
- **b** Maîtresse, j'ai oublié mon carnet de notes chez moi !
- **c** Maîtresse, j'ai oublié mon cahier chez moi !

5 Find five different words for 'pen' in French

- **a**
- **b**
- **c**
- **d**
- **e**

6 'To sit an exam' in French is...

a passer un examen
b asseoir un examen
c s'asseoir à un examen

7 How would you say to 'attend an evening class' in French? [*note: more than one answer possible*]

a assister à une classe du soir
b prendre des cours du soir
c prendre une classe le soir

8 **Un stage** in French is...

a a stage
b a level
c work experience/professional training

9 LMD – in LMD Reform – stands for...

a langues-maîtres-diplômes
b laboratoire-maîtrise-discipline
c licence-mastère doctorat

10 **La lecture** in French is...

a lecture
b reading
c lecture reading

Answers: 1 a b c d; 2 c; 3 a c; 4 c; 5 le crayon, le crayon à papier, le stylo-bille, le stylo-feutre, le stylo-plume; 6 a; 7 b; 8 c; 9 c; 10 b

5

At home

5.1 The house

Core vocabulary

house	**la maison**
at home	**chez soi**

Insight

To talk about your home, you may use either **à la maison** or **chez moi/chez nous**. There are subtle differences: I will use **à la maison** if the person I am speaking to also lives in that house, or comes from that house (such as older siblings). The expression **à la maison** is usually applied to a house where at least two people live together.

apartment/flat	**un appartement**
level	**le niveau**
studio	**le studio**
block of flats	**un immeuble**
the building	**le bâtiment**
floor/storey	**l'étage**
ground floor	**le rez-de-chaussée**
first floor	**le premier étage**
second floor	**le deuxième étage**
basement	**le sous-sol**

cellar	**la cave**
attic	**le grenier**
stairs	**l'escalier**
lift	**l'ascenseur**
garage	**le garage**
cottage	**une maison individuelle**
farm	**une ferme**
chalet	**un chalet**
villa	**une villa**
council flat/house	**un logement HLM (Habitation à Loyer Modéré)**
social housing	**un logement social/le logement social** *(as a sub-industry)*
semi-detached house	**une maison jumelle**
terrace house	**une maison en rangée**
central heating	**le chauffage central**
solar heating	**le chauffage solaire**
double glazing	**le double-vitrage**
double windows	**le double-fenêtrage**
gas	**le gaz**
electricity	**l'électricité**
oil	**le fuel** *or* **le mazout**
oil tank	**la fosse à mazout**
water	**l'eau**
telephone	**le téléphone**
mains sewerage	**le tout-à-l'égout**
septic tank	**la fosse septique**
sound proofing	**l'insonorisation**
insulation (heat, sound…)	**l'isolation (thermique, acoustique ...)**
shutter	**le volet**
roller shutter	**le store**
blind	**le store**
Venetian blind	**le store vénitien**
sliding shutter	**le volet roulant**
burglar alarm	**l'alarme antivol**
fire alarm	**l'alarme incendie**
outside	**dehors**

balcony	**le balcon**
roof	**le toit**
slate	**une ardoise**
roof tile	**une tuile**
terrace	**la terrasse**
conservatory	**le jardin d'hiver** *or* **la véranda**
garden	**le jardin**
backyard	**la cour**
gate	**la barrière**
path	**une allée**
lawn	**la pelouse**
flower bed	**la plate-bande**
vegetable garden	**le potager**
greenhouse	**la serre**
situation	**l'exposition**
view	**la vue**
stone	**la pierre**
brick	**la brique**
timber	**le bois**
concrete	**le ciment**
the main walls/framework of a building	**le gros œuvre**

Useful verbs

to buy	**acheter**
to sell	**vendre**
to put on the market	**mettre en vente**
to let	**louer**
to rent	**louer**
to advertise	**passer une annonce**
to view (a house)	**visiter**
to show (a house, a property)	**faire visiter**
to make an appointment	**prendre rendez-vous**
to lock up	**fermer à chef**
to move (house)	**déménager**
to move in	**emménager**

Useful phrases

the house overlooks the bay	**la maison donne sur la baie**
a central position	**une situation centrale**
close to all services	**à proximité du centre/des magasins**
in the town centre	**dans le centre-ville**
in a residential area	**dans un quartier résidentiel**
in the suburbs	**dans la banlieue**
in the country	**dans la campagne**
by the sea	**au bord de la mer**

5.2 Rooms

Core vocabulary

room	**la pièce**
entrance	**l'entrée** *or* **le vestibule**
kitchen	**la cuisine**
open-plan kitchen	**la cuisine américaine**

Insight

The concept of an open-plan kitchen – **une cuisine américaine** – is widespread in France, in particular in new apartments and flats. In self-contained houses you are more likely to find the traditional kitchen model – **la cuisine traditionnelle** or **la cuisine à l'ancienne** – where the various pieces of furniture and fittings don't necessarily go together and are not interior decoration/design-based.

dining room	**la salle à manger**
sitting room	**la salle de séjour** *or* **le living ...** *a direct import!*
drawing room	**le salon**
bedroom	**la chamber**

the dressing-room	**le dressing**
play room	**la salle de jeux**
bathroom	**la salle de bain**
shower room	**la salle d'eau** *or* **la salle de douche**
cloakroom	**la penderie**
toilet	**les toilettes**
study	**le bureau**
hall	**le hall** *or* **l'entrée**
landing	**le palier**
mezzanine	**la mezzanine**
stairs	**l'escalier**
step	**une marche**
utility room	**la buanderie**
junk room	**le débarras**
pantry	**la dépense**
window	**la fenêtre**
window sill	**le rebord de la fenêtre**
French window	**la porte-fenêtre**
radiator	**le radiateur**
floor	**le sol**
ceiling	**le plafond**
door	**la porte**
wall	**le mur**
partition wall	**la cloison**
central heating	**le chauffage central**
boiler	**la chaudière**
water heater	**le ballon d'eau chaude**
lock	**le verrou**
key	**la clef**
plug	**le bouchon de la bonde**

Insight

In current usage, although inappropriate, the single word **bonde** will be used to refer to **le bouchon de la bonde. La bonde**, strictly speaking, refers to the metal grill part fitted at the entrance of a drain, usually by a central screw.

socket	**la prise**
switch	**l'interrupteur**
handle	**la poignée**
door knob	**le bouton de porte**
fuse box	**la boîte à fusibles**
fuse	**le fusible**
fuse coil	**la bobine du fusible**
torch	**la torche** *or* **la lampe de poche**
power failure	**la panne d'électricité**
curtain	**le rideau**
blind	**le store**
carpet	**le tapis**
fitted carpet	**la moquette**
rug	**le tapis**
tile (floor/wall)	**le carreau**
tiling	**le carrelage**
flooring	**le revêtement de sol**
wallpaper	**le papier peint**
paint	**la peinture**
coating	**l'enduit**
coat	**la couche**
varnish	**le vernis**
paintbrush	**le pinceau**
ladder	**une échelle**
a step-ladder	**un escabeau**

Useful phrases

upstairs	**en haut** *(everyday)* **; à l'étage** *(technical)*
downstairs	**en bas** *or* **au rez-de-chaussée**
on the first floor	**au premier étage**
in the basement	**au sous-sol**
in the attic	**au grenier**
Where is ...?	**Où est ... ?**
How does it work?	**Comment est-ce que ça marche ?**

Useful verbs

to turn on/off	**allumer/éteindre**
to switch on/off	**allumer/éteindre**

5.3 Furniture and contents

Core vocabulary

In the sitting room *dans la salle de séjour*

armchair	**le fauteuil**
easy chair	**le fauteuil**
settee/sofa	**le canapé**
coffee table	**la table basse**
bookcase	**une étagère**
lamp	**une lampe**
picture	**un tableau**
television	**la télévision**
flat screen	**un écran plat**
video recorder	**le magnétoscope**
DVD player	**le lecteur DVD**
remote control	**la commande (à distance)**
Hi-Fi stereo	**une chaîne hi-fi** *(pronounced hee-fee!)*
(loud) speaker	**une enceinte**

In the bedroom *dans la chambre*

bed	**le lit**
bedside table	**la table de chevet**
chair	**la chaise**
wardrobe	**l'armoire**
chest of drawers	**la commode**
mirror	**le miroir**
built-in cupboard	**le placard**
wardrobe (both built-in and free-standing)	**la penderie**

Insight

Wardrobe, when meaning 'a set of clothes belonging to one individual' is **garderobe** – in effect the exact same word: *ward-warden* –> **garde-gardien**; and *robe* –> **robe**. A typical example of two compound words with similar meanings which have evolved differently over the centuries.

shelf	**une étagère**
bedding	**la literie**
pillow/pillow case	**l'oreiller/la taie d'oreiller**
quilt	**la couette**
quilt cover	**la housse de couette**
sheet	**le drap**
fitted sheet	**le drap-housse**

In the bathroom *dans la salle de bain*

bathroom fixtures	**les éléments de salle de bain**
bathtub	**la baignoire**
plug	**la bonde**
mirror	**le miroir**
shelf	**la tablette**
enlarging mirror	**le miroir grossissant**
bidet	**le bidet**
towel stand/rail	**le porte-serviettes**
shower	**la douche**
shower head	**la pomme de douche**
wash basin	**le lavabo**
tap	**le robinet**
hot/cold water tap	**le robinet d'eau chaude/froide**
toilet bowl	**la cuvette des toilettes**
razor	**le rasoir**
tooth brush	**la brosse à dents**
tooth paste	**le dentifrice**
shampoo	**le shampoing**
conditioner	**l'après-shampooing** *or* **le conditionneur**
hairdryer	**le sèche-cheveux**
soap	**le savon**

hand towel	**la serviette pour les mains**
bath towel	**la serviette de bain**
bath sheet	**le drap de bain**
flannel	**le gant de toilette**
deodorant	**le déodorant**

Useful phrases

Where is/are ...?	**Où est/sont ... ?**
It's on the table.	**Il/Elle est sur la table.**
under the bed	**sous le lit**
in the armchair	**sur le fauteuil**
in the cupboard/drawer	**dans le placard/le tiroir**
Can I have a clean...?	**Est-ce que je pourrais avoir un/une/des ... propre(s) ?**
How does the television/ oven work?	**Comment marche la télévision/le four ?**

Useful verbs

to do housework	**faire le ménage**
to wash	**laver**
to wash up	**faire la vaisselle**
to do the laundry	**faire la lessive**

Insight

To do a wash is **faire une lessive,** or **faire une machine;** *to wash dark things* is **faire une machine de foncé,** *to wash light-coloured things*, **faire une machine de clair;** *to wash whites*, **faire une machine de blanc.**

to clean	**nettoyer** *or* **laver**
to clean the windows	**faire les carreaux**
to vacuum	**passer l'aspirateur**
to sweep	**balayer**
to make the beds	**faire les lits**

5.4 In the kitchen

Core vocabulary

table	**la table**
chair	**la chaise**
stool	**le tabouret**
drawer	**le tiroir**
cupboard	**le placard**
shelf	**une étagère**
sink	**l'évier**
refrigerator	**le réfrigérateur**
fridge	**le frigidaire**
oven	**le four**
hot plate	**la plaque**
grill	**le grill**
dishwasher	**le lave-vaisselle**
washing machine	**le lave-linge** (*usually referred to as* **la machine**)
washing-line	**la corde à linge**
clothes-horse	**le séchoir à linge**
tumble drier	**le sèche-linge**
mixer	**le mixeur**
plate	**l'assiette**
soup plate	**l'assiette creuse**
bowl	**le bol**
dish	**le plat**
cup	**la tasse**
saucer	**la soucoupe**
mug	**le mug** *or* **le pot**
jug	**la carafe** *or* **le pichet**
teapot	**la théière**
coffee pot	**la cafetière**
sugar bowl	**le sucrier**
knife	**le couteau**
fork	**la fourchette**
spoon	**la cuillère**

Insight

The contents of **une cuillère** – also spelt **cuiller** – is called **cuillerée.** Remember **jour – journée, soir – soirée, bol – bolée,** etc. (Note: this rule does not apply to **an – année.**) **Cuillerée** will most frequently appear in recipes: **« Ajouter une cuillerée à soupe de sucre, deux cuillerées à café d'extrait de menthe, une généreuse cuillerée à soupe d'anis étoilé… »**, for example.

salt	**le sel**
salt-box, salt mill	**la salière**
pepper	**le poivre**
pepper mill	**le poivrier**
mustard	**la moutarde**
teaspoon	**la cuillère à café**
soup spoon	**la cuillère à soupe**
dessert spoon	**la petite cuillère**
serving spoon	**une cuillère pour servir**
serving spoon and fork	**le couvert de service**
carving knife	**un couteau à découper**
bread knife	**un couteau à pain**
kitchen knife	**un couteau de cuisine**
butter knife	**un couteau à beurre**
glass	**un verre**
wine glass	**un verre à vin**
champagne flute	**une flûte à champagne** *(thin and tall)*
champagne glass	**une coupe à champagne** *(shaped like an open water lily –* **comme un nénuphar***)*

Insight

It is more common to use the term **coupe à champagne** – once filled, **coupe de champagne** – for both **coupe** and **flûte.** Grand cocktail receptions tend to serve champagne in **coupes.** Otherwise, even although you speak of **une coupe à/de champagne**, you will be served champagne in most cases in a flûte. Note: you may also be served a 'baby serving' in some traditional brasseries and cafés, called… **coupette.**

water glass	**un verre à eau**
tumbler	**un gobelet**

Waste *les dechets ménagers*

rubbish	**les ordures**
leftovers	**les restes**
packaging	**un emballage**
plastic bag	**un sac en plastique**
kitchen bin/waste bin	**la poubelle de cuisine/la poubelle à ordures**
bin liner	**le sac-poubelle**
dustbin	**la corbeille à papier**
recycling	**le recyclage**
bottle bank	**le container à verres**
bulk uplift	**l'enlèvement des encombrants**
(domestic) waste collection	**l'enlèvement des ordures (ménagères)**
waste collection site/centre	**la déchetterie**
compost	**le compost**

For cleaning *pour nettoyer*

vacuum cleaner	**l'aspirateur**
broom	**le balai**
duster	**le chiffon**
brush	**la brosse**
brush and dustpan	**la balayette et la pelle**
cleaning materials	**les produits nettoyants**
scrubbing brush	**la brosse à récurer**
floor mop	**le balai laveur**
brush (broom)	**le balai-brosse**
floor cloth	**la serpillère**
detergent	**le détergent**

Useful phrases

I like/dislike cooking.	**J'aime faire/Je n'aime pas faire la cuisine.**
I don't know how to cook.	**Je ne sais pas faire la cuisine.**

I don't cook.	**Je ne fais jamais de cuisine.**
I'll do the washing up/the dishes.	**Je vais faire la vaisselle.**

Useful verbs

Cooking terms *des mots pour faire la cuisine*

mix	**mélanger**
beat	**battre**
roast	**faire rôtir**
toast	**faire griller**
bake	**faire cuire au four**
stir-fry (in a pan)	**faire revenir**
steam	**faire cuire à l'étuvée/à la vapeur**
grill	**faire griller**
barbecue	**faire cuire au barbecue**
peel	**éplucher**
cut	**couper**
slice	**couper en tranches**
chop	**couper en rondelles**

5.5 Outside

Core vocabulary

garage	**le garage**
shed	**un appentis**
footpath	**une allée**
gate	**la barrière**

In the garden *dans le jardin*

flower bed	**la plate-bande**
lawn	**la pelouse**
flower	**la fleur**
plant	**la plante**
bush	**le buisson**
shrub	**un arbuste**

tree	**un arbre**
grass	**l'herbe**
weeds	**les mauvaises herbes**
herbs	**les fines herbes**
bulb	**un oignon** *or* **un bulbe**

Trees *les arbres*

beech	**le bouleau**
chestnut	**le châtaigner**
horse chestnut	**le marronnier**
elm	**un orme**
hazel	**le noisetier**
holly	**le houx**
oak	**le chêne**
plane tree	**le platane**
sycamore	**le sycomore**
willow	**le saule**
weeping willow	**le saule pleureur**

Flowers *les fleurs*

carnation	**l'œillet**
chrysanthemum	**le chrysanthème**

Insight

Le chrysanthème is the only flower that you should not offer as a present in France. It is associated with All Souls' Day, when pots of chrysanthemums will be taken to the cemetery and placed on tombs.

daffodil	**la jonquille**
rose	**la rose**
sweet pea	**le pois de senteur**
tulip	**la tulipe**
red poppy	**le coquelicot**
poppy	**le pavot**
lily of the valley	**le muguet**
water lily	**le nénuphar** *(as in* **Les nénuphars** *by Monet)*

Garden tools ***les outils de jardinage***

fork	**une fourche**
hoe	**une houe**
spud	**la houlette**
rake	**un râteau**
spade	**une pelle** *or* **une bêche**
scraper	**le grattoir**
lawnmower	**la tondeuse**
wheelbarrow	**la brouette**
garden tractor	**le motoculteur**
basket	**le panier**
watering can	**l'arrosoir**
hose	**le tuyau d'arrosage**
sprinkler	**l'arroseur**
weedkiller	**le désherbant**
fertilizer	**le fertilisant**

Insects and pests ***les insectes et les animaux nuisibles***

ant	**la fourmi**
bee	**une abeille**
fly	**la mouche**
greenfly	**le puceron**
horsefly	**le taon**
maybug	**le hanneton**
mosquito	**le moustique**
long leg (non biting) mosquito	**le cousin**
spider	**une araignée**
harvest spider	**le faucheux**
wasp	**la guêpe**

Insight

Une taille de guêpe means *hour-glass figure.*

Garden furniture ***les meubles de jardin***

barbecue	**le barbecue**
table	**la table**
deck chair	**le transat**
lounger	**la chaise longue**

bench	**le banc**
swing	**la balançoire**
slide	**le toboggan**

Useful phrases

It needs to be weeded.	**Il faudrait désherber.**
It needs to be watered.	**Il faudrait arroser.**
The grass needs to be cut.	**Il faudrait tondre la pelouse.**
They are ripe/not ripe.	**Ils/Elles sont mûr(e)s/Ils/Elles ne sont pas mûre(e)s.**
I like gardening.	**J'aime jardiner** *or* **travailler dans le jardin.**
He/She has green fingers.	**Il/Elle a la main verte.**
I am allergic to ...	**Je suis allergique à ...**
I have been stung!	**Je me suis fait piquer !**

Useful verbs

to dig	**creuser** *or* **bêcher**
to plant	**planter**
to grow	**faire pousser**
to weed	**désherber**
to water	**arroser**
to pick	**cueillir**
to cut the grass	**tondre la pelouse**

5.6 Tools and DIY

Core vocabulary

Tools *les outils*

drill	**une perceuse**
drill bit	**la mèche**
hammer	**le marteau**
pincers	**la tenaille**

pliers	**la pince**
saw	**la scie**
chainsaw	**la scie sauteuse**
screwdriver	**le tournevis**
spanner	**la clef à molette**
staple gun	**une agrafeuse**
tape measure	**un mètre pliant** *(of wood or steel, articulated)*/**un mètre enrouleur** *(on a retractable spool)*

DIY ***le bricolage***

nail	**un clou**
bolt	**un boulon**
nut	**un écrou**
staple	**une agrafe**
brush	**une brosse**
paint brush	**un pinceau**
scissors	**les ciseaux**
sandpaper	**le papier de verre**
ladder	**une échelle**
stepladder	**un escabeau**
window pane	**la vitre**
putty	**le mastic**
window frame	**l'encadrement**
sliding window	**la fenêtre coulissante**
scaffold	**un échafaudage**

Plumbing and electricity ***la plomberie et l'électricité***

pipes and ductings	**la plomberie**
pipe, duct	**un tuyau**
drain	**l'écoulement** *(m)*, **l'évaculation** *(f)*
tap	**un robinet**
wire	**un fil électrique**
bulb	**une ampoule**
fuse	**le fusible**
socket	**la prise**
switch	**une interrupteur**

Useful phrases

Can you fix it?	**Est-ce que vous pouvez le réparer ?**
to fix/mend	**réparer**
DIY shop	**le magasin de bricolage**
DIY-ers' paradise	**le paradis des bricoleurs ...**

Insight

... This could be the name of a shop where DIY-ers would find everything they need – **où les bricoleurs seraient certains de trouver leur bonheur** (from: **trouver son bonheur**)

Useful verbs

to DIY	**bricoler** *or* **faire du bricolage**
to fix something to a wall	**accrocher quelque chose**
to screw	**visser...** *incidentally, screw you (pardon my French, but for knowledge's sake...) does not translate as* **visse toi !**
to unscrew	**dévisser**
to hammer	**taper avec un marteau**
to nail	**clouer**
to drill	**percer**
to fasten	**attacher**
to cut	**couper**
to rub down (sandpaper)	**passer au papier de verre**
to paint	**peindre**
to plane	**aplanir** *or* **égaliser**
to glue	**coller**
to solder	**souder**
to weld	**souder**
to assemble, to mount	**assembler, monter** (*Note: wall-mounted =* **mural***; e.g. wall-mounted heater =* **un radiateur mural**)

TEST YOURSELF

À vous !

A mini stock-taking exercise on the unit you have just worked on

1 'A residential area' in French is...
  a une aire résidentielle
  b une ère résidentielle
  c une zone résidentielle
  d un quartier résidentiel

2 *Emménager* in French means...
  a to move out
  b to move in
  c to move house

3 'I will help you do the washing up' in French may be... [*note: more than one answer possible*]
  a Je vais vous aider à laver les vaisselles
  b Je vous aiderai à laver les vaisselles
  c Je vais vous aider à laver la vaisselle
  d Je vais vous aider à faire les vaisselles
  e Je vous aiderai à faire la vaisselle

4 How would you say in French 'three teaspoons of mint liqueur'?
  a Trois cuillerées de liqueur de menthe
  b Treize cuillerées à soupe de liqueur de mente
  c Trois cuillerées à café de liqueur de menthe

5 'To chop carrots' in French is...
  a couper des carottes en dés
  b couper des carottes en rondelles
  c couper des carottes en tranches

6 How would you say 'She has green fingers' in French?
  a Elle a des doigts verts.
  b Elle a la main verte.
  c Elle a les pouces verts.

7 'Shower head' in French is...
  a la tête de douche
  b la poire de douche
  c la pomme de douche
  d la douchette
  e la douche-tête

8 How would you say 'Our house overlooks the estuary' in French?
  a Notre maison regarde sur l'estuaire
  b Chez nous regarde sur l'estuaire
  c Chez nous se penche sur l'estuaire
  d Notre maison donne sur l'estuaire

9 Give the names of five different rooms in the house in French, with their articles, starting with...
  a s (masculine)
  b s (feminine)
  c c (feminine)
  d b (masculine)
  e b (feminine)

10 'To DIY' in French is...
  a dihawaïer
  b déboulonner
  c déboutonner
  d bricoler
  e barboter

Answers: 1 d; 2 b; 3 c e; 4 c; 5 b; 6 b; 7 c; 8 d; 9 a le salon, b la salle à manger ou la salle de jeux ou la salle de bains, c la cuisine, d le bureau, e la buanderie; 10 d

6

Entertaining and food

6.1 Issuing an invitation and making arrangements

a party	**une fête** *or* **une soirée** *(if it is taking place in the evening)*

Insight

Le soir > la soirée: une soirée – a party that will take place in the evening *and* last all evening. Similarly, **le jour > la journée; le matin > la matinée.**

birthday	**un anniversaire**
anniversary	**un anniversaire**
engagement	**les fiançailles**
wedding	**le mariage**
celebration	**la fête**
Silver wedding	**les noces d'argent**
Golden wedding	**les noces d'or**
invitation	**une invitation**
reply	**une réponse**
acceptance	**une acceptation**
refusal	**un refus**
excuse	**une excuse**
thank you letter	**une lettre de remerciement**
cake	**un gâteau**

champagne	**le champagne**
to toast	**porter un toast à ...** *or* **lever son verre à la santé de ...**
present	**un cadeau**
cheers!	**à la vôtre !** *or* **à la bonne vôtre !** *or* **à la tienne !** *or* **Chin !** *(pronounced 'tschinn')* *or* **Santé !** *to which, in Switzerland, one will reply*: **Sensible !**

Useful phrases

Let's have a party.	**Et si on organisait une fête ?** *or* **Si on faisait une fête** *(colloquial)* **?**
Let's dance.	**Et si on dansait ?**
I would like to propose a toast.	**Je propose de porter un toast.**
I would like to thank our hosts.	**J'aimerais remercier nos hôtes/notre hôte/notre hôtesse.**
I've got a hangover.	**J'ai mal aux cheveux** *or* **J'ai la gueule de bois.**

Useful verbs

to have a party	**faire la fête**
to eat	**manger**
to drink	**boire**
to toast (the bride)	**porter un toast (à la mariée)**
to enjoy onseself	**s'amuser**
to overindulge/have too much	**trop boire/trop manger**
to get drunk	**trop boire** *or* **se soûler**
to feel sick	**se sentir mal** *or* **avoir envie de vomir**

6.2 Dinner

Core vocabulary

dinner	**le dîner**
menu	**la carte** *or* **le menu** *(the latter refers to a set menu)*
pre-dinner drink	**un apéritif**

Insight

Naturally, **l'apéritif** is not restricted to dinner time. Note that in France, whisky will be offered as an apéritif, rather than as a **digestif** – post-dinner drink. A classic among the non-alcoholic apéritifs is tomato juice, traditionally served with celery salt. Delicious also with the juice from a whole pressed lemon!

starter	**l'entrée** *or* **le hors-d'œuvre**
soup	**la soupe**
fish	**le poisson**
main course	**le plat principal** *(often referred to as* **le plat***)*
dessert	**le dessert**
cheese	**le fromage**
coffee	**le café**
after-dinner drinks (brandy)	**le digestif**

Drinks *les boissons*

soft drink	**une boisson sans alcool**
tomato juice	**un jus de tomate**
pineapple juice	**un jus d'ananas**
water	**l'eau**
mineral water	**une eau minérale**
fizzy	**pétillante** *or* **gazeuse**
still	**plate**
aperitif	**un apéritif**
cocktail	**un cocktail**
sherry	**un xérès** *or* **un porto**
gin and tonic	**un gin tonic**
red wine	**le vin rouge**
white wine	**le vin blanc**
champagne	**le champagne**
brandy	**un alcool fort (un cognac, un calvados, une mirabelle,** *etc.***)**

Insight

Drinks and food originating from a specific area, town, village or region will often be called after it. When this happens, the name is no longer capitalized, e.g. **la Champagne** (a region): **le champagne; Bordeaux** (a city): **le bordeaux;** Cognac (a town): **le cognac; Camembert** (a village): **le camembert; Calvados** (an administrative area): **le calvados; la Brie** (a region between Paris and Champagne): **le brie,** etc.

However, **une mirabelle** is called after the fruit it is made from and originates in the Lorraine region (border with Luxembourg and Germany).

liqueur **une liqueur**

***Les entrées* or *hors-d'œuvres* starters**

A few examples:

une douzaine d'escargots	*a dozen snails grilled in garlic and parsley butter*
œuf cocotte à la truffe	*an egg baked in the oven in a ramekin, with crème fraîche, Cornish clotted-cream and double-cream, herbs and shavings of truffles*
jambon de pays	*raw/cured/smoked ham on the bone, thinly sliced*
pâté chaud de caille	*a boned quail baked in a puff pastry casing*
turban de saumon	*mousse-type dish laced with salmon strips marinated in lemon juice*

***Les soupes* soups**

A few examples:

potage de laitue	*smooth lettuce and cream soup*
soupe au potiron	*smooth pumpkin and cream soup*

soupe froide au thon *a kind of liquid salsa with red tuna, tomatoes, goat's cheese, olive oil and basil*

soupe du pêcheur *literally, 'fisherman's soup'– its ingredients will vary depending on the season and the region*

bouillabaisse *fish soup from Marseilles*

***Les plats* main courses**

A few examples:

***Les poissons* fish**

filet de carpe au pouligny Saint-Pierre *carp fillet in a crème fraîche and goat's cheese sauce*

lotte à la basquaise *monkfish with tomatoes, sweet chillies, garlic, onions and olive oil*

truite meunière *pan-fried trout served in a butter and crème fraîche sauce*

filet de sandre au lard *pikeperch fillet wrapped in a thin layer of bacon*

turbot au bouzy rouge *turbot with a red wine sauce from the Champagne region*

***Les viandes* meat**

ris de veau au riesling *calves' sweetbreads in a dry white wine and cream sauce*

tête de veau gribiche *various veal offals served with a 'gribiche' sauce*

râbles de lapin aux figues *pan-fried saddle of rabbit and figs in a cinnamon and honey sauce*

magrets de canard au citron vert, joue et queue de bœuf sauce marchand de vin *duck cutlets in a lime sauce, beef tail and cheek in a red wine and shallot sauce*

***Les légumes* vegetables**

les pommes de terre *potatoes*

les frites (une frite) *chips*

les chips *crips*

Insight

Attention: un faux ami ! *chips* – **frites,** *crisps* – **chips.** Crisps in France – **les chips** – are typically reserved for a **pique-nique.**

les haricots verts	*green beans*
les épinards	*spinach*
les navets	*turnips*
les carottes	*carrots*
une mousse de céleri	*celeriac mousse*
une mousse de carotte	*carrot mousse*
une mousse de poireaux	*leek mousse*
une purée de petits oignons	*spring onion sauce*
une salade verte	*green salad*
le riz	*rice*

Les fromages cheese

Insight

There is a saying that France has as many cheese varieties as there are days in a year: 365! Try the cheeses of any region you visit: they will be at their best. Indeed, 'real' cheese doesn't like travelling… hence the ubiquitous pasteurized camembert and solid brie to be found in most shops and supermarkets.

Les desserts desserts

A few examples:

blanc-manger	*coconut mixed and whipped with cream, served chilled*
chocolaté aux griottines	*chocolate sponge cake with chocolate cream and baby morello cherries*
poires au vin et aux épices	*pears with wine and spices*
moëlleux aux framboises	*a sponge-type cake with an almond and raspberries filling*
coupe de marrons	*a sweet chestnut cream served on a meringue base*
les glaces et les sorbets	*ice-cream and sorbets*

Drinks les boissons

coffee (black)	**un café**
coffee (white)	**un café avec du lait**
espresso	**un expresso**
cappuccino	**un cappuccino**
latte	**le café au lait**
coffee with milk	**un café avec un peu de lait**
sugar	**le sucre**
sweetener	**une sucrette**
without sugar	**sans sucre**
decaffeinated coffee	**un café décaféiné**
tea	**le thé**
China tea	**le thé de Chine**
herbal tea	**une tisane**
fruit tea	**un thé parfumé à ...**
green tea	**le thé vert**
with lemon	**avec une rondelle de citron**
with milk	**avec du lait**

Useful phrases

I have a special diet.	**Je suis au régime.**
I am allergic to ...	**Je suis allergique à ...**
I don't eat ...	**Je ne mange pas de ...**
I can't eat ...	**Je ne peux pas manger de ...**
I am a vegan.	**Je suis végétalien(ne).**
I am a vegetarian.	**Je suis végétarien(ne).**
I am following a gluten-free diet.	**Je suis** (from **suivre) un régime sans gluten.**
I am diabetic.	**Je suis diabétique.**
May I offer you something to drink? (pre-dinner/lunch)	**Je vous offre un apéritif ?** *or* **Je vous offre quelque chose à boire ?**
Anyone for a (pre-dinner) drink?	**Je sers l'apéritif !** *(a good way to 'round up' your guests and other members of the family for dinner!)*

Would you like a drink (in a restaurant) ?	**Prendrez-vous l'apéritif ?** *or* **Je vous sers un apéritif ?**

Useful verbs

to like/dislike	**aimer/ne pas aimer**
to eat	**manger**
to drink	**boire**
to prefer	**préférer**
to love	**adorer**

6.3 Meals

Core vocabulary

meal	**le repas**
mealtimes	**l'heure des repas**
breakfast	**le petit-déjeuner**
elevenses	**la pause café**
lunch	**le déjeuner**
afternoon tea	**le thé, le goûter**

Insight

Le goûter is usually for children and fast-growing adolescents. Served at primary school at around 4 pm, it consists typically of some bread and a chocolate bar, with a drink of milk or fruit juice. At home, it also consists – typically – of bread, jam and chocolate bars, with fruit juice, or milk, or 'sirops à l'eau' – a fruit-crush with added water – that come in many different flavours. A 'luxury goûter' might consist of a **pain aux raisins** or a **pain au chocolat** bought from a **boulangerie** on the way home.

dinner	**le dîner**
supper	**le souper**

Breakfast *le petit-déjeuner*

cereal	**les céréales**
wheat	**le blé** and **le froment**
oats	**l'avoine**
barley	**l'orge**
rye	**le seigle**
bran	**le son**
muesli	**le müsli**
milk	**le lait**
semi-skimmed milk	**le lait demi-écrémé**
skimmed milk	**le lait écrémé**
soya milk	**le lait de soja**
goat's milk	**le lait de chèvre**
ewe's milk	**le lait de brebis**
cream	**la crème**
yoghurt	**le yaourt**
bacon	**le bacon**
eggs	**les œufs**
scrambled	**brouillés**
poached	**pochés**
soft boiled	**à la coque**
fried	**sur le plat**
hard boiled	**durs**

Insight

You may find **des œufs durs** on the bar in traditional brasseries and cafés, displayed on a small, carousel-shaped holder, together with a salt dispenser in the centre, to which customers can help themselves. It is a way of stilling your appetite – hard-boiled eggs are said to be good for that! – to help you to wait until lunchtime.

sausages	**les saucisses**
tomatoes	**les tomates**
mushrooms	**les champignons**
fried	**frit(e)s**
grilled	**grillé(e)s**

tinned	**en boîte**
baked beans	**des flageolets à la sauce tomate en boîte**
pancake	**une crêpe**
maple syrup	**le sirop d'érable**
ham	**le jambon**
salami	**le salami**
cheese	**le fromage**
bread	**le pain**
white bread	**la baguette, le pain de deux livres,** etc.
wholemeal	**complet**
sliced	**tranché**
organic	**bio**
roll	**un petit pain individuel**
croissant	**un croissant**

Insight

The name **croissant** comes from the moon: **la lune croissante,** *the waxing moon* (and **décroissante,** *waning moon*). **Un croissant de lune** is that particular shape of the moon when it waxes – or wanes – like **le croissant** that you eat.

Danish pastries	**les viennoiseries** e.g. **un pain au chocolat, un pain aux raisins, un croissant à la frangipane,** etc.
butter	**le beurre**
margarine	**la margarine**
low-fat spread	**le beurre sans matières grasses**
jam	**la confiture**
marmalade	**la confiture d'oranges**
honey	**le miel**
peanut butter	**le beurre de cacahuètes**
tea	**le thé**
coffee	**le café**
milk	**le lait**
milk with coffee ('latte')	**le café au lait**

Insight

Le café au lait is the traditional breakfast drink in France. It is served in a large bowl, and consists of perhaps two parts milk to one part coffee, with or without sugar. It may also be drunk at dinner time on the farm, with large chunks of bread in it.

cold milk	**le lait froid**
hot milk	**le lait chaud**
hot chocolate	**le chocolat chaud**
fruit juice	**le jus de fruit**
orange juice	**le jus d'orange**
freshly-squeezed orange juice	**une orange pressée**

Useful phrases

I don't eat breakfast.	**Je ne petit-déjeune jamais** *or* **Je ne prends jamais de petit déjeuner.**
I only eat …	**Je ne mange que …**
I don't drink milk.	**Je ne bois pas de lait.**
I have my breakfast at …	**Je petit-déjeune à …** *or* **Je prends mon petit déjeuner à …**

6.4 Snacks

burger	**un burger**
cheeseburger	**un cheeseburger**
hamburger	**un hamburger**
fishburger	**un fishburger**
yoghurt	**un yaourt**
biscuit	**un petit gâteau**
chocolate biscuit	**un petit gâteau au chocolat**
piece of cake	**une tranche/une part de gâteau**

Insight

The English slang term *piece of cake* would be **fastoche** in French (from **'facile'**) or **les doigts dans le nez** (literally: the fingers in the nose … not the most elegant of phrases, I concede!)

bun	**un petit pain**
sweets	**des bonbons**
snacks	**les en-cas** *or* **sur le pouce**
sandwich	**un sandwich**
in brown bread	**avec du pain complet**
in white bread	**avec du pain blanc**
in a roll	**dans un petit pain individuel**
with mayonnaise	**avec de la mayonnaise**
without mayonnaise	**sans mayonnaise**

Useful phrases

Can I offer you a cup of coffee?	**Je vous offre un café ?**
How do you take it?	**Qu'est-ce que vous mettez dedans ?**
With milk or without milk?	**Avec ou sans lait ?**
Do you take sugar?	**Vous prenez du sucre ?**
Have you got a sweetner?	**Est-ce que vous avez des sucrettes ?**
Would you like a biscuit?	**Voulez-vous un petit gâteau ?**
I am on a diet.	**Je suis au régime.**
I watch what I eat.	**Je fais attention à ce que je mange.**
I keep an eye on my figure.	**Je fais attention à ma ligne.**
I don't take …	**Je ne prends pas de …**
It's too hot/cold/spicy.	**C'est trop chaud/froid/épicé.**
It isn't cooked properly.	**Ce n'est pas assez cuit.**
It is delicious!	**C'est délicieux !**

6.5 Fruit and vegetables

Core vocabulary

Fruit *les fruits*

apple	**la pomme**
cooking apple	**une pomme à compote**
dessert apple	**une pomme à couteau**
apricot	**un abricot**
banana	**une banane**
grape red/white	**le raisin rouge/blanc**
cherry	**la cerise**
melon	**le melon**
peach	**la pêche**
pear	**la poire**
plum	**la prune**
raspberry	**la framboise**
rhubarb	**la rhubarbe**
strawberry	**la fraise**
watermelon	**la pastèque**

Vegetables *les légumes*

artichoke	**un artichaut**
aubergine	**une aubergine**
bean	**le haricot**
green bean	**le haricot vert**
beetroot	**la betterave**
broccoli	**le broccoli**
brussels sprout	**le choux de Bruxelles**
cabbage	**le choux**
red cabbage	**le choux rouge**
carrot	**la carotte**
cauliflower	**le choux-fleur**
chicory	**une endive**
celery	**le céleri (en branches)**
celeriac	**le céleri rave**

courgette	**la courgette**
cucumber	**le concombre**
garlic	**l'ail**
leek	**le poireau**
lentils	**les lentilles**
lettuce	**la laitue**
mushroom	**le champignon**
olive	**l'olive**
onion	**l'oignon**
potato	**la pomme de terre**
sweet potato	**la patate douce**
pumpkin	**le potiron**
radish	**le radis**
shallot	**une échalote**
spring onion	**un oignon grelot**
sweetcorn	**le maïs**
corn on the cob	**un épi de maïs**
turnip	**le navet**
tomato	**la tomate**
spinach	**les épinards**
watercress	**le cresson**

Citrus fruits *les agrumes*

clementine	**la clémentine**
grapefruit	**le pamplemousse**
lemon	**le citron**
lime	**le citron vert**
orange	**une orange**
tangerine	**la mandarine**

Berries *les baies*

blackcurrant	**le cassis**
blueberry/bilberry	**la myrtille**
cranberry	**une airelle**
gooseberry	**une groseille à maquereaux**
redcurrant	**une groseille**

Exotic fruits *les fruits exotiques*

avocado	**un avocat**
coconut	**une noix de coco**
date	**la datte**
fig	**la figue**
kiwi	**le kiwi**
mango	**la mangue**
passion fruit	**le fruit de la passion**
pineapple	**un ananas**

Nuts *les noix*

almond	**une amande**
brazil	**une noix du Brésil**
cashew	**une noix de cajou**
hazel	**une noisette**
peanut	**une cacahuète**
pistachio	**une pistache**
walnut	**une noix**

6.6 Fish and meat

Core vocabulary

Fish *les poissons*

anchovy	**un anchois**
cod	**la morue** *or* **le caubillaud**
haddock	**le haddock**
hake	**le colin**
herring	**le hareng**
halibut	**le flétan**
mackerel	**le maquereau**
plaice	**la plie**
red mullet	**le rouget**
salmon	**le saumon**
sardine	**la sardine**
sea bass	**le bar**

sea bream	**la dorade**
skate	**la raie**
sole	**la sole**
tuna	**le thon**
whiting	**le merlan**
eel	**une anguille**
jelly fish	**une méduse**
octopus	**la pieuvre**
squid	**la seiche**

Seafood *les fruits de mer*

clam	**la palourde**
cockle	**une coque**
common crab	**le tourteau**
crab	**un crabe**
crayfish	**une écrevisse**
gambas	**les gambas**
langoustine	**la langoustine**
lobster	**un homard**
mussel	**la moule**
oyster	**une huître**
prawn	**le bouquet**
shellfish	**les coquillages**
shrimp	**la crevette**

Freshwater fish *les poissons de rivière*

perch	**la perche**
pike	**le brochet**
pikeperch	**le sandre**
trout	**la truite**
rainbow trout	**la truite saumonée**

Meat *la viande*

beef	**le bœuf**
lamb	**l'agneau**
pork	**le porc**
veal	**le veau**
ham	**le jambon**

liver	**le foie**
kidney	**le rognon**

a sausage made of chitterlings, eaten cold in thin slices	**une andouille**
a smaller sausage than **une andouille** *served cooked*	**une andouillette**
white pudding	**le boudin blanc**
black pudding	**le boudin noir**
a spicy, thin sausage from the Mediterranean, served hot	**la merguez**

Poultry *les volailles*

capon	**le chapon**
chicken	**le poulet**
turkey	**la dinde**
duck	**le canard**
fowl	**la poule**
goose	**une oie**
partridge	**la perdrix**
pigeon	**le pigeon**
quail	**la caille**

Game *le gibier*

grouse	**le coq de bruyère**
hare	**le lièvre**
pheasant	**le faisan**
rabbit	**le lapin**
venison	**le chevreuil**
wild boar	**le sanglier**

***La charcuterie* cold cuts, mostly from pork**

salami	**le salami**
a thin, dry kind of salami	**le saucisson sec**
a terrine made of pork fat and meat, originally from the area of Le Mans (also known for its Formula 1 24-hour circuit race)	**les rillettes**

a dish made of pork, baked in the oven. Served cold with bread.	**une terrine de ...**
cooked ham	**le jambon blanc ou de Paris**
cured and smoked ham	**le jambon fumé**
a regional variation of the above	**le jambon de pays**
a smooth terrine	**le pâté**

6.7 Some recipe terms

to make a cake	**faire un gâteau**
to bake	**faire de la pâtisserie**
puff pastry	**la pâte feuilletée**
short crust	**la pâte brisée**
shortbread	**la pâte sablée**
ingredients	**les ingrédients**
flour	**la farine**
self-raising flour	**la farine auto-levante**
raising agent (baking powder)	**la levure**
cornflour	**la maïzena**
sugar	**le sucre**
butter	**le beurre**
salt	**le sel**
vanilla/almond essence	**l'extrait de vanille/d'amande**
melted chocolate	**le chocolat fondu**
grated lemon rind	**l'écorce de citron râpée**
the zest of an orange	**le zeste d'une orange**
chopped walnuts	**les noix écrasées**
grated chocolate	**le chocolat râpé**
weighing scales	**la balance de cuisine**
mixing bowl	**le bol du mixeur**
wooden spoon	**la cuillère en bois**
mixer	**le mixeur**
grater	**la râpe**
sieve	**le chinois**

baking tin — **le moule à gâteau**
oven — **le four**
oven glove — **un gant de cuisine**
pot holder — **la manique**
saucepan — **la casserole**
casserole — **le faitout** *or* **la cocotte**

TEST YOURSELF

À vous !

A mini stock-taking exercise on the unit you have just worked on

1 'To have a hangover' in French is...
[*note: more than one answer possible*]
- **a** avoir mal par-dessus la tête
- **b** avoir mal aux cheveux
- **c** avoir une migraine
- **d** avoir la gueule de feutre
- **e** avoir la gueule de bois

2 Please give four possible ways of giving a toast in French
- **a**
- **b**
- **c**
- **d**

3 A good way to entice everyone to come to dinner in French may be...
[*note: more than one answer possible*]
- **a** Vous serez privés de dessert !
- **b** Venez prendre un drink !
- **c** Je sers l'apéritif !
- **d** Je vais servir l'apéritif dans le jardin !
- **e** Je vous sers des drinks ?

4 How would you say 'the four o'clock meal for children' in French?
- **a** le chocolat-thé
- **b** le goûter
- **c** le thé pour les enfants

5 La pastèque means...
- **a** a small pastry
- **b** coconut liqueur
- **c** watermelon

6 How would you say 'Do you have some sweeteners?' in French?
[*note: more than one answer possible*]
  a Est-ce que vous avez du sucre sans sucre ?
  b Auriez-vous du faux sucre ?
  c Est-ce que auriez des sucrettes ?

7 'A soft drink' in French is...
[*note: more than one answer possible*]
  a une boisson douce
  b un vin doux
  c une boisson légère
  d une boisson sans alcool
  e une boisson non alcoolisée
  f un drink soft

8 How would you say 'It is delicious' in French?
  a C'est délicious !
  b C'est délicieux !
  c C'est merveilleux !

9 Kidneys, when served at a French table, would be...
  a les reins
  b les foies
  c les rognons
  d les rognottes

10 Les **viennoiseries** are...
  a Viennese starters
  b Viennese pastries
  c Danish pastries
  d Vienna cakes

Answers: 1 b e; 2 à la vôtre/à la bonne vôtre/à la tienne/santé/chin; 3 c d; 4 b; 5 c; 6 a b c; 7 d e; 8 b; 9 c; 10 c

7

In the town

7.1 The town plan and the sights

Core vocabulary

About town *vivre en ville*

bank	**la banque**
cash dispenser	**le distributeur de billets (de banque)**
ATM (automatic telling machine)	**DAB (distributeur automatique de billets)**
bus station	**la gare routière**
train station	**la gare ferroviaire**
car park	**le parking**
ticket issuing machine	**un horodateur**
parking meter	**le parcmètre**
cinema	**le cinéma**
football ground	**le terrain de football**
rugby ground	**le terrain de rugby**
hospital	**l'hôpital**
clinic	**la clinique**
hotel	**un hôtel**
library	**une bibliothèque**
market	**le marché**
opera house	**l'opéra**
post office	**la poste**
public toilets	**les toilettes publiques**

swimming pool	**la piscine**
theatre	**le théâtre**
tourist office	**l'office du tourisme**
town hall	**la mairie** *or* **l'hôtel de ville** *(in larger cities)*
underground station	**la station de métro**
bus stop	**l'arrêt de bus**
tram stop	**l'arrêt de tramway**
law court	**le tribunal** *or* **le palais de justice**
police station	**le commissariat**

The sights ***les endroits à visiter***

bridge	**le pont**
castle	**le château**
place of worship	**lieu de culte**
cathedral	**la cathédrale**
chapel	**la chapelle**
church	**une église**
temple	**le temple**
mosque	**la mosquée**
synagogue	**la synagogue**
fountain	**la fontaine**
gardens	**le jardin public**
monument	**le monument**
museum	**le musée**
old town	**la vieille ville**
park	**le parc**
river	**la rivière**
square	**la place**
public gardens (small)	**le square**

Insight

In most cases, the English *square* translates as **la place** in French. However, in some instances, the English *square* is the equivalent of the French **square** – London squares such as Cavendish Square or Gordon Square would be referred to as **des squares**; whereas Trafalgar or Leicester Square would qualify as **des places**. The difference lies in the size and the garden/landscaped element.

statue	**la statue**
area/neighbourhood	**le quartier**
region	**la région**
town	**la ville**
new town	**la ville nouvelle**
constituency, ward	**la circonscription**
city council	**le conseil municipal** *or* **la municipalité** *or* **la Ville** *(with capital)*
council offices	**les services municipaux**
built-up area	**une zone construite**
suburb	**la banlieue** *or* **les faubourgs**
town centre	**le centre** *or* **le centre-ville**
industrial zone	**une zone industrielle**
enterprise zone	**une pépinière d'entreprise**
commercial zone	**une zone commerciale**
opening times	**les heures d'ouverture**
open	**ouvert(e)**
closed	**fermé(e)**
holidays	**les vacances**
bank holiday	**le jour férié**
annual holiday	**les congés annuels**

Useful verbs

to meet someone (to have arranged/agreed to meet)	**retrouver/se retrouver**

Insight

To meet may also be translated as **rencontrer**. Heads of state who meet, **se rencontrent**; **rencontrer** is also used when referring to a neighbour you may see every morning on your way to work; and also when you speak of your first meeting with someone in your life, e.g. **Nous nous sommes rencontrés à Toulouse, place du Capitole, en 1976.**

to look for	**chercher**
to be situated	**se trouver**

Useful phrases

I am looking for the rue des tissandiers.	**Excusez-moi, je cherche la rue des tissandiers.**
Could you possibly tell me please where the nearest underground is?	**Pourriez-vous m'indiquer la station de métro la plus proche, s'il-vous-plaît ?**
Shall we meet in front of the train station?	**On se retrouve devant la gare ?**
Where is it?	**C'est où ?**
in the centre	**dans le centre**
on (name) street	**dans la rue** *(name)*
next to the post office	**à côté de la poste**
very near the university campus	**tout près du campus universitaire**
opposite the Central European bank	**en face de la Banque des pays d'Europe centrale**
on the market place	**sur la place du marché**
just as you come out of the underground station	**juste à la sortie du métro**
very near your office	**à deux pas de ton bureau** *(literally: two steps away from your office)*

7.2 Getting around town

Core vocabulary

road	**la route**
street	**la rue**
lane	**une allée**
avenue	**une avenue**
pavement	**le trottoir**
gutter	**le caniveau**

pedestrian crossing	**le passage pour piétons** *or* **le passage piétons**
pedestrian zone	**la zone piétonnière** *or* **la zone piétonne**
traffic lights	**les feux (de la circulation)**
crossing lights	**les feux (de la circulation)**
traffic warden	**l'agent de la circulation**
'green man'	**le 'petit bonhomme vert'**
subway (foot passage)	**le passage souterrain pour piétons**

How do I get into town? ***comment faire pour aller en ville*** **?**

by car	**en voiture**
by bus	**en bus**
by tram	**en tramway**
by subway (metro)	**en métro**

Parking the car ***se garer***

in a car park	**dans un parking**
multi-storey car park	**dans un parking aérien**
underground car park	**dans un parking souterrain**
full	**complet**
spaces	**libre**
entrance	**entrée**
ticket machine	**le distributeur de tickets**
change	**la monnaie**
credit card	**la carte de crédit**
ticket	**le ticket**
exit	**la sortie**
barrier	**la barrière**
one-way system	**le système à sens unique**

Useful phrases

crossing the road	**traverser la rue**
use the crossing	**traverser au passage pour piétons**
don't cross	**ne pas traverser**
There's a car coming!	**Voilà une voiture !**

wait for the green man	**attendre que le feu passe au vert pour les piétons**
I am looking for a parking space	**Je cherche une place (de stationnement** *or* **pour me garer)** *or* **Je cherche à me garer**
I have been going round and round for almost one hour	**Je tourne en rond depuis presqu'une heure**

Asking for help *demander son chemin*

Excuse me …	**Excusez-moi** *or* **pardon madame** *or* **pardon monsieur**
Can you tell me …	**Pourriez-vous m'indiquer ...**
How to get to the station?	**La gare, s'il-vous-plaît ?**
Where is the nearest car park?	**Excusez-moi, je cherche un parking ?**
When is the next bus?	**Pardon madame/monsieur, pourriez-vous me dire à quelle heure est le prochain bus ?**

Useful verbs

to walk	**marcher**
to cross	**traverser**
to turn left/right	**tourner à gauche/à droite**
to go straight on	**aller/continuer tout droit**
to run	**courir**
to drive	**aller (en voiture, à moto, à vélo)**
to take the bus	**prendre le bus**
to catch the bus	**attrapper le bus**
to miss the bus	**rater le bus**

7.3 Shops and shopping

Core vocabulary

shop	**le magasin**
bakery	**la boulangerie**

butcher	**la boucherie**
meat products/game caterer	**la charcuterie**
cake shop	**la pâtisserie**
chemist's/pharmacy	**la pharmacie**
clothes shop	**le magasin de vêtements –** *colloquial:* **une boutique de fringues**
flower shop	**le fleuriste**
hairdresser's	**le salon de coiffure**
market	**le marché**
shoe shop	**le magasin de chaussures**
sports shop	**le magasin de sport**
confectioner's/sweetshop	**la confiserie**
hyper-/supermarket	**l'hyper-/le supermarché**
shopping centre	**le centre commercial**
shopping mall	**la galerie marchande**
department store	**le grand magasin**
health food store	**le magasin diététique**
newsagent's	**le marchand de journaux** *or* **la maison de la presse**
optician	**l'opticien**
dry cleaner's	**le pressing**
travel agent	**l'agence de voyage**
store guide	**le plan du magasin**
escalator	**l'escalier roulant**
lift	**l'ascenseur**
ground floor	**le rez-de-chaussée**
first floor	**le premier étage**
basement	**le sous-sol**
department	**le rayon**
bedding	**le linge de maison**
fashion	**la mode**
sportswear	**le sportswear**
leather goods	**le cuir**
electrical (household) goods	**l'électro-ménager**
lingerie/hosiery	**la lingerie**
paperware	**la papeterie**
accessories	**les accessoires**
jewellery	**la bijouterie**

toiletries	**la parfumerie et les soins de beauté**
sales person	**le vendeur, la vendeuse**
cash desk	**la caisse**
changing room	**la cabine d'essayage**
price	**le prix**
deposit	**les arrhes** *or* **un accompte**
loyalty card	**la carte de fidélité**
sales	**les soldes**
discount	**la démarque**

Insight

La démarque refers to the discount applied to items on sale. When the sales period reaches its end – sales periods are strictly regulated in France – you may see signs announcing une **« 2e démarque ! »** – a further discount. Note: **démarque** → **démarquer**, *a discounted item* → **un article démarqué.**

Useful phrases

How much does it cost?	**Combien ça coûte ?**
How are you paying?	**Vous payez** *or* **vous réglez comment ?**

Insight

Régler – *to settle*, and **le règlement** – *settlement* are used in French exactly as they are in English: *to settle a bill* – **régler l'addition**, or **une facture** (*invoice*); to settle a dispute (*amicably, out of court*) – **régler un différend** (**à l'amiable**).

Are you paying cash?	**Vous payez** *or* **réglez en liquide ?**
Do you have the right change?	**Auriez-vous l'appoint ?**
Will you wrap it as a gift?	**Vous pouvez me faire un paquet cadeau, s'il-vous-plaît ?**

Useful verbs

to buy	**acheter**
to sell	**vendre**

to look for	**chercher**
to pay	**payer** *or* **régler**
to pay at the cash desk	**payer** *or* **régler** *or* **passer à la caisse**
to prefer	**préférer**
to go shopping	**aller faire des courses** *or* **aller faire les magasins**

Insight

Aller faire les courses refers to going shopping for food; **aller faire des courses** may refer to food but also to any other items.

to order	**commander**
to deliver	**livrer**
to window shop	**faire du lèche-vitrine**
to pay a deposit	**verser un accompte** *or* **des arrhes**
to be out of stock	**être en rupture de stock**

7.4 At the supermarket

Core vocabulary

food department	**le rayon alimentation**
fruit and vegetables	**les fruits et les légumes**
dairy produce	**les produits laitiers**
frozen foods	**les surgelés**
cleaning materials	**les produits d'entretien**
electrical goods	**l'électro-ménager**
household appliances	**l'électro-ménager**
CDs, videos, DVDS	**les CD, les vidéos, les DVD**
wines and spirits	**les vins et spiritueux**
drinks	**les boissons**
bottle of water	**une bouteille d'eau**
jar of jam	**un bocal de confiture**
box of paper hankies	**une boîte de mouchoirs en papier**
tin of tomatoes	**des tomates en boîte**

packet of biscuits	**un paquet de petits gâteaux**
tube of toothpaste	**un tube de dentifrice**

A shopping list *une liste des courses*

coffee	**le café**
tea bags	**les sachets de thé**
loose tea	**le thé en vrac**
chocolate drink powder	**le chocolat en poudre**
yoghurt	**le yaourt**
juice	**le jus**
milk	**le lait**
water	**l'eau**
cereals	**les céréales**
sugar	**le sucre**
flour	**la farine**
rice	**le riz**
pasta	**les pâtes**
instant meals	**les plats tout préparés**
microwaveable meals	**les plats micro-ondes**
detergent	**le détergent**
for the washing machine	**la lessive**
for the dishwasher	**la poudre lavante pour le lave-vaisselle**
for the washing up	**le produit vaisselle**
stain remover	**le détachant**
polish	**le produit lustrant**
shopping trolley	**le caddy**
basket	**le panier**
cash machine	**le distributeur de billets**
checkout	**la caisse**

Useful verbs

to weigh	**peser**
to ask (the assistant) to weigh	**faire peser**
to look for	**chercher**
to find	**trouver**

to deliver	**livrer**
ask for items/shopping to be delivered	**demander à se faire livrer**

Useful phrases

Where is/are the...?	**Où est le/la ... ? Où sont les ... ?**
In the... department/aisle	**Dans le rayon/l'allée ...**
Where is the gardening section?	**Où se trouve le rayon jardinage ?**
On the row with the...	**Dans le même rayon que .../ Dans la même allée que ...**
At the far end.	**Tout au bout.**
On the left/right hand side.	**À gauche./À droite** *or* **Sur votre gauche./Sur votre droite.**
Is there a restaurant?	**Est-ce que vous avez un restaurant ?**
What time do you shut?	**À quelle heure fermez-vous ?**
Are you open on a Sunday?	**Est-ce que vous êtes ouverts le dimanche ?**
Yes, we open on Sunday mornings, from 9 till noon.	**Oui, nous ouvrons le dimanche matin, de 9 heures à midi.**
Yes, we are open from 11 am onwards.	**Oui, nous sommes ouverts à partir de 11 heures.**

7.5 At the post office and the bank

Core vocabulary

letter box	**la boîte aux lettres**
post (letters and parcels in general)	**le courrier**
letter	**la lettre**
packet	**le petit paquet**
parcel	**le paquet**
postcard	**la carte postale**

writing paper	**le papier à lettres**
envelope	**une enveloppe**
a pre-stamped envelope	**une enveloppe affranchie**
pen (ballpoint)	**un stylo**
stamp	**un timbre**
postman (woman)	**le postier, la postière**
money	**l'argent**
cash	**la monnaie**
exact change	**l'appoint**
coin	**la pièce (de monnaie)**
note	**le billet (de banque)**
cheque book	**le chéquier**
credit card	**la carte de crédit**
bank card	**la carte bancaire**
phone card	**la carte téléphone**
printed matter	**un formulaire**
recorded delivery	**un envoi en recommandé**
overnight delivery	**un envoi sous 24 heures**
air mail	**par avion**
email	**un courriel** *or* **un email** *or* **un mèl**

Insight

Courriel is a contraction of **courrier électronique**. It is used in formal, professional environments: international firms, research institutes, and government agencies/departments. **Mèl** and **email** are used in professional circles, but also in more personal/friendly communication.

a cash transfer	**un virement bancaire**
date	**la date**
amount	**le montant**
signature	**la signature**
bank reference code	**le code banque**
sort code	**le code guichet**
bank account number	**le numéro de compte**
credit card number	**le numéro de carte**
expiry date	**la date d'expiration**

balance	**le solde**
credit	**le solde créditeur**
debit	**le solde débiteur**
loan	**l'emprunt** *(from the perspective of the borrower)* **le prêt** *(from the perspective of the lender)*
mortgage	**un emprunt/prêt sur hypothèque** *or* **hypothécaire**

Useful phrases

Insert your card.	**Insérez votre carte.**
Type in your PIN	**Composez votre code confidentiel.**
Wait ... we are processing your request.	**Patientez ... nous traitons votre demande.**
Remove your card.	**Reprenez votre carte.**
Take your money.	**Prenez les billets.**
Take the receipt.	**N'oubliez pas votre facturette.**
Fill in the form.	**Remplissez le formulaire.**
Go to the counter/cash desk.	**Allez au guichet/à la caisse.**
Where do I have to sign?	**Où est-ce qu'il faut que je signe ?**
How much does it cost to send this to ...?	**Combien ça coûte pour envoyer ça à ... ?**
By air mail.	**Par avion.**

Useful verbs

to cash	**encaisser**
to deposit	**déposer**
to transfer	**virer**
to sign	**signer**
to fill in	**remplir**
to stop a payment	**faire opposition**

TEST YOURSELF

À vous !

A mini stock-taking exercise on the unit you have just worked on

1 **Un horodateur** in French is…
  a an hourly-rate-based ATM
  b a ticket-issuing machine
  c a parking attendant

2 How would you say 'library' in French?
  a une librairie
  b une libraire
  c une bibliothèque

3 How would you say 'We met by chance at a conference' in French?
[*note: more than one answer possible*]
  a Nous nous sommes retrouvés à une conference – quelle chance !
  b Nous nous sommes rencontrés par hasard à une conférence.
  c Nous nous sommes revus par hasard à un congrès.
  d Nous nous sommes rencontrés par chance à un congrès.
  e Nous nous sommes rencontrés par hasard à un congrès.

4 How would you say in French 'Let's meet at 7 pm at Mado's.'
[*note: more than one answer possible*]
  a On se rencontre à 7 heures du soir chez *Mado*.
  b On se retrouve à 19 heures chez *Mado*.
  c On se retrouve à 7 heures chez *Mado*.
  d On se voit à 7 heures chez *Mado*.
  e On se rencontre à 19 heures chez *Mado*.

5 'I am waiting for the green man', the title of my friend's new play, may be translated as…
  a En attendant le petit bonhomme vert
  b J'attendrai toujours le petit bonhomme vert

c En attendant que le feu se transforme en vert
d J'attends que le feu passe au vert

6 'An item in the sale' in French may be...
[*note: more than one answer possible*]
a un article en solde
b un article en vente
c un article démarqué

7 **Le code guichet** in French is ...
a sort code
b international account reference code
c bank code

8 **Un caddy**, in a French shopping context, is...
a a caddy
b a trolley
c a wheelie-basket

9 How could you say in French 'I would like to pay by credit card'?
[*note: more than one answer possible*]
a J'aimerais régler par carte de crédit
b Je souhaiterais payer avec ma carte de crédit
c J'aimerais payer par carte de crédit

10 'Household goods department/aisle' in French is...
a le département Biens de ménage
b la rangée Biens domestiques
c le rayon électro-ménager
d le département électro-ménager

Answers: 1 b; 2 c; 3 b e; 4 b c d; 5 d; 6 a c; 7 a; 8 b; 9 a b c; 10 c

8

In the country

8.1 The countryside

Core vocabulary

In the countryside *à la campagne*

field	**le champ**
meadow	**la prairie**
(foot)path	**le sentier**
hill	**la colline**
mountain	**la montagne**
stream	**le cours d'eau**
river	**la rivière**
lake	**le lac**
pond	**un étang**
valley	**la vallée**
grass	**l'herbe**
plant	**la plante**
wild flower	**la fleur sauvage**
moss	**la mousse**
fungi	**le champignon**
fern	**la fougère**
bush	**le buisson**
copse	**le taillis**
tree	**un arbre**

wood	**le bois**
forest	**la forêt**
hedge	**la haie**
fence	**la barrière**
ditch	**le fossé**
gate	**la barrière** *(for a field)* ; **le portail** *(for an estate)*
stile	**le tourniquet**
bridge	**le pont**
ford	**le gué**
waterfall	**la chute d'eau**
weir	**le barrage**
water mill	**le moulin à eau**
reservoir	**le réservoir**
dam	**la retenue**
hydro electric power station	**le barrage hydro-électrique**
flood	**une inondation**

Useful phrases

Where shall we go?	**Où allons-nous ?**
What shall we do?	**Qu'est-ce qu'on fait ?**
What about...	**Ça vous dit ...**
... going for a walk?	**... d'aller faire une balade ?**
... going fishing?	**...d'aller à la pêche ?**

Insight

Naturally, *What about + ing?* – **Ça vous dit de** + verb? may be used in all kinds of situations – in the country, in the town, planning a holiday: *What about going to Brussels this weekend?* **Ça vous dit d'aller à Bruxelles, ce week-end ?** *What about* ... can also be translated with **Et si on** + imperfect... e.g. **Et si on allait à Bruxelles ce week-end ?** to which you may reply – as one of those taking part in the discussion of the plans – **Et si on allait plutôt à Barcelone ?** to suggest an alternative.

Useful verbs

to go for a walk	**aller se promener** *or* **aller faire une balade**
to go hill-walking	**aller faire une randonnée** *or* **partir en randonnée**
to go swimming	**aller se baigner**

Insight

Aller nager is used if, for example, you are sunbathing by the pool and decide that you will go into the pool for a swim.

to go hiking	**aller faire une randonnée/de la randonnée**
to ride a bike	**faire du vélo**
to go fishing	**aller à la pêche**
to go and pick mushrooms	**aller chercher des champignons**

8.2 In the mountains

Core vocabulary

hill	**la colline**
mountain	**la montagne**
mountain range	**la chaîne montagneuse**
mountain pass	**le col**
mountain path	**le sentier**
mountain hut/refuge	**le refuge de montagne**
cable car	**le téléphérique**
summit	**le sommet**
the weather	**le temps**
cloudy	**nuageux**
rainy	**pluvieux**
sunny	**ensoleillé**
dry	**sec**
windy	**venté**
easy	**facile**

moderately difficult	**moyennement difficile**
difficult	**difficile**
extreme	**extrême**
peak	**le pic**
rock face	**la face rocheuse**
slope	**la pente**
gorge	**la gorge**
cave	**le gouffre**
route	**la voie**
climbing equipment	**l'équipement d'escalade**
rope	**la corde**
harness	**le harnais**
karabiner	**le mousqueton**
nut	**un coinceur**
jamming	**le coincement**
pick axe	**le piolet**
rucksack	**le sac à dos**
torch	**la torche**
stove	**le poêle**
dried food	**les aliments séchés**
waterproofs	**les vêtements imperméables**
wedging	**le coinçage**
penknife, Swiss knife	**le couteau de poche, le couteau suisse**
flask	**une gourde**
thermos flask	**une thermos**
water bottle	**la bouteille d'eau**
sleeping bag	**le sac de couchage**
tent	**la tente**

Useful verbs

to climb	**grimper, escalader**
to abseil	**descendre en rappel**
to bivouac	**bivouaquer**
to hike	**randonner**
to rock climb	**escalader**
to ice climb	**faire de l'escalade dans les glaciers**

Useful phrases

What is the forecast?	**Que dit la météo ?/Qu'est-ce qui a été prévu, comme temps ?**
How difficult is it?	**Quel est le degré de difficulté ?**
How long does it take?	**Ça prend combien de temps ?**

8.3 At the seaside

Core vocabulary

seaside	**le bord de la mer**
sea	**la mer**
ocean	**l'océan**
wave	**la vague**
harbour	**le port**
port	**le port**
beach	**la plage**
sand	**le sable**
quicksand	**les sables mouvants**
sandy beach	**une plage de sable**
sand dune	**la dune**
cliff	**la falaise**
shell	**le coquillage**
pebble	**le galet**
pebble beach	**une plage de galets**
rock	**le rocher**
little island	**un îlot**
island	**une île**
jetty	**la jetée**
pier	**un embarcadère**
quay	**le quai**
pontoon	**le ponton**
reef	**la barre**
surf	**le ressac**
foam	**l'écume**
spray	**les embruns**

shore, coast	**la côte**
estuary	**l'estuaire**
cape	**le cap**
promontory	**le promontoire**
peninsula	**la péninsule**
sailing boat	**le bateau à voile**
sail	**la voile**
rowing boat	**le bateau à rames**
oar	**la rame**
oarlock	**la dame de nage**
yacht	**le yacht**
dinghy	**le canot**
motor boat	**le bateau à moteur**
ferry boat	**le ferry**
car ferry	**le ferry**
cruiser	**le bateau de croisière**
liner	**le transatlantique**
pilot	**le pilote**
navigation	**naviguer**
starboard	**tribord**
port side	**bâbord**
bow	**la proue**
stern	**la poupe**
buoy	**la bouée**
lighthouse	**le phare**
mast	**le mât**
anchor	**l'ancre**
automatic pilot	**le pilote automatique**
ropes	**les gréments**
high tide	**la marée haute**
low tide	**la marée basse**
sea-level	**le niveau de la mer**
calm	**calme**
choppy	**agitée**
rough	**forte**
gale warning	**un avis de coup de vent**

Useful verbs

to row	**ramer**
to sail	**faire de la voile**
to motor	**naviguer au moteur**
to cast off	**appareiller** *or* **larguer les amarres**
to tie up	**s'amarrer**
to drop anchor	**jeter l'ancre**

Useful phrases

When is high/low tide?	**La mer est haute/basse à quelle heure ?**
Where can I moor?	**Où est-ce que je peux mouiller ?** *or* **Où est-ce que je peux jeter l'ancre ?**

8.4 Working in the country

Core vocabulary

agriculture	**l'agriculture**
bee keeping	**l'apiculture**
horticulture	**l'horticulture**
wine growing	**la viniculture**
forestry	**la sylviculture**
farming	**l'agriculture**
market gardening	**les cultures maraîchères**
farmhouse	**la (maison de) ferme**
barn	**la grange**
stables	**l'écurie**
cattle shed	**une étable**
cattle	**le bétail**
cow	**la vache**
heifer	**le bœuf**
bull	**le taureau**
calf	**le veau**

sheep	**le mouton**
ewe	**la brebis**
ram	**le bélier**
lamb	**un agneau**
pig	**le cochon**
boar	**le verrat**
piglet	**le porcelet**
goat	**la chèvre**
nanny	**la bique**
billy	**le bouc**
kid	**le chevreau**
poultry	**les volailles**
chicken	**le poulet**
hen	**la poule**
cockerel	**le coq**
capon	**le chapon**
duck	**le canard**
duckling	**le caneton**
goose	**une oie**
gosling	**un oison**
turkey	**la dinde**
turkey cock	**le dindon**
turkey poult	**le dindonneau**
pheasant	**le faisan**
hen pheasant	**la faisanne**
sheep dog	**le chien de berger**
guard dog	**le chien de garde**
dog	**le chien**
bitch	**la chienne**
puppy	**le chiot**
cat	**le chat**
pussy	**la chatte**
kitten	**le chaton**
crops	**les cultures**
hay	**le foin**
hay stack	**une meule de foin**
roll	**un rouleau**
ball	**une balle**

straw	**la paille**
bee keeper	**l'apiculteur**
farmer	**le fermier/la fermière,** *or* **l'agriculteur/l'agricultrice** *or* **le cultivateur/la cultivatrice** *or* **l'exploitant/(e) agricole**
farm worker	**l'ouvrier/l'ouvrière agricole**
horticulturalist	**l'horticulteur/l'horticultrice**
vet	**le/la vétérinaire**
wine grower	**le viticulteur/la viticultrice** *or* **l'éleveur (de vin)**

Insight

In the French world of wine you speak of **un éleveur.** On a Bordeaux wine bottle, you may read **élevé dans nos chais** – literally: *brought up in our sheds* or **Marine et Pierre Dessadieu, éleveurs à Pauillac.**

vineyard	**la vigne**
vines	**les ceps**
grapes	**les raisins**
grape picking	**les vendanges**
fruit growing	**l'arboriculture** *or* **la culture fruitière**
olive grove	**une oliveraie**

Farm equipment ***le matériel agricole/les machines agricoles***

tractor	**le tracteur**
trailer	**la remorque**
plough	**la herse**
combine harvester	**la moissonneuse-batteuse**
harvester	**la moissonneuse**
hay baler	**la botteleuse**
milking machine	**la trayeuse**
generator	**le groupe électrogène**

Useful verbs

to cultivate, to grow (large-scale)	**cultiver**
to plant	**planter**
to spread fertilizer	**épandre** *or* **faire l'épandage**
to weed	**désherber**
to harvest	**récolter**
to package	**emballer**
to feed	**nourrir**
to milk	**traire**
to breed	**élever**
to sow	**scier**
to pick	**cueillir**
to harvest	**récolter**
to pick grapes	**vendanger,** *or* **faire les vendanges**

Useful phrases

Beware of the dog/bull.	**Attention, chien méchant !/ Attention au taureau !**
Please shut the gate.	**Veuillez refermer la barrière derrière vous.**
electric fence	**la barrière électrique**
No entry	**Entrée interdite**

TEST YOURSELF

À vous !

A mini stock-taking exercise on the unit you have just worked on

1 'High tide today is at noon' in French is…
[note: *more than one answer possible*]
- **a** Aujourd'hui, la mer est haute à midi.
- **b** Aujourd'hui, la marée sera haute à midi.
- **c** Aujourd'hui, la marée haute est à midi.
- **d** Aujourd'hui, la haute mer est à midi.

2 Please give the nouns of five activities carried out in the countryside, each ending in **culture**:
- **a** l'... culture
- **b** l'... culture
- **c** l'... culture
- **d** la... culture
- **e** la... culture

3 How would you say 'to milk the cows' in French?
- **a** allaiter les vaches
- **b** laiter les vaches
- **c** retraire les vaches
- **d** traire les vaches

4 How would you say in French 'Please shut the gate'?
- **a** Veuillez refermer le barreau.
- **b** Veuillez refermer la barrière derrière vous.
- **c** Veuillez refermer le barreau derrière vous.

5 Please translate the following five suggestions for weekend activities into French:
- **a** What about going to the Isle of Lewis?
- **b** What about going to a concert at the Vienna Opera House?
- **c** What about going to the movies?
- **d** What about meeting for brunch on Sunday?

6 'What is the weather forecast?' in French may be...
[*note: more than one answer possible*]
- **a** Que dit la météo ?
- **b** Quel temps va-t-il faire ?
- **c** Qu'est-ce que dit la météo ?
- **d** Qu'est-ce qui a été prévu comme temps ?

7 **Randonner** in French is...
[*note: more than one answer possible*]
- **a** to hike
- **b** to go hill-walking
- **c** to random
- **d** to roam

8 **Un avis de coup de vent** in a French maritime context is...
- **a** wind notification
- **b** wind alert
- **c** gale alert
- **d** gale warning

9 'Quicksand' in French is...
- **a** le sable filant
- **b** le sable mouvant
- **c** les sables mouvants
- **d** les sables en quick

10 'Vineyard' in French is...
[*note: more than one answer possible*]
- **a** la cour à vin
- **b** le clos à vins
- **c** la vigne
- **d** le vignoble

Answers: 1 a b c; 2 l'apiculture/l'agriculture/l'horticulture/la sylviculture/la viniculture; 3 d; 4 b; 5 a Ça vous dirait d'aller sur l'île de Lewis/à Lewis ? *or* Et si on allait sur l'île de Lewis/à Lewis ? b Ça vous dirait d'aller au concert à l'Opéra de Vienne ? *or* Et si on allait à l'Opéra de Vienne ? c Ça vous dirait d'aller au cinéma ? *or* Et si on allait au cinéma ? d Ça vous dirait de se retrouver pour bruncher dimanche ? *or* Et si on se retrouvait pour bruncher dimanche ?; 6 a b c d; 7 a b; 8 d; 9 c; 10 c d

9

Hobbies and sports

9.1 Hobbies

Core vocabulary

acting	**faire du théâtre**
cooking	**faire la cuisine**
dancing	**danser**
modern	**danser en boîte**
ballroom	**danser les danses de salon**
DIY	**bricoler**
drawing	**dessiner**
gardening	**jardiner**
going for a walk	**aller se promener**
going out (socially)	**sortir**
horse riding	**monter à cheval**
listening to music	**écouter de la musique**
meeting people	**voir des gens** *or* **rencontrer des gens**
painting	**peindre**
photography	**faire de la photo**
playing tennis/football	**jouer au tennis/au foot**
pottery	**faire de la poterie**
reading	**lire**
sailing	**faire de la voile**
sewing	**faire de la couture**
singing	**chanter**

sport	**faire du sport**
walking	**marcher**
watching films	**regarder des films**
watching television	**regarder la television**
go to the movies	**aller au cinéma**
writing	**écrire**

Insight

Aller au cinéma, colloquially, becomes **aller au cinoche** : **« Et si on allait au cinoche, ce soir ? »** Another colloquial way to make that suggestion is **« Et si on se faisait une toile, ce soir ? »** Note: **se faire**, may be used – still colloquially, between friends – to say a number of things: **se faire un petit resto** (literally 'to do oneself a little restaurant' – **resto** being the common abbreviation for restaurant). **« Ça vous dirait de vous faire un petit resto ? » « Ça vous dirait de vous faire un cinoche ? »**. This is the opposite of the formal *May I invite you to dinner?* **« Permettez-moi de vous inviter à dîner »**.

Outdoor pursuits *faire des choses en plein air*

birdwatching	**observer les oiseaux**
fishing	**aller à la pêche**
hunting	**aller à la chasse**
shooting	**faire du tir**
rambling	**partir en randonnée**

Indoor games *jeux de société*

playing chess	**jouer aux échecs**
playing cards	**jouer aux cartes**
playing bridge	**jouer au bridge**
playing party games	**jouer à des jeux de société**
happy families	**jouer au jeu des 7 familles**
bingo	**jouer au bingo**
jigsaw puzzle	**faire des puzzles**
dominoes	**jouer aux dominos**
draughts	**jouer aux dames**
darts	**jouer aux fléchettes**
billards	**jouer au billard**

snooker	**jouer au billard américain**
table football	**jouer au baby-foot**
crosswords	**faire des mots croisés**
making music	**faire de la musique**
playing in an orchestra	**jouer dans un orchestre**
singing in a band	**chanter dans un groupe**
singing in a choir	**chanter dans une chorale**
singing in a choir (grander)	**faire partie d'un chœur**
playing an instrument	**jouer d'un instrument**
piano	**du piano**
guitar (acoustic or electrical)	**de la guitare (sèche** *or* **électrique)**
violin	**du violon**
viola	**de l'alto**
trumpet	**de la trompette**
drums	**faire de la batterie**
to attend	**aller à**
to be a member of	**être membre de**
to be interested in	**s'intéresser à**
to be keen on	**beaucoup aimer** *or* **adorer**
to enjoy	**bien aimer**
to meet	**retrouver** *or* **se retrouver** *or* **faire la connaissance de**
to spend time doing something	**passer du temps à faire quelque chose**

Useful phrases

What do you do in your free time?	**A quoi passez-vous votre temps libre ?** *or* **Qu'est-ce que vous faites, dans votre temps libre ?**
Do you like …?	**Est-ce que vous aimez … ?**
I like meeting people.	**J'aime bien faire la connaissance de nouvelles personnes** *or* **J'aime bien sortir rencontrer des gens.**
I belong to a sailing/chess club.	**Je fais partie d'un club de voile/de joueurs d'échecs.**
We meet every Thursday night.	**Nous nous retrouvons tous les jeudi soirs.**

It's interesting.	**C'est intéressant.**
It's fantastic.	**C'est fantastique** *or* **C'est super.**
It's boring.	**C'est pas très intéressant.**
I am interested in astronomy.	**Je m'intéresse à l'astronomie** *or* **L'astronomie m'intéresse beaucoup.**
I go to cooking/baking classes.	**Je prends des cours de cuisine/des cours de pâtisserie.**

9.2 Sports

Core vocabulary

Ball games ***les jeux d'équipe***

football — **le football,** *referred to as* **« le foot ».**

Insight

Note that there are no single inverted commas in French; the only type, used both to quote and indicate direct speech/dialogue, is the chevron type: **le football**, commonly called **« le foot ».**

ball	**le ballon**
team	**l'équipe**
goal	**le but**
game	**le match**
football ground	**le terrain de foot**
score	**le score**
rugby	**le rugby**
player	**le joueur**
pitch	**le terrain de rugby**
basketball	**le basket**
basket	**le panier**
volleyball	**le volley**
net	**le filet**
hand-ball	**le handball –** *short:* **le hand**

Insight

Remember that the 'h' is never pronounced in French – 'le hand' with an adequate French accent would sound more like an 'euh' -> 'euhand' -> leuhand.

hockey **le hockey**
hockey stick **la crosse**
hockey puck **le palet**
golf **le golf**
golf club **le club de golf**
golf course **le parcours de golf**
green **le green**
hole **le trou**
bunker **le bunker**

Racket games *les jeux de raquettes*

tennis **le tennis**
tennis racquet **la raquette de tennis**
tennis court **le court de tennis**
tennis ball **la balle de tennis**
tennis player **le joueur de tennis**
badminton **le badminton**
net **le filet**
shuttlecock **le volant**
squash **le squash**
squash court **le court de squash**
squash racquet **la raquette de squash**

Martial arts *les arts martiaux*

boxing **la boxe**
judo **le judo**
karate **le karaté**
tae-kwando **le taïkwando**
wrestling **la lutte**

Athletics *l'athlétisme*

running **la course**
cross country **le cross**

high jump	**le saut en hauteur**
hurdles	**la course de haies**
track	**la piste**
lane	**le couloir**
timer	**le chronomètre**

Keep fit ***la mise en forme***

aerobics	**l'aérobic**
gymnastics	**la gymnastique**
fitness, working out	**le fitness**

Insight

In France, 'a gym' is called **une salle** or **un club de mise en forme** ou **une salle de fitness** or **un club/un centre de fitness.** My friends in Canada call it **le gym: « Bon, je vais au gym ! »** *Right, I am going to the gym !*

jogging	**le jogging**
machines (for muscle sculpting/working out)	**les appareils (de musculation)**
muscle sculpting	**le culturisme**
running	**courir**
weight lifting	**l'haltérophilie**
working out	**faire de la muscu(lation)** *or* **aller dans une salle** *or* **dans un club**
yoga	**le yoga**

Useful verbs

to win	**gagner**
to lose	**perdre**
to draw	**être ex-æquo**
to box	**boxer** *or* **faire de la boxe**
to jog	**faire du jogging**
to run	**courir**
to work out	**aller dans une salle** *or* **dans un club** *or* **faire du fitness**

Useful phrases

I like doing ...	**J'aime bien faire de/du/de la/des ...**
I don't like ... at all.	**J'ai horreur de ...**
I used to do that/it a lot.	**J'en ai beaucoup fait ...**
... not any more, though.	**... mais plus maintenant.**
I am not much into sports.	**Je ne suis pas très « sport »** *or* **Je ne suis pas trèsporté(e) sur le sport.**

Insight

Colloquially, to say that something is not 'your thing', you may say, almost word for word: **ça, c'est pas mon truc**. Thus: **Le sport, c(e n)'est pas mon truc**. For emphasis, add **du tout** – *at all* – at the end: **Le sport, c'est pas mon truc du tout !** And for pronunciation practice, you can repeat **du tout** three times: **du tout du tout du tout !**

9.3 More sports

Core vocabulary

Water sports ***les sports nautiques***

canoeing	**faire du canoë**
kayaking	**faire du canoë-kayak**
kayak	**le canoë-kayak**
canoe	**le canoë**
paddle	**la pagaie**
diving (deep sea)	**la plongée sous-marine**
wet suit	**une combinaison en néoprène/une combinaison isothermique**
dry suit	**une combinaison étanche**
gas bottle	**la bouteille d'oxygène**
mask	**le masque**
flippers	**les palmes**
snorkel	**le tuba**
rowing	**faire de l'aviron**

boat	**le bateau**
oar	**l'aviron**
sailing	**faire de la voile**
sail	**la voile**
hull	**la coque**
surfing	**faire du surf**
surf board	**la planche**
wind surfing	**la planche à voile**
wind surfer	**le planchiste**
sand yachting	**le char à voile**
yachting	**faire du yacht**
yacht	**un yacht** *or* **un bateau de plaisance**
dinghy	**un canot à moteur**
swimming	**la natation** *(competition – local as well as Olympic) otherwise* **nager**
breast stroke	**la brasse**
front crawl	**le crawl**
butterfly	**le papillon**
backstroke	**le dos crawlé**
diving	**plonger**
swimming pool	**la piscine**
lane	**la ligne d'eau**
length	**la longueur**
diving board	**le plongeoir**
swimming cap	**le bonnet de bain**
swimming costume	**le maillot de bain**
goggles	**les lunettes de natation**
archery	**le tir à l'arc**
bow	**l'arc**
arrow	**la flèche**
target	**la cible**
cycling	**le cyclisme**
racing bike	**un vélo de course**
mountain bike	**un vélo tout-terrain (un VTT – pronounce vétété)**
bike	**un vélo**
handlebars	**le guidon**
saddle	**la selle**

fencing	**l'escrime**
foil	**le fleuret**
mask	**le masque**
sword	**l'épée**
horse riding	**l'équitation**
saddle	**la selle**
bridle	**la bride**
stirrup	**l'étrier**
riding hat	**la bombe**
crop	**la cravache**
jodphurs	**la culotte de cheval**

Insight

The shape of jodphurs – two elephant ears dangling on the outsides of the thighs – has given rise to the name of this piece of clothing being used to refer to the unattractive fatty protruberances at the back and side of the thighs.

roller skating	**le roller**
skates	**les patins à roulettes** *or* **les rollers** *(modern)*
blades	**les rollerblades**
skateboarding	**le skateboard**
skateboard	**le skateboard**
rock climbing	**l'escalade**
mountaineering	**la montagne**
climbing	**l'escalade**
climbing boots	**les chaussures d'escalade**
climbing shoes (for walls)	**les chaussons d'escalade (pour murs/parois)**
rope	**la corde**
rucksack	**le sac à dos**
(indoor) climbing wall	**le mur d'escalade**
skiing	**faire du ski**
ski	**un ski**
pole	**le bâton**
binding	**la fixation**
piste	**la piste**

downhill skiing	**le ski de piste**
cross-country skiing	**le ski de fond**
off-piste	**le (ski) hors piste**
snowboarding	**faire du surf des neiges**
snowboard	**le surf**
sledging	**faire de la luge**
sledge	**la luge**
ice skating	**faire du patin à glace**
skates	**les patins**
ice rink	**la patinoire**
figure skates	**les patins à glace**
hockey skates	**les patins de hockey**

Useful phrases

I enjoy doing …	**J'aime bien faire du/de la …**
I am good at …	**Je suis bon/bonne en …**
I am not good at …	**Je ne suis pas bon/bonne en …**
I am hopeless at …	**Je suis nul/nulle en …**

TEST YOURSELF

À vous !

A mini stock-taking exercise on the unit you have just worked on

1 'A baking class' in French is...
 a des cours de cuisine
 b des cours de gâteau
 c des cours de pâtisserie
 d une classe de tartes

2 Please give the nouns of five hobbies/activities using **faire du/de la...** (e.g. **faire de la voile** – *sailing*)
 a
 b
 c
 d
 e

3 How would you say in French 'to play an instrument'?
 a jouer un instrument
 b jouer avec un instrument
 c jouer d'un instrument

4 How would you say in French 'to attend every (sports) event'? [*note: more than one answer possible*]
 a attendre toutes les rencontres
 b assister à toutes les rencontres
 c aller à toutes les rencontres

5 'I am interested in martial arts' in French is...
 a Je suis intéressé(e) dans les arts martiaux.
 b Les sports martiaux sont intéressés.
 c Je suis intéressé(e) auprès des arts martiaux.
 d Je suis intéressé(e) par les arts martiaux.
 e J'intéresse les arts martiaux.
 f Les arts martiaux m'intéressent.

6 Etre ex-æxquo means...
  a to be on par
  b to draw
  c to be eliminated

7 How would you say in French 'to be hopeless at...'?
  a être désespérant à
  b être désespéré(e) de
  c être nul/nulle en
  d être sans espoir

8 'Dry suit' in French is...
  a une combinaison sèche
  b un costume de bain sec
  c un ensemble étanche
  d une combinaison étanche

9 How would you say in French that...
  a fencing is not your thing
  b fencing is not your thing at all
  c ... not at all, not at all, not at all? (for the latter part of your answer, you are required to say your answer out loud!)

10 Un VTT is...
  a un vélo de transport touristique
  b un vélo de trekking transfrontalier
  c un vélo tout-terrain
  d un vélo terrain-traceur

Answers: 1 c; 2 faire du canoë-kayak/faire de la planche à voile/faire du cross/faire du ski/faire de la randonnée etc.; 3 c; 4 b c; 5 d f; 6 b; 7 c; 8 d; 9 L'escrime, c'est pas mon truc; l'escrime, c'est pas mon truc du tout; l'escrime, c'est pas mon truc du tout, du tout, du tout !; 10 c

10

Clothing

10.1 Garments and styles

Core vocabulary

Ladies' fashion *la mode femme*

blouse	**un corsage** *or* **un chemisier**
cardigan	**un cardigan** *or* **une veste de laine**
dress	**une robe**
evening dress	**une robe du soir**
stole	**une étole**
sundress	**une robe d'été**
wide-brimmed hat	**une capeline**
jacket	**une veste**
long jacket	**une veste longue**
short jacket	**une veste courte**
jersey	**un pull fin**
shorts	**un short**
skirt	**une jupe**
suit	**un costume** *or* **un tailleur**
trouser suit	**un tailleur-pantalon**
trousers	**un pantalon**
palazzo trousers	**un pantalon papillon**
lingerie	**la lingerie**
underwear	**les sous-vêtements**

Insight

Les sous-vêtements are also referred to as **les dessous** (for a woman). While **les sous-vêtements** carry a practical, functional dimension, **les dessous** are more frivolous; as in **des dessous affriolants**, *tempting/enticing underwear*.

bra	**le soutien-gorge**
panties	**le slip** *or* **la petite culotte** *or* **simply la culotte**
g-string	**un string**
slip	**une combinaison** *(if laced) or* **un fond de robe** *(if very simple)*
stocking(s)	**le(s) bas**
tights	**un collant**
underskirt	**un jupon**
nightie	**une chemise de nuit**
pyjamas	**un pyjama**
negligee	**un négligé**

Men's fashion *la mode homme*

blazer	**un blazer**
jacket	**un veston** *or* **une veste**
dinner jacket	**une veste habillée**
tuxedo	**un smoking**
jeans	**un jean**
jumper	**un pull** *or* **un chandail**
shirt	**une chemise**
shorts	**un short**
sock	**une chaussette**
suit	**un costume** *or* **un complet**
sweatshirt	**un sweat-shirt**
T-shirt	**un tee-shirt**
tie	**une cravate**
bow tie	**un nœud papillon**
trousers	**un pantalon**
belt	**une ceinture**
braces	**les bretelles**
waistcoat	**le gilet**
briefs	**un slip**

boxer shorts	**un caleçon**
vest	**un maillot de corps** *or* **un marcel** *(from the original brand name, in the 19th century)*
pyjamas	**un pyjama**
outerwear	**les vêtements du dessus**
coat	**le manteau**
wax jacket	**une veste de chasse**
duffel coat	**le duffle-coat**
raincoat	**un imperméable**
sports jacket	**le blouson**
trenchcoat	**le trench**
jacket	**la veste**
hat	**le chapeau**
cap	**la casquette**
balaclava	**la cagoule**

Insight

La cagoule, *balaclava*, can be worn to keep warm under your bike helmet as well as for robbing banks! Thus: **Trois gangsters cagoulés ont fait irruption dans l'agence en début d'après-midi.**

scarf	**l'écharpe**
glove	**le gant**
mitt	**la moufle**

Useful verbs

to wear	**porter**
to put on	**enfiler/mettre**
to fit	**aller**
Does it fit?	**Ça vous va ?**
to suit	**aller**
It suits you, really.	**Ça vous va vraiment bien.**
It fits perfectly.	**Ça tombe impeccablement** *(e.g. a tailor-made jacket)*

Useful phrases

I will be wearing ...	**Je vais mettre ...**
a dark suit	**un ensemble noir**
a coat and hat	**un manteau et un chapeau**
a sweatshirt, jeans and trainers	**un sweat-shirt, un jean et des baskets**
What will you be wearing?	**Qu'est-ce que vous allez mettre/ porter ?**
Which size are you?	**Vous faites du combien ?** *or* **Quelle taille faites-vous ?**
It is too short.	**C'est trop court.**
too wide	**trop large**
too long	**trop long**
too tight	**trop étroit/serré**
Have you got anything bigger/smaller?	**Auriez-vous quelque chose de plus grand/de plus petit ?**
Would you have the same one size bigger/smaller?	**Auriez-vous la taille au-dessus/au-dessous ?**
Would you have the same in a different colour?	**Auriez-vous la même chose d'une autre couleur ?**
It suits you./It doesn't suit you.	**Ça vous va très bien./Ça ne vous vas pas.**

10.2 The garment

Core vocabulary

Measures and parts ***Mesures et parties du vêtement***

measurements **les mesures**

Insight

To take someone's measurements is **prendre les mesures de quelqu'un**. If you decide to have your wedding dress made by a seamstress, she may say: **« Je vais prendre vos mesures »**. Note, however, that **prendre la mesure de quelqu'un**, in

(Contd)

the singular, means to assess someone for what they really are, e.g. **Il n'avait pas pris la mesure de son adversaire,** *He misjudged his opponent.*

tape measure	**le mètre ruban**
length	**la longueur**
width	**la largeur**
height	**la hauteur**
size	**la taille**
collar	**le col**
neck	**le col** *or* **l'ouverture**
shoulder	**l'épaule**
sleeve	**la manche**
cuff	**le poignet**
chest	**la poitrine**
waist	**la taille**
hips	**les hanches (la)**

Fabric *le tissu*

cotton	**le coton**
corduroy	**le velours côtelé**
fur	**la fourrure**
fake fur	**la fausse fourrure**
jersey	**la maille**
leather	**le cuir**
linen	**le lin**
satin	**le satin**
silk	**la soie**
suede	**le daim**
synthetic fibre	**la fibre synthétique**
tweed	**le tweed**
velvet	**le velours**
dévoré	**le velours dévoré**
wool	**la laine**
checked	**à carreaux**
hound's tooth (small)	**pied-de-poule**
hound's tooth (large)	**pied-de-coq**
floral	**à fleurs**

multicolour	**multicolore**
patterned	**imprimé**
pleated	**plissé**
plain (one colour)	**uni**
spotted	**à pois**
striped	**à rayures**
button	**le bouton**
fastener	**la fermeture**
needle	**une aiguille**
ribbon	**le ruban**
scissors	**les ciseaux**
sewing machine	**la machine à coudre**
velcro	**le velcro**
zip	**la fermeture éclair** *or* **le zip**
lining	**la doublure**
detergent	**la lessive**
detergent for wool	**la lessive liquide pour lainages**
fabric softener	**un adoucissant à linge**
soap powder	**la lessive**
dry cleaner's	**le pressing**

Useful verbs

to wash	**laver**
to dry	**faire sécher**
to dry clean	**nettoyer à sec**
to have something dry cleaned	**donner quelque chose à nettoyer**
to iron	**repasser**
to mend	**réparer** *or* **racommoder**
to soak	**faire tremper**

Useful phrases

I have lost a button.	**J'ai perdu un bouton.**
Can I get this laundered?	**Est-ce que je peux vous donner ça à nettoyer ?**
How long will it take?	**Ça prendra combien de temps ?**

When will it be ready?	**Ça sera prêt quand ?**
Can you remove this stain?	**Est-ce que vous pensez pouvoir faire partir cette tache ?**
Can you sew this button on?	**Est-ce que vous pouvez recoudre ce bouton ?**
Can you take it in?	**Est-ce que vous pouvez le/la reprendre ?**
Can you shorten it?	**Est-ce que vous pouvez le/la raccourcir ?**
This garment must be dry cleaned.	**Nettoyage à sec uniquement.**
This garment can be machine washed.	**Lavable en machine.**
Handwash only.	**Lavage à la main uniquement.**
Don't use bleach.	**Ne pas utiliser d'eau de Javel sur ce vêtement.**

10.3 Special occasions

Core vocabulary

Going to work *aller travailler*

coat	**une blouse**
uniform	**un uniforme**
apron	**un tablier**
overall	**une combinaison**
dungarees	**une salopette**

It's raining! *Il pleut !*

raincoat	**un vêtement de pluie** *or* **un imperméable**
rain hat	**un chapeau de pluie**
waterproof trousers	**un pantalon imperméable**
rubber boots	**des bottes de pluie**
umbrella	**un parapluie**

It's cold! ***Il fait froid !***

anorak	**un anorak**
walking boots	**des chaussures de marche**
thick socks	**des grosses chaussettes**
woollen hat	**un bonnet (en laine)**

Insight

In Scotland, you may hear the French word 'bonnet' used to refer to a woollen hat.

gloves	**des gants**

On the beach ***à la plage/sur la plage***

swimming costume	**un maillot de bain**
bikini	**un bikini**
topless bikini	**un monokini**
trunks	**un slip de bain**
flippers	**les palmes**
goggles	**les lunettes de natation**
snorkel	**le tuba**
flip-flops	**des claquettes**
sun cream	**de la crème solaire**
sun oil	**de l'huile solaire**
sun hat	**un chapeau de soleil**

A night on the town ***une soirée en ville***

evening dress	**la tenue de soirée**
formal dress	**la tenue habillée**
casual dress	**la tenue décontractée**
high heels	**les talons hauts**

Playing the game ***l'équipement de sport***

baseball hat	**une casquette de baseball**
polo shirt	**un polo**
shorts	**un short**
socks	**des chaussettes**
trainers	**des baskets/des chaussures de sport**

Accessories *les accessoires*

jewellery	**les bijoux**
bracelet	**le bracelet**
brooch	**la broche**
earrings	**les boucles d'oreille**
dangling earrings	**les pendants d'oreille**
necklace	**le collier**
ring	**l'anneau/la bague**
watch	**la montre**
silver	**l'argent**
gold	**l'or**
platinum	**la platine**
diamond	**le diamant**
emerald	**l'émeraude**
ruby	**le rubis**
sapphire	**le saphir**
semi-precious stone	**une pierre semi-précieuse**

Useful verbs

to get dressed	**s'habiller**
to get undressed	**se déshabiller**
to put on	**mettre**
to slip into	**enfiler**
to take off	**enlever**
to tie one's shoelaces	**faire/mettre ses lacets**
to wear	**porter**
to accessorize	**accessoiriser**

Useful phrases

He/She always looks ...	**Il/Elle a toujours l'air ...**
casual	**décontracté(e)**
fashionable	**à la mode**
smart	**élégant(e)**
unfashionable	**démodé(e)**
untidy	**négligé(e)**

10.4 Footwear

Core vocabulary

The shoe shop *le magasin de chaussures*

shoes	**les chaussures**
hosiery	**la bonnetterie**
socks	**les chaussettes**
stockings	**les bas**
tights	**le collant**
I am looking for a pair of boots with a side zip.	**Je cherche une paire de bottes qui se ferment sur le côté.**
I am looking for a pair of court shoes with a very low heel.	**Je cherche une paire d'escarpins avec un tout petit talon.**
Which size are you?	**Quelle taille faites-vous ?** *or* **Du combien chaussez-vous ?**
I am a size six.	**Je chausse du 39.**
May I try them on?	**Je peux les essayer ?**
boot	**la botte**
clog	**le sabot**
court shoe	**un escarpin bas**
flip-flops	**les claquettes (la)** *or* **les tongs (le)**
mocassin	**le mocassin**
pump	**un escarpin**
sandal	**la sandale**
shoe	**la chaussure**
slip on	**un mocassin** *or* **une chaussure basse**
slipper	**une pantoufle** *or* **un chausson**
tennis shoe	**une tennis**
trainer	**une basket** *or* **une chaussure de sport**
wellington/rubber boot	**une botte en caoutchouc** *or* **une botte de pluie**
wader	**la cuissarde**
ballet shoe	**le chausson de danse**

half point	**les demi-pointes**
point shoes	**les pointes**
climbing boot	**la chaussure** *or* **le chausson d'escalade**
cycling shoe	**le cycliste**
dancing shoe	**la chaussure de bal**
diving boot	**le chausson de plongée**
flipper	**la palme**
ski boot	**la chaussure de ski**
snowboard boot	**la botte de surf**
safety/steel-toed boot	**la chaussure de sécurité/à bout renforcé**
walking boot	**la chaussure de marche**
leather	**le cuir**
rubber	**le caoutchouc**
synthetic	**le synthétique**
shoe polish	**le cirage**
shoe cleaner	**le cireur**
shoe protector	**un enduit protecteur**
shoe stretcher	**un embauchoir**
chiropody	**la chiropodie**
massage	**le massage**
reflexology	**la réflexologie**
foot	**le pied**
toe	**un orteil**
ankle	**la cheville**
sole	**la semelle**
toe nail	**un ongle de pied**
arch of the foot	**la voûte plantaire**

Useful verbs

to try shoes on	**essayer des chaussures**
to put on one's shoes	**mettre ses chaussures**
to take off one's shoes	**enlever ses chaussures**
to get blisters	**se faire des ampoules**
to break one's shoes in	**faire ses chaussures**

Insight

I'd better break these shoes in before wearing them to the End of Year Ball! **Il vaut mieux que je fasse ces chaussures avant de les porter au bal du Bout de l'An !**

to polish one's shoes	**cirer ses chaussures**

Useful phrases

bare foot	**pieds nus**
I have got sore feet.	**J'ai mal aux pieds.**
I have got blisters.	**J'ai des ampoules.**
Have you got a plaster?	**Auriez-vous un pansement ?**
Please remove your shoes in the house.	**Veuillez enlever vos chaussures dans la maison.**
What shoe size are you?	**Du combien chaussez-vous ?**
These shoes are comfortable/ uncomfortable.	**Ces chaussures sont confortables/ pas très confortables.**
These shoes hurt my feet.	**Ces chaussures me font mal aux pieds.**

TEST YOURSELF

À vous !

A mini stock-taking exercise on the unit you have just worked on

1 **Un marcel** in French means…
- **a** docker
- **b** boxer
- **c** vest

2 Please give the nouns for five types of coat:
- **a**
- **b**
- **c**
- **d**
- **e**

3 How would you say 'It really suits you' in French?
- **a** Ça vous suit réellement
- **b** Ça vous va réellement
- **c** Ça vous va vraiment bien
- **d** Ça vous suit vraiment bien

4 **Un complet** in French is…
- **a** a suit
- **b** complete evening dress
- **c** a raincoat

5 'Would you have the same one in a bigger size?' in French is… [*note: more than one answer possible*]
- **a** Auriez-vous la même chose en plus grand ?
- **b** Auriez-vous une grande taille ?
- **c** Auriez-vous la taille au-dessous ?
- **d** Auriez-vous la taille au-dessus ?
- **e** Auriez-vous la même chose une taille au-dessus ?

6 Give the names of five types of footwear in French.

a

b

d

e

7 How would you say in French 'the arch of the foot'?

a l'arche du pied

b le coup de pied

c la voûte plantaire

d la voûte podologique

8 **Une ampoule** in French may be...
[*note: more than one answer possible*]

a a blister

b a lightbulb

c a shoelace

d a hat

9 **Faire tremper** in French means...

a to exchange

b to soak

c to dry clean

e to hand wash

10 'Evening dress' in French is...
[*note: more than one answer possible*]

a une robe du soir

b une tenue du soir

c une tenue de soirée

d une robe de soirée

Answers: 1 c; 2 un manteau/un blouson/un imperméable/un trench/une veste/etc.; 3 c; 4 a; 5 d e; 6 les chaussures/les escarpins/les claquettes/les sandales/les bottes de pluie/etc.; 7 c; 8 a b; 9 b; 10 a c d

11

Travel

11.1 Travel

Core vocabulary

journey	**le voyage** *or* **le trajet**

Insight

For example, you may see written on train tickets **trajet aller retour**, *return journey*, or **aller simple**, *single journey*.

itinerary	**l'itinéraire**
route	**l'itinéraire**
map	**la carte**
journey or travel	**le voyage** – *professionally:* **le déplacement**
travel agency	**l'agence de voyages**
overland	**par voie de terre**
by air	**par air**
by sea	**par mer**
by rail	**par voie ferrée**
by train	**en train**
by plane	**en avion**
by coach	**en car**

Insight

Coach is **un car** on the road and **une voiture** when it refers to part of a train.

by car	**en voiture**
by hire car	**en voiture de location**
by boat	**en bateau**
by ferry	**en ferry**
by bike	**en vélo**
on horseback	**à cheval**
on foot	**à pied**
timetable/schedule	**les horaires**
ticket	**le ticket** *or* **le billet**

Insight

'ticket' v. **'billet'**

There is no rule differentiating between the use of **ticket** or **billet**: either can be used interchangeably. Thus: **Le ticket de bus, le ticket de métro, le ticket de tram(way); le billet de train, le billet d'avion, le billet de bateau.** Usage rules.

booking	**la réservation**
reservation	**la réservation**
online booking	**la réservation en ligne**
arrival	**l'arrivée**
departure	**le départ**
scheduled arrival/departure	**arrivée prévue/départ prévu**

Useful verbs

to travel	**voyager** *or* **se déplacer** *(in a work context)*
to go	**aller**
to sail	**aller/venir en bateau**
to fly	**aller/venir en avion**
to drive	**aller/venir en voiture**
to tour	**faire le tour de .../visiter**
to arrive	**arriver**
to leave	**quitter**

Useful phrases

Can you help me, please?	**Pourriez-vous m'aider, s'il-vous-plaît ?**
I'm lost.	**Je me suis perdu(e).**
How do I get to ...?	**Pourriez-vous m'indiquer ... ?**
What is the best way to go to ...?	**Quel est la meilleure façon d'aller à ... ?**
Is it far?	**C'est loin ?**
How far is it?	**C'est à quelle distance ?**
How long does it take?	**Je vais mettre combien de temps ?**
I travel a lot for my job.	**Je me déplace beaucoup pour mon travail.**

11.2 Travel by train

Core vocabulary

station	**la gare (ferroviaire)**
station master	**le chef de gare**
booking office	**le guichet** *or* **le centre de réservations** *(the latter in a large station)*
timetable	**les horaires**
ticket	**le billet (de train)**
single ticket	**un aller simple**
return ticket	**un aller-retour**
second class	**en seconde**
first class	**en première**
full price	**plein tarif**
concession	**tarif réduit**
proof of concession	**une carte de réduction**
arrivals	**arrivées**
departures	**départs**
indicator board	**le tableau**
information	**l'information** *or* **les renseignements**
waiting room	**la salle d'attente**
platform	**le quai**

subway	**le métro**
stairs	**l'escalier**
escalator	**l'escalier roulant**
conveyor	**le tapis roulant**
lift	**l'ascenseur**
train	**le train**
high speed train (360 km/h)	**le TGV (train à grande vitesse)**
express, intercity-type trains	**le train corail or l'Intercités**
slower, local/regional train	**le TER (Train Express Régional)** – *pronounced*: **téheair –** *'in one go', no pauses between the respective letters*
coach	**la voiture** *or* **le wagon**
non smoking	**non-fumeurs**
smoking	**fumeurs**

Insight

As public space is becoming increasingly non-smoking throughout Europe – including in France, where it took 15 years to implement (the so-called **Loi Evin** was passed in…1991!) – you may want to look for the sign **Espace fumeurs** if you are dying for a cigarette.

first class	**première classe**
second class	**seconde classe**
buffet	**le buffet** *or* **la voiture-bar**
trolley	**le buffet ambulant** *or* **le service de vente ambulante** *(the latter being the official designation)*
personnel	**le personnel**
guard	**le chef de bord**
ticket inspector	**le contrôleur**
train driver	**le mécanicien**
traveller	**le voyageur**
level crossing	**le passage à niveau**
railway track	**les rails** *or* **la voie**
signals	**les signaux**
luggage	**les bagages**

suitcase	**la valise**
suitcase on wheels	**la valise à roulettes**
left luggage	**la consigne**

Useful verbs

to book a ticket	**réserver une place** *or* **sa place** *or* **son billet**
to make a reservation	**réserver** *or* **prendre une réservation**

Useful phrases

Do I have to change?	**Est-ce qu'il faut que je change ?**
Is the train on time?	**Est-ce que le train est à l'heure ?**
How late is the train?	**Le train a combien de retard ?**
Will I miss the connection?	**Est-ce que je vais avoir ma correspondance ?**
Is there a car park at the station?	**Est-ce qu'il y a un parking dans la gare ?**
Which platform does it leave from?	**Il part de quel quai ?**
Is this the train for …?	**C'est le train pour … ?**
Excuse-me, but this is my seat.	**Je suis désolé(e), mais c'est ma place.**
I have a reservation.	**J'ai une réservation.**
How often does it run?	**Quelle est la fréquence des passages ?**
Which line do I need for …?	**Je prends quelle ligne pour aller à … ?**

11.3 Travel by plane

airport	**l'aéroport**
car park	**le parking**
departures	**les départs**
checking in	**s'enregistrer**
desk	**le desk** *or* **l'enregistrement**
ID	**une pièce d'identité**

hand luggage	**un bagage à main**
cabine luggage	**un baggage cabine**
luggage search	**une fouille des bagages**
security check	**le contrôle de sécurité**

Which class? ***en quelle classe ?***

economy	**économie**
business	**classe affaires**
first	**première classe**
ticket	**un billet**
passport	**le passeport**
ID document	**la pièce d'identité**
passport photograph	**une photo d'identité**
credit card	**une carte de crédit**
green card	**une « green card » (un permis de travail pour travailler aux États-Unis)**
boarding card	**la carte d'embarquement**
departure lounge	**la salle d'embarquement**
executive lounge	**le salon Classe Affaires**
information	**l'information** *or* **les renseignements**
announcement	**une annonce**
flight	**le vol**
gate	**la porte**
delay	**le retard**
taking off	**le décollage**
plane	**un avion**
aircraft	**un appareil**
row	**la rangée**
seat	**la place**
window seat	**la place côté fenêtre**
aisle seat	**la place côté couloir**
seat belt	**la ceinture**
life jacket	**le gilet de sauvetage**
emergency exit	**la sortie de secours**
overhead locker	**le compartiment à bagages**
toilet	**les toilettes**
arrivals	**les arrivées**
landing	**l'atterrissage**

landing card	**la carte de débarquement**
baggage reclaim	**l'arrivée des bagages**
customs	**la douane**
duty	**la taxe**
pilot	**le/la pilote**
co-pilot	**le/la co-pilote** *or* **le commandant de bord** *(on commercial carriers)*
mechanics	**le mécanicien/la mécanicienne**
steward	**le steward**
stewardess	**la stewardesse** *or* **l'hôtesse**

Useful verbs

to board	**embarquer**
to leave/depart	**partir**
to take off	**décoller**
to fly	**être en vol**
to arrive	**arriver**
to land	**atterrir**
to navigate	**naviguer**
to put the seat back	**incliner son siège**
to put the seat upright	**remettre son siège en position verticale**
to stow the table	**remonter sa tablette**
to experience turbulence	**traverser des turbulences**

Useful phrases

The plane is delayed.	**L'avion a du retard.**
The plane is delayed by 25 minutes.	**L'avion a 25 minutes de retard.**
Your flight leaves from gate ...	**Votre vol partira de la porte ...**
Please will you return to your seats and fasten your seat-belts.	**Veuillez regagner votre place et attacher votre ceinture.**
We are flying at an altitude of ...	**Nous naviguons à une altitude de ...**
At a speed of...	**À la vitesse de ...**
Can I have ...?	**Est-ce que je pourrais avoir ...**
earphones	**des écouteurs**

a blanket	**une couverture**
a pillow	**un oreillet**
a drink of water	**un verre d'eau**
My luggage is missing.	**Je ne retrouve pas mon bagage/mes bagages.**

11.4 Travel by car

Core vocabulary

car	**la voiture**
estate car	**le break**
four wheel drive/off-road car	**un quatre/quatre – un 4 X 4**
sports car	**une voiture de sport**
convertible	**un coupé décapotable**
electric	**une voiture électrique**
hybrid	**une voiture hybride**
automatic	**une boîte automatique**
manual	**une boîte manuelle**
It has ...	**C'est ...**
three/five doors	**une trois/cinq portes**
16 valves	**à 16 pistons**
pedal	**la pédale**
accelerator	**un accélérateur**
brake	**le frein**
clutch	**un embrayage**
windscreen	**le pare-brise**
gears	**les vitesses**
gear lever	**le levier de vitesse**
steering wheel	**le volant**
handbrake	**le frein à main**
indicator	**le clignotant**
lights	**les feux**
headlamps	**les phares**
side lights	**les codes**
on full	**en plein phares**

on dip	**en codes**
speedometer	**le compteur de vitesse**
mileometer	**le compteur de kilomètres**
petrol gauge	**la jauge d'essence**
interior	**l'intérieur**
seat	**le siège**
safety belt	**la ceinture de sécurité**
leg room	**la place pour les jambes**
glove compartment	**la boîte à gants**
visor/sunshield	**le pare-soleil**
wing mirror	**le rétroviseur extérieur (gauche/droit)**
rear mirror	**le rétroviseur**
heating	**le chauffage**
air conditioning	**la climatisation**
wheel	**la roue**
tyre	**le pneu**
valve	**la valve**
tyre pressure	**la pression des pneus**
jack	**le crick**
spare wheel	**la roue de secours**
exterior	**l'extérieur**
boot	**le coffre**
bumper	**le pare-choc**
number plate	**la plaque d'immatriculation** *or* **minéralogique**
fog lights	**les feux de brouillard**
rear lights	**les feux arrière**
exhaust	**le pot d'échappement**
battery	**la batterie**
radiator	**le radiateur**
getting technical	**techniquement ...**
ignition	**le démarrage**
spark plug	**la bougie**
water hose	**l'arrivée d'eau**
oil pressure	**le niveau d'huile**
fan belt	**la courroie du ventilateur**
windscreen wiper	**l'essuie-glace**
warning light	**le warning**

Useful verbs

to drive	**conduire**
to drive from A to B	**aller de A à B en voiture**
to put one's lights on	**allumer ses lumières**
to turn one's lights off	**éteindre ses lumières**
to put one's indicator on	**mettre son clignotant (à gauche/ à droite)**
to give way	**laisser passer**
to overtake	**doubler**

Useful phrases

You have left your lights on.	**Tu as laissé tes lumières allumées.**
How do I adjust the seat?	**Comment est-ce que je règle mon siège ?**

11.5 The road

country road	**une route de campagne**
main road	**une grand'route**
one-way road	**une route à sens unique**
dual carriageway	**une route à quatre voies**
motorway	**une autoroute**
toll	**le péage**

Insight

In France, most motorways are subject to a toll. Both the toll and the tollbooth are referred to as **le péage**. In Brittany, motorways are free. If you are not in a rush to get to your destination, the best way to discover France – and avoid paying tolls that may amount to quite a sum if you do a lot of driving! – is to take **les routes nationales** and **les routes départementales**, which are well maintained.

motorway lane	**une voie**
inside lane	**la voie rapide**
outside lane	**la voie lente**
central reservation	**la bande médiane (matérialisée)**
access road	**la bretelle d'accès**
junction	**la sortie**
intersection	**le carrefour** *or, for a motorway*, **l'échangeur**
crossroads	**le carrefour**
roundabout	**un rond-point**
bridge	**le pont**
toll bridge	**le pont à péage**
level crossing	**le passage à niveau**
traffic lights	**les feux (de la circulation)**
road works	**les travaux**
emergency traffic lights	**les feux d'urgence**
diversion	**la déviation**
road signs	**les panneaux de signalisation**
hard shoulder	**l'accotement**
speed limit	**la limitation de vitesse**
speed camera	**la caméra**
driving licence	**un permis de conduire**
insurance	**une assurance**
car registration card	**la carte grise**
fine	**une amende**
road tax	**la vignette**

Services *les services*

garage	**le garage**
petrol station	**la station essence**
petrol	**l'essence**
diesel	**le gazole**
unleaded petrol	**l'essence sans plomb**
air	**l'air**
water	**l'eau**
oil	**l'huile**
oil change	**le changement d'huile**
emergency dlane	**la bande d'arrêt d'urgence**

emergency services	**les services d'urgence**
breakdown	**une panne**

Useful verbs

to speed	**faire de la vitesse**
to accelerate	**accélérer**
to slow down	**ralentir**
to brake	**freiner**
to break down	**tomber en panne**

Useful phrases

The road surface is …	**Le revêtement de la route est …**
good/bad	**en bon état/en mauvais état**
smooth/uneven	**lisse/abîmé**
bumpy	**irrégulier**
I have broken down.	**Je suis en panne.**
The car is overheating.	**Le moteur chauffe anormalement.**
The engine has stopped.	**Le moteur a calé.**
I have a puncture.	**J'ai un pneu creuvé.**
The silencer has blown.	**Le pot d'échappement a explosé.**

TEST YOURSELF

À vous !

A mini stock-taking exercise on the unit you have just worked on

1 'Unleaded petrol' in French is...
- **a** le pétrole déplombé
- **b** le pétrole sans plomb
- **c** l'essence déplombée
- **d** l'essence sans plomb

2 'We will drive to the Côte d'Azur' in French is...
- **a** Nous conduirons à la Côte d'Azur
- **b** Nous conduirons jusqu'à la Côte d'Azur
- **c** Nous irons sur la Côte d'Azur en voiture
- **d** Nous irons en voiture à la Côte d'Azur

3 'A return ticket' in French is...
[*note: more than one answer possible*]
- **a** un ticket retour
- **b** un aller-retour
- **c** un billet aller-retour
- **d** un billet retour
- **e** un ticket aller-retour

4 TGV stands for...
- **a** train en gare ou en pleine voie
- **b** train à grande vitesse
- **c** train garé hors voie

5 'To miss one's connection' in French is...
[*note: more than one answer possible*]
- **a** manquer sa correspondance
- **b** rater sa correspondance
- **c** perdre sa correspondance

6 **La carte d'embarquement** means....

a landing card
b embarking card
c boarding card

7 How would you say in French 'My luggage is missing'? [*note: more than one answer possible*]

a Mon bagage me manque
b Mon bagage manque
c Il manque mon bagage
d Je ne retrouve pas mon bagage
e Je ne retrouve pas mes bagages
f Je manque mes bagages

8 **La carte grise** in French is:

a a French green card
b a car registration card
c a speeding boarding card

9 You have broken down and you are calling from **une borne d'appel d'urgence** on the motorway. What will you say?

a Je suis cassé(e)
b Je suis arrêté(e) sur l'autoroute.
c Je suis en panne
d Ma voiture s'est cassée.

10 **La consigne** is...

a consignment services
b left luggage
c consignor's office

Answers: 1 d; 2 c; 3 b c e; 4 b; 5 a b; 6 c; 7 d e; 8 b; 9 c; 10 b

12

Tourism

12.1 Where to go

Core vocabulary

tourism industry	**l'industrie du tourisme**
travel agents	**une agence de voyage**
brochure	**une brochure** *or* **un dépliant**
tourist	**un(e) touriste**
excursion	**une excursion**
tour	**un voyage** *or* **un itinéraire**
coach trip	**une excursion en car**
guided visit or tour	**une visite guidée**
cruise	**une croisière**
holiday resort	**un village de vacances**
seaside	**le bord de la mer**
sea, sand and sun	**la mer, la plage et le soleil**
mountains and lakes	**les lacs et les montagnes**
countryside	**la campagne**
adventure holidays	**partir à l'aventure**
winter sports	**les sports d'hiver**
ski resort	**une station de ski**
outdoor pursuits	**les activités de plein-air**
summer holiday	**les grandes vacances**
school holiday	**les vacances scolaires**
to go on holiday	**partir en vacances**

12.2 What to take

Core vocabulary

luggage (a piece of)	**les bagages (un bagage)**
suitcase	**la valise**
travel bag	**le sac de voyage**
rucksack, backpack	**le sac à dos**
overnight bag	**le sac de week-end**
hand luggage	**un bagage à main**
cabin luggage	**un bagage cabine**
passport	**le passeport**
visa	**le visa**
ticket	**le billet** *or* **le ticket**
insurance	**l'assurance**
driving licence	**le permis de conduire**
credit card	**la carte de crédit**
currency	**la monnaie** *or* **la devise**

Insight

La monnaie and **la devise** mean the same thing: *currency*. However, **la monnaie** is used mostly in informal, everyday dealings, whereas **la devise** is used in the financial world to refer to foreign currencies, e.g. investments in currencies – **placements en devises.** It will also be the heading on the currency board in a bank or a bureau de change. Also remember: **la monnaie** means change: **Auriez-vous la monnaie ?** Would you have the exact change? and **Auriez-vous de la monnaie ?** Would you have some change?

traveller's cheque	**le chèque de voyage**
emergency phone number	**un numéro d'appel d'urgence**
laptop	**un ordinateur portable**
mobile phone	**un téléphone portable**
sponge bag/toilet bag	**la trousse de toilette**
soap	**le savon**
toothbrush	**la brosse à dents**

toothpaste	**le dentifrice**
mouthwash	**le rinçage bucal** *or* **un elixir dentaire**
razor	**le rasoir**
nail scissors	**les ciseaux à ongles**
nail file	**la lime à ongle**
nailbrush	**la brosse à ongles**
tweezers	**la pince à épiler**
shampoo	**le shampooing**
conditioner	**l'après-shampoing**
hairbrush	**la brosse à cheveux**
comb	**le peigne**
hair-dryer	**le sèche-cheveux** *or* **le séchoir à cheveux**
face/day/night cream	**la crème pour le visage/de jour/de nuit**
hand cream	**la crème pour les mains**
cleanser	**le soin nettoyant**
toner	**le soin tonifiant**
moisturiser	**le soin hydratant**
sun cream	**la crème solaire**
waterproof sun cream	**une crème solaire qui résiste à l'eau**
after-sun cream	**une crème après-soleil**
SPF – sun protection factor	**IPS – un indice de protection solaire**
sun block	**un écran (solaire) total**
wardrobe	**une armoire** *or* **une penderie**
coat hanger	**le cintre**
iron	**le fer à repasser**

Useful verbs

to pack	**faire ses bagages/sa valise/son sac**
to unpack	**défaire ses bagages/sa valise/son sac**
to fold	**plier**
to unfold	**déplier**
to hang up	**accrocher**

to wash	**laver**
to dry clean	**faire nettoyer**
to take to the drycleaner's	**donner au pressing**
to mend	**réparer** *or* **racommoder**
to iron	**repasser**
to press	**presser**

Useful phrases

I have lost my luggage.	**J'ai perdu mes bagages/ma valise/ mon sac.**
I can't find …	**Je ne retrouve pas …**
Have you got a …?	**Auriez-vous … ?**
Where can I get a …?	**Où est-ce que je peux trouver … ?**
Where is the nearest drycleaner's?	**Où se trouve le pressing le plus proche ?**

12.3 Where to stay

Core vocabuary

accommodation	**le logement** *or* **l'hébergement**
two-star hotel	**un hôtel deux étoiles**
three-star hotel	**un hôtel trois étoiles**
luxury hotel	**un hôtel de luxe**
inn	**un petit hôtel (de charme)**
farm guestroom	**une chambre à la ferme**
holiday house	**une maison de vacances**
youth hostel	**une auberge de jeunesse**
camp site	**un camping**
caravan site	**un caravaning**
entrance	**l'entrée**
reception	**la réception**
bill	**la note**

Insight

La note or **l'addition**? Well... this is very much a matter of personal choice and perhaps also local influences. A rule of thumb is that **la note** is used more for hotel bills; whereas both **la note** and **l'addition** can be used in restaurants.

stairs	**l'escalier**
lift	**l'ascenseur**
restaurant	**le restaurant**
breakfast room	**la salle du petit déjeuner**
fitness room	**la salle de mise en forme/l'espace beauté**
pool	**la piscine**
hot tub	**le sauna**
staff	**le personnel**
day/night porter	**le portier de jour/de nuit**
manager	**le gérant**
receptionist	**le/la réceptionniste**
chamber maid/man	**la femme de chambre/le garçon d'étage**
single room	**une chambre simple**
double room	**une chambre double**
twin-bedded room	**une chambre twin** *or* **une chambre à deux lits**

Insight

The use of **une chambre à deux lits** or **une chambre twin** will depend on the 'internationality' of the hotel in which you have chosen to stay. The more international the hotel, the more you will come across, and be able to use, English terms.

family room	**une chambre familiale**
with shower	**avec douche**
with bathroom	**avec bain**
with toilet	**avec toilettes**
with phone	**avec le téléphone**
with television	**avec la télévision**

with internet connection	**avec un point d'accès Internet** *or* **avec accès à l'Internet**
with a balcony	**avec balcon**
with a sea view	**avec vue sur la mer**
with air conditioning	**climatisée**

Useful phrases

Have you got anything ...?	**Auriez-vous quelque chose de ... ?**
bigger/smaller	**plus grand/plus petit**
cheaper/better	**moins cher/mieux**
quieter	**de plus tranquille ?**
Do you have a non-smoking room?	**Avez-vous une pièce non-fumeurs ?**
It is too noisy.	**C'est trop bruyant.**
The shower doesn't work.	**La douche ne marche pas.**
There is no hot water.	**Il n'y a pas d'eau chaude.**
There is no plug in the basin/bath.	**Le lavabo/la baignoire n'a pas de bouchon de bonde.**

12.4 Camping and caravaning

Core vocabulary

camp site	**le camping**
caravan	**la caravane**
camping car	**le camping car**
RV (recreational vehicle; camper van)	**le mobile home** *(Remember: h is never pronounced in French – so* **le mobile home** *pronounced with a genuine French accent will sound something like:* **leuhmobiloooom)**
trailer	**la remorque**
hook-up	**un attelage**

tent	**la tente**
site	**le site**
hard standing for a caravan	**un emplacement matérialisé pour caravane**
a flat site	**un site plan**
a shady site	**un site ombragé**
facilities	**les équipements**
electricity	**l'électricité**
water	**le point d'eau**
running water	**l'eau courante**
drinking water	**l'eau potable**
water tap	**le robinet**
washrooms	**les sanitaires**
toilets	**les toilettes**
showers	**les douches**
wash basins	**les lavabos**
hairdryer	**le sèche-cheveux**
cooking area	**l'espace cuisine**
gas ring	**la plaque de gaz**
sink	**un évier**
washing machine	**la machine à laver**
drier	**le sèche-linge**
drying area	**la pièce pour le séchage**
restaurant	**le restaurant**
self-service restaurant	**le self**
bar	**le bar**
shop	**la boutique** *or* **le magasin**
swimming pool	**la piscine**
paddling pool	**la pataugeoire**
children's play area	**l'aire de jeux pour les enfants**
swings	**les balançoires**
slide	**le toboggan**
roundabout	**le tourniquet**
tent pegs	**les sardines/les piquets**
guy rope	**la corde de tente**
groundsheet	**le tapis de sol**
fly sheet	**le double-toit**

canopy	**un auvent**
sleeping bag	**le sac de couchage**
torch	**la torche**
pocket lamp	**la lampe de poche**
blanket	**la couverture**
gas cooker	**le réchaud à gaz**
gas bottle	**la bouteille de gaz**

Useful verbs

to tow	**remorquer**
to park	**se garer**
to put up a tent	**monter une tente**
to take down a tent	**démonter une tente**
to hook up	**accrocher/atteler**
to get wet	**prendre l'eau**
to wash/do the laundry	**faire la lessive**
to wash up	**faire la vaisselle**
to dry	**sécher**

Useful phrases

Can you help me?	**Est-ce que vous pourriez m'aider, s'il-vous-plaît ?**
I don't understand how the dryer works.	**Je ne comprends pas comment marche le sèche-linge.**
Where is ...?	**Où se trouve ... ?**
Is there electricity/water ...?	**Est-ce qu'il y a l'électricité/un point d'eau ?**
Is there shade?	**Est-ce que c'est ombragé ?**
Do you have ...?	**Est-ce que vous avez ... ?**
When is the shop open?	**Quelles sont les heures d'ouverture de la boutique/du magasin ?**
Where can I get ...?	**Où est-ce que je peux trouver ... ?**

12.5 What are you going to do?

Core vocabulary

an activity holiday	**des vacances actives**
We want to go …	**Nous voulons aller …**
We intend to go …	**Nous avons l'intention d'aller …**
We are thinking about going …	**Nous pensons aller …**
canyoning	**faire du canyoning**
swimming	**nous baigner**
diving	**faire de la plongée**
water skiing	**faire du ski nautique**
surfing	**faire du surf**
windsurfing	**faire de la planche à voile**
walking	**marcher**
hiking	**faire de la randonnée**
climbing	**faire de l'escalade**
gliding	**faire du vol à voile**
paragliding	**faire du parapente**
abseiling	**faire du rappel**
to do sport	**faire du sport**
to play tennis	**jouer au tennis**
to play volleyball	**jouer au volley**
to go bike riding	**faire des randonnées à vélo**
We want to see …	**Nous voulons aller voir …**
We intend to see …	**Nous avons l'intention d'aller voir …**
We are thinking about seeing …	**Nous pensons aller voir**
monuments	**les monuments**
the castle	**le château**
an 18th century castle	**un château du XVIIIe siècle**
an archeological site	**un site de fouilles archéologiques**
an ancient monument	**un monument ancien**
an historic building	**un bâtiment historique**
the scenery	**l'environnement** *or* **la campagne** *or* **la vue** *or* **le panorama**

We want ...	**Nous voulons ...**
We intend ...	**Nous avons l'intention de ...**
to have a good time	**nous amuser**
to have a rest	**nous reposer**
to relax	**nous détendre**
enjoy the sea, beach and sea	**profiter de la mer, de la plage et du soleil**
to do nothing	**ne rien faire**
to be waited on	**nous faire servir**
In winter I like to go ...	**L'hiver, j'aime aller ...**
skiing	**faire du ski**
snowboarding	**faire du surf**
sledging	**faire de la luge**
ice skating	**faire du patin à glace**
ice climbing	**faire de l'escalade dans les glaciers**

Useful phrases

What is there to see/do?	**Qu'est-ce que vous me/nous conseillez de voir/faire ?**
Is it suitable for...	**Est-ce que ça convient à...**
elderly people?	**des personnes âgées ?**
younger people?	**des jeunes ?**
children?	**des enfants ?**
I like to go and find some sun.	**J'aime aller au soleil.**

12.6 On the beach

Core vocabulary

sea	**la mer**
coast	**la côte**
beach	**la plage**
bay	**la baie**
shore	**la côte**
sand	**le sable**

rock	**le rocher**
rock pool	**la flaque dans les rochers**
seashell	**le coquillage**
tide	**la marée**
high tide	**la marée haute**
low tide	**la marée basse**
wave	**la vague**
private/public beach	**une plage privée/publique**
beach bar	**un bar de plage**
windbreak	**le coupe-vent**
shelter	**un abri**
parasol	**le parasol**
lounger	**la chaise longue**
deck chair	**le transat**
air mattress	**le matelas pneumatique**
shower	**la douche**
beach towel	**la serviette de plage**
bath sheet	**un drap de bain**
swimming costume	**le maillot de bain**
trunks	**le slip de bain**
bikini	**le bikini**
topless bikini	**le monokini**
sun lotion	**la lotion solaire**
sun block	**un écran total**
sun glasses	**les lunettes de soleil**
rubber ring	**une bouée**
arm bands	**des flotteurs pour les bras**
sandcastle	**le château de sable**
bucket	**le seau**
spade	**la pelle**
kite	**le cerf-volant**
snorkel	**le tuba**
flippers	**les palmes**
wet suit	**une combinaison en néoprène/une combinaison isothermique**
dry suit	**une combinaison étanche**
inflatable	**gonflable**

pump	**une pompe**
surfboard	**une planche**
surfer	**le surfer**
windsurf	**la planche à voile**
windsurfer	**le véliplanchiste**

Insight

In my view, the best surf spots in France – **les meilleurs spots de surf** – are: l'Almannare, on the Western side of **la presqu'île de Giens** (the Giens peninsula) on the Mediterranean coast; and Biarritz, in the south of the Bay of Biscay – **le golfe de Gascogne** – in the Basque Country, close to the Spanish border.

jetski	**la moto marine**
waterski	**le ski nautique**
fish	**le poisson**
shell	**le coquillage**
octopus	**la pieuvre**
squid	**la seiche**
mussel	**la moule**
scallop	**la coquille Saint-Jacques**
shrimp	**la crevette**
jellyfish	**la méduse**

Useful verbs

to snorkel	**faire de la plongée**
to sunbathe	**prendre un bain de soleil/se faire dorer au soleil**
to relax	**se détendre**
to play	**jouer**
to dig	**creuser**
to dive	**plonger**
to sting	**piquer**
to be stung	**se faire piquer**
to waterski	**faire du ski nautique**

Useful phrases

The tide is in/out.	**La mer est haute/basse.**
The tide is coming in/out.	**La mer monte/descend**
It is safe for bathing/swimming.	**On peut se baigner sans danger.**
Bathing/swimming permitted.	**Baignade autorisée.**
I have been stung by a jellyfish – it hurts!	**Je me suis fait piquer par une méduse : ça brûle !**
He/She is out of her depth.	**Il/Elle n'a plus pied.**
He/She can't swim.	**Il/Elle ne sait pas nager.**
He/She needs help.	**Il faut aller l'aider/lui porter secours.**
Help!	**Au secours !**

12.7 At sea

Core vocabulary

canoe	**le canoë**
jetski	**la moto marine**
motor boat	**le canot à moteur**
outboard	**le hors-bord**
RIB (rigid inflatable boat)	**le canot pneumatique**
dinghy	**un canot pneumatique/un dinghy**
rowing boat	**un canot à rames**
sailing dinghy	**un dinghy**
waterski	**le ski nautique**
yacht	**le yacht**
emergency services	**le poste de secours**
mayday	**MayDay**
SOS	**SOS**
lifeboat	**le canot de sauvetage**
lifejacket	**le gilet de sauvetage**
rescuer	**le sauveteur en mer**
flare	**la fusée**

weather forecast	**les prévisions météo** *(short for* **météorologiques***)*
shipping forecast	**la météo marine**
weather report	**le bulletin météo**
calm sea	**mer calme/peu agitée**
rough sea	**mer agitée**
wind force	**le vent de force**
gale force	**un avis de coup de vent**
rain	**la pluie**
poor visibility	**visibilité réduite**
good visibility	**bonne visibilité**
fog	**le brouillard**
equipment	**l'équipement**
compass	**la boussole**
GPS (global positioning system)	**le GPS (le système de positionnement par satellite)**

Insight

The European Union is developing a concurrent positioning system – due to be piloted in 2010 and fully operational by 2013 – called Galileo.

sail	**la voile**
hull	**la coque**
cabin	**la cabine**
berth	**la couchelte**
wheel	**le gouvernail**
harbour	**le port**
port	**le port**
lighthouse	**le phare**
starboard	**tribord**
port side	**bâbord**
bow	**la proue**
stern	**la poupe**
mooring	**le mouillage**
chain	**la chaîne**
anchor	**l'ancre**

Useful verbs

to sail	**faire de la voile**
to navigate	**naviguer**
to steer	**barrer**
to tie up/moor	**s'amarrer/mouiller**
to anchor	**descendre l'ancre**
to rescue	**porter secours**
to be rescued	**être secouru**

12.8 The great outdoors

Insight

The great outdoors in French is **les sports de l'extrême.** If this is your thing – **si c'est votre truc** – go to the Great Outdoors Exhibition in Toulouse, in the South West of France, next autumn – **le Salon des Sports et de l'Extrême.**

Core vocabulary

rucksack	**le sac à dos**
sleeping bag	**le sac de couchage**
ground mat/mattress	**le matelas**
torch	**la torche**
penknife	**le couteau de poche/le couteau suisse**
compass	**la boussole**
map	**la carte**
water bottle	**la gourde**
camping stove	**le réchaud de camping**
match	**une allumette**
lighter	**le briquet**
gas container	**la bouteille de gaz**
billycan	**la gamelle**
bowl	**le bol**

knife/fork/spoon	**un couteau/une fourchette/une cuillère**
plate	**une assiette**
mug	**un mug** *or* **une chope**
emergency ration	**une ration de secours**
dried food	**des aliments séchés**
dried fruit	**des fruits secs**
nuts	**des noix**
chocolate	**du chocolat**
transceiver (for snow rescue)	**un émetteur-récepteur radio**
mobile phone	**un téléphone portable**
battery	**la batterie** *or* **la pile – « la pile »** *refers to the AA-type batteries one buys off the shelf*
charger	**le chargeur**
plug	**la prise**
waterproofs	**un équipement imperméable**
spare clothing	**des vêtements de rechange**
rope	**une corde**
climbing harness	**un harnais d'escalade**
climbing gear	**un équipement d'escalade**
karabiner	**le mousqueton**
crampons	**les crampons**
nut	**le coinceur**
wedging	**le coinçage**
boots	**les chaussures d'escalade**
ice axe	**le piolet**

Useful phrases

I have got sore feet.	**J'ai mal aux pieds.**
I have got blisters.	**J'ai des ampoules./Je me suis fait des ampoules.**
My hands are frozen.	**J'ai les mains gelées.**
Have you got spare socks for me?	**Est-ce que tu as/vous avez des chaussettes de rechange pour moi ?**

Would you have some plasters for me?	**Auriez-vous des pansements pour moi ?**
Does anyone have some antiseptic cream?	**Est-ce que quelqu'un aurait de la crème antiseptique ?**
Have you got something for ...	**Est-ce que vous auriez quelque chose pour ...**
I have been stung by/I have been bitten by a wasp/bee/mosquito.	**Je me suis fait piquer par une guêpe/une abeille/un moustique.**

Insight

If bitten by a mosquito (or stung by a wasp or a bee) you may say: **« Oh, la vache ! Je me suis fait piquer par un moustique ! »** Literally: 'Hey, the cow! I have been bitten by a mosquito!' Please note that **'la vache'** is an exclamation that is slang, yet not vulgar.

TEST YOURSELF

À vous !

A mini stock-taking exercise on the unit you have just worked on

1 'SPF' in French is **IPS**; it stands for...
- **a** indicateur partagé de soleil
- **b** indicateur de potion solaire
- **c** indice de protection contre le soleil
- **d** indicateur de protection contre le soleil
- **e** indice de protection solaire

2 'A bike ride' in French is...
[*note: more than one answer possible*]
- **a** un tour à vélo
- **b** une balade à vélo
- **c** une randonnée à vélo
- **d** une expédition en vélo

3 If you wanted to say to your friends departing for the Mediterranean, in French, 'Enjoy the sun!' you might say...
- **a** Jouissez du soleil !
- **b** Enjouez le soleil !
- **c** Profitez du soleil !
- **d** Absorbez le soleil !

4 **Est-ce que ça convient à des enfants** ? means...
- **a** Is it convenient for children to come along?
- **b** Is it suitable for children?
- **c** Is it convenient if we bring the children?

5 **Le coquillage** in French is...
- **a** cockle
- **b** cockle-picking
- **c** shellfish

6 How would you say 'I have been stung by a jellyfish' in French? [*note: more than one answer possible*]

- **a** Je me piqué(e) avec un poisson-gelée
- **b** Je viens de me piquer avec un poisson-gelée
- **c** Je viens de me faire piquer par une méduse
- **d** Je me suis fait piquer par une méduse
- **f** J'ai été piqué(e) par une méduse

7 'The drycleaners' in French is…

- **a** les nettoyeurs secs
- **b** les nettoyeurs à sec
- **c** le nettoyage à sec
- **d** le pressing

8 'To sunbathe' in French may be…
[*note: more than one answer possible*]

- **a** se faire rôtir au soleil
- **b** se faire dorer au soleil
- **c** se faire bronzer au soleil
- **d** se faire ensoleiller
- **e** s'ensoleiller
- **f** se faire griller au soleil

9 You are just back from a long walk in the frozen countryside, and your feet are frozen. What will you say?

- **a** Mes pieds sont congelés.
- **b** J'ai les pieds froids.
- **c** J'ai les pieds gelés.
- **d** J'ai les orteils gelés.

10 The name of the GPS developed by the European Union is…

- **a** Archimedes
- **b** Galileo
- **c** Michelangelo

Answers: 1 d; 2 a b c d; 3 c; 4 b; 5 c; 6 c d e; 7 d; 8 b c; 9 c; 10 b

13

Health

13.1 The face

Core vocabulary

skin	**la peau**
head	**la tête**
face	**le visage**
hair	**les cheveux** (*singular:* **un cheveu**)
body hairs	**les poils** (*singular:* **un poil**)
forehead	**le front**
ear	**une oreille**
eye	**un œil** (*plural* **des yeux**)
eyebrow	**un sourcil**
eyelash	**un cil**
eyelid	**la paupière**
nose	**le nez**
nostril	**la narine**
cheek	**la joue**
chin	**le menton**
mouth	**la bouche**
lip	**la lèvre**
tongue	**la langue**
tooth	**la dent**
neck	**le cou**
beard	**la barbe**
a goatee	**le bouc**

moustache	**la moustache**
glasses	**des lunettes**
contact lens	**une lentille de contact**
hard/soft lens	**une lentille de contact dure/souple**
disposable lenses	**des lentilles jetables**
short-sighted	**myope**
long-sighted	**hypermétrope** *or* **presbyte** *(if this happens as one ages)*

The five senses *les cinq sens*

hearing	**l'ouïe**	*to hear*	**entendre**
sight	**la vue**	*to see*	**voir**
smell	**l'odorat**	*to smell*	**sentir**
taste	**le goût**	*to taste*	**goûter**
touch	**le toucher**	*to touch*	**toucher**

Useful verbs

to wink	**cligner de l'œil** *or* **faire un clin d'œil**
to flutter one's eyelashes	**battre des paupières**
to sleep	**dormir**
to smile	**sourire**
to laugh	**rire**
to frown	**plisser le front**
to talk	**parler**
to shout	**crier**
to cry	**pleurer**
to snore	**ronfler**
to hiccup	**avoir le hoquet**
to cough	**tousser**
to pull faces	**faire des grimaces**
to yawn	**bâiller**
to have a beard	**porter une barbe** *or* **porter la barbe**
to have a moustache	**porter la moustache**
to have a goatee	**porter le bouc**

to wear glasses	**porter des lunettes**
to have a facial	**se faire faire un nettoyage de peau**
to have your hair done	**aller chez le coiffeur**
to have a nose job	**se faire refaire le nez**
to have plastic surgery	**subir une opération de chirurgie esthétique**
to have wrinkles	**avoir des rides**
to have a nice smile	**avoir un beau/joli sourire**

Useful phrases

I have a headache.	**J'ai mal à la tête.**
toothache	**le mal de dents**
earache	**le mal aux oreilles**
My nose is bleeding/I have a nose bleed.	**Je saigne du nez.**
My eyes are sore.	**J'ai mal aux yeux.**

13.2 The body

Core vocabulary

limb	**le membre**
collarbone	**la clavicule**
shoulder	**une épaule**
arm	**le bras**
elbow	**le coude**
wrist	**le poignet**
hand	**la main**
finger	**le doigt**
thumb	**le pouce**
forefinger	**un index**
middle finger	**le majeur**

Insight

L'index et le majeur – the first and middle fingers – are used to make a rude sign which hails from a 'rude' (the French **rude** meaning *rough*) period; namely, the 100 Years War (1337–1453) between France and England: before the battle, the English archers used to mock their adversary by showing them these two fingers which were used to handle the crossbow and which would be cut off any Frenchmen who were taken prisoner.

ring finger	**un annulaire**

Insight

L'annulaire owes its name to **l'anneau**, *the ring*, and in particular, the wedding ring. In the Catholic tradition, the wedding ring is worn **à l'annulaire gauche**; and in Protestant traditions, **à l'annulaire droit.**

little finger	**un auriculaire**

Insight

Auriculaire comes from the Latin **auricularius** means 'relating to the ear'. This was the finger used to clean one's ears – hence its name.

fingernail	**un ongle**
body	**le corps**
chest	**la poitrine**
breast	**le sein**
nipple	**une aréole**
rib cage	**la cage thoracique**
rib	**la côte**
waist	**la taille**
hip	**la hanche**
abdomen	**un abdomen**
bottom	**le derrière**
buttock	**la fesse**
pubis	**le pubis**

sexual organ	**un organe sexuel**
penis	**le pénis** *or* **la verge**
testicle	**la testicule**
balls	**les bourses**
vagina	**le vagin**
vulva	**la vulve**
leg	**la jambe**
thigh	**la cuisse**
knee	**le genou**
calf	**le mollet**
ankle	**la cheville**
foot	**le pied**
toe	**un orteil**
big toe	**le gros orteil**
arch	**la voûte plantaire**
heel	**le talon**
back	**le dos**
lower back	**le bas du dos**
front	**le devant**
side	**le côté**

Internal organs ***les organes internes***

brain	**le cerveau**
stomach	**un estomac**
throat	**la gorge**
lung	**le poumon**
kidney	**le rein**

Insight

Note that *kidney*, **le rein**, is called **le rognon** when served as a dish.

heart	**le cœur**
blood	**le sang**
vein	**une veine**
artery	**une artère**
blood transfusion	**une transfusion sanguine**
blood donor	**un donneur sanguin**

blood type	**le groupe sanguin**
intestine	**un intestin**
small intestine	**l'intestin grêle**
large intestine	**le gros intestin**
skeleton	**le squelette**
bone	**un os**
joint	**une articulation**
nervous system	**le système nerveux**
nerve	**le nerf**
circulation	**la circulation**
blood pressure	**la tension**
breathing	**la respiration**
digestion	**la digestion**

Useful verbs

to feel	**sentir**
to touch	**toucher**
to stroke	**caresser**
to massage	**masser**
to hold	**tenir**
to embrace	**serrer dans ses bras**
to kick	**donner un coup de pied**
to walk	**marcher**
to run	**courir**
to jump	**sauter**

Useful phrases

I have stomach ache.	**J'ai mal au ventre.**
heart burn	**mal à l'estomac**
indigestion	**une indigestion**
high/low blood pressure	**une tension haute/une tension basse**
My foot/hand/leg hurts.	**J'ai mal ... au pied/à la main/à la jambe.**

13.3 I need a doctor

Core vocabulary

doctor	**le médecin**
appointment	**le rendez-vous**
surgery	**le cabinet médical**

Diseases *maladies*

a cold	**un rhume**
flu (influenza)	**la grippe**
measles	**la rougeole**
mumps	**les oreillons**
German measles	**la rubéole**
chickenpox	**la varicelle**
tonsillitis	**les végétations**
cough	**la toux**
sore throat	**mal à la gorge**
hypertension	**l'hypertension**
constipation	**la constipation**
diarrhoea	**la diarrhée**
polio	**la polio**
hepatitis	**l'hépatite**
rabies	**la rage**
typhoid	**la typhoïde**
cholera	**le choléra**
yellow fever	**la jaunisse**
malaria	**la malaria**
cancer	**le cancer**
multiple sclerosis	**la sclérose en plaques**
AIDS	**le Sida**
HIV infection	**la séropositivité**
HIV positive	**être séropositif/séropositive**

Useful phrases

I am allergic to …	**Je suis allergique …**
penicillin	**à la pénicilline**
nuts	**aux noix**
cats	**aux chats**
I have a pain …	**J'ai des douleurs …**
It hurts.	**Ça me fait mal.**
I have broken a leg.	**Je me suis cassé la jambe.**
I have fractured a rib.	**Je me suis fêlé une côte.**
I don't feel well.	**Je ne me sens pas bien.**
I can't sleep/eat/walk…	**Je n'arrive pas à dormir/manger/ marcher …**
I want to go to the toilet.	**Il faut que j'aille aux toilettes.**
I feel sick/nauseous.	**Je me sens mal./J'ai mal au cœur.**
I feel dizzy.	**J'ai la tête qui tourne.**
I have got spots.	**J'ai des boutons.**
I have been bitten/stung.	**Je me suis fait piquer.**
I have hay fever.	**J'ai le rhume des foins.**
I have asthma.	**Je suis asthmatique** *or* **Je fais de l'asthme.**
He/She needs an inhaler.	**Il lui faut un inhalateur.**
He/She is handicapped/ paraplegic	**Il/Elle est handicapé(e)/ paraplégique**
I have broken my leg/ankle/wrist.	**Je me suis cassé la jambe/la cheville/le poignet.**
Go to bed early.	**Couchez-vous tôt.**
Take more exercise.	**Faites plus d'exercice.**
Eat less.	**Mangez moins.**
Avoid smoky rooms.	**Évitez les endroits enfumés.**

Treatment *les remèdes*

an injection/a jab for …	**un vaccin contre …**
immunization	**la vaccination** *or* **l'immunisation**
innoculation	**une injection**
health certificate	**un certificat médical**

examination	**un examen**
x-ray	**la radio (graphie)**
radiation	**la radiation**
scan	**le scanner**
diagnostic ultrasound	**une échographie**
MRI – Magnetic Resonance Imaging	**une IRM (Image par Résonnance Magnétique)**
plaster	**le plâtre**
crutch	**la béquille**
walking stick	**la canne**
wheelchair	**le fauteuil roulant**
medication	**un médicament**
pill	**un cachet** *or* **un comprimé**
painkiller	**un analgésique**
vitamin supplement	**un supplément vitaminique**
cure	**une cure**
homeopathic remedy	**un remède homéopathique**
exercise	**de l'exercice**
physiotherapy	**la kinésithérapie**
rest	**le repos**
sleep	**le sommeil**

In the hospital *à l'hôpital*

hospice	**un hospice**

Insight

L'hospice used to mean a monastery or a hotel. The most famous 'hospices' nowadays in France are **les hospices de Beaune**, in Burgundy. The wine auctions held there every year on the third Sunday in November, perpetuate the charitable tradition of the hospices: the profits are used exclusively to support the work – medical, religious and secular – of the hospices.

hospital	**un hôpital**
clinic	**une clinique**

Insight

In France, the difference between **un hôpital** and **une clinique** is that **l'hôpital** is publicly funded and organized as a public service whereas **la clinique** is privately run by medical practitioners who are also the founders and partners of the business.

department	**le service**
emergency	**les urgences**
emergency doctor	**un/e urgentiste**
doctor	**le/la médecin**
nurse	**un infirmier/une infirmière**
ward	**le service**
bed	**le lit**
anaesthesia	**l'anesthésie**
general	**une anesthésie générale**
local	**une anesthésie locale**
surgery	**la chirurgie**
operation	**l'opération**
operating theatre	**la salle d'opération**

13.4 Family planning

family planning	**le planning familial**
to have intercourse	**avoir des rapports sexuels**
contraception	**la contraception**
contraception method	**une méthode contraceptive/un moyen de contraception**
a condom	**un préservatif/une capote** *(very informal, short for* **'une capote anglaise'** *or… French letter)*

Insight

The French for the preservatives found in processed food is **conservateur**. Beware! Note that *preserves* are **les conserves**. My grandmother would announce, several times throughout the summer as vegetables and fruit turned ripe: **« Je vais faire des conserves ! »**

the pill	**la pilule/une pilule contraceptive**
coil	**un stérilet**
diaphragm	**un diaphragme**
morning-after pill	**la pilule du lendemain**
abortive pill	**la pilule abortive**
abortion	**un avortement**
termination of pregnancy	**IVG – Intervention Volontaire de Grossesse**
vasectomy	**une vasectomie**
ovariectomy	**une ovariectomie**

TEST YOURSELF

À vous !

A mini stock-taking exercise on the unit you have just worked on

1 'Body hair' in French is...
- **a** les cheveux corporels
- **b** les poils de corps
- **c** les poils
- **d** les cheveux

2 'I winked at her' in French is...
[*note: more than one answer possible*]
- **a** Je lui ai fait une œillade
- **b** Je lui ai cligné de l'œil
- **c** Je lui fais un clin d'œil
- **d** Je lui ai cligné
- **e** Je lui ai fait un clin d'œil

3 'My nose is bleeding/I have a nose bleed' in French is...
- **a** mon nez saigne
- **b** J'ai saigné du nez
- **c** J'ai le nez saignant
- **d** Je saigne du nez

4 Please give the names of the five fingers of the hand in French, starting with the thumb:
- **a**
- **b**
- **c**
- **d**
- **e**

5 'I broke my left leg' in French is...
- **a** J'ai cassé ma jambe gauche
- **b** Je m'ai cassé la jambe gauche
- **c** Je me suis cassé la jambe gauche

6 How would you say 'I can't sleep' in French?
[*note: more than one answer possible*]
a Je n'arrive pas à dormir
b Je ne peux pas dormir
c Je n'arrive pas à m'endormir

7 **Un conservateur** in French, in a food context, is…
a a conservative diet
b a food preservative
c a freezing agent

8 IVG in French stands for…
a Invention vénérienne de grossesse
b Invention vernaculaire de grossesse
c Intervention de vérification de grossesse
d Intervention volontaire de grossesse

9 'A painkiller' in French is…
[*note: more than one answer possible*]
a un tueur de douleurs
b un analgésique
c un antalgique
d un anti-douleur

10 'The big toe' in French is…
[*note: more than one answer possible*]
a le gros doigt
b le gros doigt de pied
c le gros orteil
d le grand orteil
e le grand doigt de pied

Answers: 1 c; 2 b e; 3 d; 4 1 le pouce/2 l'index/3 le majeur/4 l'annulaire/5 l'auriculaire ou le petit doigt; 5 c; 6 a c; 7 b; 8 d; 9 b c d; 10 b c

14

The wider world

14.1 Countries, continents and regions

world	**le monde**
earth	**la terre**
globe	**le globe**

Insight

Beware! The English 'global' is in French **international**, or **mondial**. The French 'global' would be the equivalent of 'general', looked at in a general way/as a whole. Thus: *globalization*, in French, is **la mondialisation**.

atlas	**l'atlas**
Africa	**l'Afrique**
America	**l'Amérique**
North America	**l'Amérique du Nord**
Central America	**l'Amérique centrale**
South America	**l'Amérique du Sud**
Latin America	**l'Amérique latine**
Asia	**l'Asie**
Oceanie	**l'Océanie**
Australia	**l'Australie**
Polynesia	**la Polynésie**
Micronesia	**la Micronésie**
Melanesia	**la Mélanésie**

New Zealand	**la Nouvelle Zélande**
Europe	**l'Europe**
Arctic	**l'Arctique**
North Pole	**le pôle Nord**
Antarctic	**l'Antarctique**
South Pole	**le pôle Sud**
The Near East	**le Proche-Orient**
Middle East	**le Moyen-Orient**
Far East	**l'Extrême-Orient**
southern hemisphere	**l'hémisphère Sud**
northern hemisphere	**l'hémisphère Nord**
India	**l'Inde**
China	**la Chine**
Japan	**le Japon**

The countries of Europe ***les pays européens***

*Countries followed by an asterisk are Member States of the European Union

Scandinavia	**La Scandinavie**
Denmark	**le Danemark***
Finland	**la Finlande***
Norway	**la Norvège**
Sweden	**la Suède***
Iceland	**l'Islande**
Benelux	**le Bénélux**
Belgium	**la Belgique***
Netherlands	**les Pays-bas***
Luxembourg	**le Luxembourg***
Iberian Peninsula	**la péninsule ibérique**
Spain	**l'Espagne***
Portugal	**le Portugal***
British Isles	**les îles britanniques**
United Kingdom	**le Royaume-Uni***
England	**l'Angleterre**
Scotland	**l'Écosse**
Northern Ireland	**l'Irlande du Nord**
Wales	**le Pays de Galles**

Bulgaria	**la Bulgarie***
Greece	**la Grèce***
Turkey	**la Turquie**
Cyprus	**Chypre***
Germany	**l'Allemagne***
Poland	**la Pologne***
France	**la France***
Ireland	**l'Irlande***
Austria	**l'Autriche***
Italy	**l'Italie***
Czech Republic	**la République tchèque***
Slovakia	**la Slovaquie***
Hungary	**la Hongrie***
Romania	**La Roumanie***
Slovenia	**la Slovénie***
Switzerland	**la Suisse**
Lichtenstein	**le Lichtenstein**
Monaco	**la principauté de Monaco**
Malta	**l'île de Malte***

Baltic Republics ***les républiques baltes***

Latvia	**la Lettonie***
Lithuania	**la Lithuanie***
Estonia	**l'Estonie***

Europe and European institutions
l'Europe et les institutions européennes

European Union, EU	**l'Union européenne, UE**
Common Market	**le marché commun**
European Communities, EC	**les Communautés européennes, CE**
European Economic Community, EEC	**la Communauté économique européenne, CEE**
Common Agricultural Policy, CAP	**la politique agricole commune, la PAC**
European Economic Area, EEA	**l'espace économique européen, EEE**
euro	**l'euro**
Council of the European Union	**le Conseil de l'Europe**

European parliament	**le Parlement européen**
European Commission	**la Commission européenne**
European Court of Justice	**la Cour de justice de l'Union européenne**
Central European Bank	**la Banque centrale européenne**
European Court of Auditors	**la Cour européenne d'auditeurs**
Economic and Social Committee	**le Comité économique et social**
Committee of the Regions	**le Comité des régions**

14.2 The high seas

Core vocabulary

The points of the compass *les quatre points cardinaux*

north	**le nord**
south	**le sud**
east	**l'est**
west	**l'ouest**

The oceans *les océans*

Atlantic	**l'océan atlantique**
Indian	**l'océan indien**
Pacific	**l'océan pacifique**
Arctic	**l'océan glacial arctique**
Antarctic	**l'océan glacial antarctique**

Seas *les mers* **(some of them!)**

Mediterranean	**la mer méditerranée**
North Sea	**la mer du Nord**
Baltic	**la mer baltique**
Red Sea	**la mer rouge**
Dead Sea	**la mer morte**
English Channel	**la mer de la Manche**

navigation	**la navigation**
longitude	**la longitude**

latitude	**la latitude**
equator	**l'équateur**
tropics	**les tropiques**
time zone	**le fuseau horaire**
bay	**la baie**
Bay of Biscaye	**Le golfe de Gascogne**
island/isle	**une île**
peninsula	**la péninsule**
canal	**le canal**
Suez canal	**le canal de Suez**
Panama canal	**le canal de Panama**
strait	**le détroit**
Strait of Gibraltar	**le détroit de Gibraltar**
current	**un courant**
Gulf stream	**le golf stream**
tide	**la marée**
ferry	**le ferry**
liner	**le transatlantique**
cruise ship	**le navire de croisière**
tanker	**le pétrolier**
container ship	**le porte-conteneurs**
hazard	**le risque**
iceberg	**un iceberg**
shipping	**le transport**
shipping forecast	**la météo marine**
weather report	**le bulletin météo(rologique)**
storm	**une tempête**
gale	**un coup de vent**
gale force 10 (on the Beaufort scale)	**un coup de vent de force 10 (sur l'échelle de Beaufort)**
rough sea	**mer agitée à forte**
calm sea	**mer calme/à peu agitée**

Useful verbs

to board	**embarquer**
to embark	**embarquer**

to load	**charger**
to disembark	**désembarquer**
to unload	**décharger**

14.3 The weather forecast

Core vocabulary

weather forecast	**les prévisions méteorologiques** *or* **le bulletin metéo** *or* **la météo**
rain	**la pluie**
drizzle	**le crachin**
light drizzle	**la bruine**
shower	**une averse**
snow	**la neige**
wind	**le vent**
fog	**le brouillard**
mist	**la brume**
sun	**le soleil**
hail	**la grêle**
sleet	**la neige fondue**
thunder	**le tonnerre**
thunderstorm	**un orage**
lightning	**la foudre**
flash of lightning	**un éclair**
ice	**la glace**
frost	**la gelée**
white frost	**la gelée blanche**

Useful phrases

today	**aujourd'hui**
tomorrow	**demain**
over the next few days	**pour les jours à venir**

It's raining.	**Il pleut.**
it's sunny	**il y a du soleil**
it's warm	**il fait chaud**
it's cold	**il fait froid**
it's overcast	**le temps est couvert**
it's humid	**il fait humide**
it's mild	**il fait doux**
it's dry	**il fait sec**
it's wet	**le temps est pluvieux**
The weather is getting worse.	**Le temps ne va pas s'améliorer.**
improving	**le temps va s'améliorer**
You can expect ...	**Vous pouvez vous attendre à ...**
light/strong winds	**des vents légers/forts**
gales	**des coups de vent**
storms	**de la tempête**
sunny intervals	**des apparitions du soleil** *or* **le soleil fera son apparition**
morning mist	**la brume matinale**
fog patches	**des nappes de brouillard**
difficult driving conditions	**les conditions de circulation sont difficiles**
risk of flooding	**risque d'inondations**
Floods are forecast.	**Des inondations sont prévues.**
The temperature is rising/falling.	**Les températures augmentent/chutent.**
climate change	**le changement climatique**
Sea levels are rising.	**Le niveau de la mer monte** *or* **on assiste à l'élévation du niveau de la mer**
global warming	**le réchauffement climatique**
greenhouse effect	**l'effet de serre**

TEST YOURSELF

À vous !

A mini stock-taking exercise on the unit you have just worked on

1 'The Far East' in French is...
  a le loin oriental
  b le lointain Orient
  c l'Extrême-Orient

2 'The Netherlands' in French is...
  a les Plats-Pays
  b les pays Inférieurs
  c les Pays-Bas

3 'Wales' in French is...
  a Les Galles
  b Le Pays de Galles
  c Les Galles

4 Le **golfe de Gascogne** in English is...
  a The Gulf of Gascony
  b The Bay of Gascony
  c The Bay of Biscay

5 'Shipping forecast' in French is...
  a les projections de transport maritime
  b les projections de transport
  c les previsions de transport maritime
  d la météo marine
  e la météo maritime

6 **La bruine** refers to...
  a a heavy rainfall
  b a heavy drizzle
  c a light drizzle

7 'Greenhouse gases' in French are...
- **a** les gaz de serres
- **b** les gaz cataclysmiques
- **c** les gaz à effet de serre
- **d** les gaz à effets verts

8 'It is sleeting' in French is...
- **a** Il pleut de la neige
- **b** Il pleut de la neige mouillée
- **c** Il tombe de la neige fondue

9 'Risk of flooding' in French is...
- **a** risque d'inondations
- **b** risque de courants
- **c** risque de débordements

10 'Global warming' in French is...
[*note: more than one answer possible*]
- **a** le chauffage mondial
- **b** le réchauffement international
- **c** le réchauffement climatique
- **d** le réchauffement de la planète

Answers: 1 c; 2 c; 3 b; 4 c; 5 d; 6 c; 7 c; 8 c; 9 a; 10 c d

15

Government and society

15.1 Politics and government

Politics *la politique*

government	**le gouvernement**
state	**un état** *(often capitalised –* **l'État***)*
democracy	**la démocratie**
state of law	**un état de droit**
dictatorship	**la dictature**
monarchy	**la monarchie**
parliamentary monarchy	**la monarchie parlementaire – par exemple, le Royaume-Uni**
federalism	**le fédéralisme**
devolution	**la dévolution**
French Republic	**la République française**

Insight

The Laws of 1982–1983 **(lois Deferre)** have led to France's regions (22 in total) becoming more autonomous. This process is called **la décentralisation**, and the resulting focus on regions is called **la régionalisation.**

President	**le président (de la République)**
Head(s) of state(s)	**le chef de l'Etat** *or* **un chef d'État (les chefs d'État)**

Prime Minister	**le premier ministre**
Head of Government	**le chef du gouvernement**
Cabinet	**le cabinet**
Minister of the Interior	**le ministre de l'Intérieur**
Defence Minister	**le ministre de la Défense**
Chancellor of the Exchequer	**le ministre des Finances**
Justice Minister	**le ministre de la Justice**
Parliament	**le parlement**
Chamber	**la chambre**
Lower chamber	**la chambre basse** *(in France,* **l'Assemblée Nationale***)*
Higher chamber	**la chambre haute** *(in France,* **le Sénat***)*
member of elected parliament	**le/la député(e)**
member of the higher chamber	**le sénateur/la sénatrice**
constituency, ward	**la circonscription**
election	**les élections**
vote	**le vote/le suffrage**
Ministry	**le ministère**
Foreign Office	**le ministère des Affaires étrangères**
Home Office	**le ministère de l'Intérieur**
Ministry of Education	**le ministère de l'Éducation**

The armed forces ***les forces armées***

army	**l'armée**
soldier/tank/to march	**le soldat/un tank/marcher**
navy	**la marine**
sailor/warship/to sail	**le marin/le navire de guerre/faire route**
airforce	**l'armée de l'air**
airman/jet fighter/to fly	**le pilote/le pilote de chasse/voler**
police force	**la police**
policeman/police car/to arrest	**le policier/un véhicule de police/arrêter**
the war against terrorism	**la lutte anti-terroriste**
the war against organized crime	**la lutte anti-gangs** *or* **la lutte contre le crime organisé**
terrorist attack	**un attentat**

suicide bomber	**un attentat-suicide à la bombe**
sea to air missile	**missile mer-air**

Useful verbs

to speak	**parler**
to make a speech	**faire un discours**
to canvass	**faire du démarchage électoral/ faire (sa) campagne**
to debate	**débattre de ...**
to vote	**voter**
to pay taxes	**payer des impôts**
to defend	**défendre**
to fight against	**lutter contre**
to guard	**garder**
to protect	**protéger**
to spy	**espionner**

15.2 Services and officialdom

Core vocabulary

police	**la police**
emergency services	**les services d'urgences**
ambulance	**SAMU (Service d'Aide Médicale d'Urgence)**
fire brigade	**les pompiers**
telephone failure/break down	**les dérangements**
directory enquiries	**les renseignements**
electricity	**EDF (Electricité de France)**
gas	**GDF (Gaz de France)**
water	**les services de l'eau**
utilities	**les énergies**
local authority	**la collectivité**
city council	**la municipalité** *or* **la Ville**
local council	**le conseil municipal**

town/city councillor	**le conseiller/la conseillère municipal/e**
mayor	**le maire/la mairesse** *or* **madame le maire**
town hall	**la mairie**
city chambers	**l'hôtel de ville** *(larger cities)*
roads department	**les services de la voirie**
public transport	**les transports en commun**
tourist office	**l'office du tourisme**
council offices	**les services municipaux**
job centre	**l'agence pour l'emploi**
social services	**les services sociaux**
inland revenue	**les services des impôts/le fisc/ le Trésor public**
tax	**un impôt/une taxe**
tax payer	**le/la contribuable**
council tax/rates	**les impôts locaux**
bureaucracy	**la bureaucratie**
the small print	**les petits caractères**
civil service	**la fonction publique**
civil servant	**le/la fonctionnaire**
council/local civil servant	**un agent des collectivités locales**
paperwork	**la paperasserie**
pass	**un laisser-passer**
permit	**un permis**
residence permit	**un permis de séjour**
receipt	**un reçu**
proof of address	**un justificatif de domicile**
driving licence	**un permis de conduire**
insurance	**une assurance**
policy	**la police** *or* **le contrat d'assurance**
cover	**la couverture**
household insurance	**une assurance habitation**
medical insurance	**une assurance médicale**
insurer	**un assureur**
insured	**un(e) assuré(e)**
medical check	**un check up** *or* **un examen médical complet**
solicitor	**un notaire** *or* **un avocat**

lawyer	**un juriste** *or* **un avocat**
criminal offence	**un délit** *or* **une infraction**
civil offence	**un délit civil**
court	**un tribunal**
sentence	**une peine/une condamnation**
fine	**une amende**
imprisonment	**une incarcération/ l'emprisonnement**

Useful phrases

I have come regarding ...	**Je viens vous voir au sujet de ...**
I don't understand.	**Je ne comprends pas.**
I didn't know that ...	**Je ne savais pas que ...**
I have already supplied you with this document.	**Je vous ai déjà fourni ce document.**
I need help.	**J'ai besoin d'aide.**
Is there anyone who can help me?	**Quelqu'un serait-il en mesure de m'aider ?** *or* **Quelqu'un pourrait-il m'aider ?**
When are the offices open?	**Quelles sont les heures d'ouverture des bureaux ?**
Where do I need to go to get ...?	**Où faut-il que je m'adresse pour ... ?**
What do I need?	**De quoi est-ce que j'ai besoin** *or* **Qu'est-ce qu'il me faut (comme papiers/comme documents/ comme justificatifs** *etc.*) **?**
Where can I get it?	**Où est-ce que je peux le trouver ?**
It hasn't been stamped.	**Vous n'avez pas le tampon.**

15.3 Money

Core vocabulary

money	**l'argent**
currency	**la monnaie**
dollar	**un dollar US/un dollar canadien**

sterling	**une livre sterling**
euro	**un euro**
cash	**le liquide**
change	**la monnaie**
bank	**la banque**
bank account	**le compte en banque** *or* **bancaire**
current account	**le compte courant** *or* **le compte-chèques**
deposit	**un versement** *or* **un dépôt**
account number	**le numéro de compte**
sort code	**le code agence**
cheque book	**le chéquier**
cheque	**le chèque**
credit card	**la carte de crédit**
signature	**la signature**
loan	**le prêt** *(lender's perspective)*; **l'emprunt** *(borrower's perspective)*
overdraft	**le découvert**
overdraft interests	**les intérêts de découvert** *or* **la comission de dépassement**
overdraft limit	**la facilité de caisse**
bank transfer	**un virement**
in credit	**créditeur**
in debit/in the red	**débiteur/dans le rouge/à découvert**

Insight

When your account is overdrawn, you may say: **« Mon compte est débiteur »** or **« Je suis dans le rouge »** or **« Je suis à découvert »** or **« Mon compte est à découvert ».**

debt	**la dette**
bankruptcy	**la faillite**
mortgage	**l'emprunt hypothécaire**

Stocks and shares *les titres et les actions*

stock market	**la Bourse/une place boursière**
foreign exchange	**le marché des changes**
price	**le prix**
dividend	**le revenu** *or* **le dividende**

profit	**les bénéfices**
loss	**la perte**
inflation	**l'inflation**
accounts	**les comptes**
accountant	**le/la comptable**
annual accounts	**les comptes annuels**
income tax	**l'impôt sur le revenu**

Useful verbs

to win	**gagner**
to lose	**perdre**
to make a loss	**perdre**
to make a gain	**faire un bénéfice**
to buy/sell shares	**acheter/vendre des actions**
to trade	**négocier**
to save	**faire des économies**
to apply	**faire une demande**
to be accepted	**voir sa demande acceptée**
to be refused	**voir sa demande refusée**

15.4 National holidays

Core vocabulary

Holidays *les vacances*

school holidays	**les vacances scolaires**
paid holidays	**les congés payés**
public holidays	**les jours fériés**
summer holidays	**les vacances d'été**
national holidays	**les fêtes nationales**

- le **14 juillet** : called 'Bastille Day' in English, is *the* national French holiday. It celebrates the burning, on 14 July 1789, of the Bastille prison – the symbol of monarchy par excellence – in Paris.

- le 11 **novembre**: commemorates the end of World War I on 11 November 1918.
- le **8 mai**: commemorates the armistice that put an end to World War II on 8 May 1945.
- le 1er **mai**: (1 May, Labour Day) with traditional workers' associations and union marches.

Insight

1 May is also the day when you buy a sprig of lily-of-the-valley – **le muguet** – for a friend or a loved one: **« le jour du muguet »**.

- Good Friday: Vendredi Saint
- **Pâques**: Easter
- **le lundi de Pâques**: Easter Monday.
- **le jeudi de l'ascension**: Ascension.
- **le lundi de Pentecôte**: Pentecost Monday
- **la Toussaint** (1 November – All Saints' Day)
- **Noël**: Christmas, 25 December.
- **le Nouvel An**: New Year.
- **la Saint-Sylvestre**: 31 December

Insight

On 24 December and 31 December the French tuck into **le réveillon** – a succulent and opulent meal that will last well into the night. Thus: **le réveillon du Jour de l'An** actually starts the night before 1 January.

15.5 Environmental issues

Core vocabulary

environment	**l'environnement**
environmentalist	**un(e) environnementaliste**
environmental issues	**les questions d'environnement**

environmental health	**la santé environnementale**
public health	**la santé publique**
housing	**le logement/l'habitat**
energy efficiency	**l'efficience énergétique**
architect	**un(e) architecte**
builder	**l'entrepreneur**
town planner, urbanist	**un(e) urbaniste**
planning permission	**le permis de construire**
building regulations	**la règlementation en matière de construction**
services	**les services publics**
water	**l'eau**
electricity	**l'électricité**
sewage	**le tout-à-l'égout**
water	**l'eau**
water level	**le niveau d'eau**
drinking water	**l'eau potable**
water supply	**l'alimentation en eau**
well	**le puits**
irrigation	**l'irrigation**
ecology	**l'écologie**
ecosystem	**un écosystème**
erosion	**l'érosion**

Foodstuffs *les aliments*

genetically modified	**les aliments génétiquement modifiés**
organic	**la culture biologique** *(short:* **bio)**

Insight

You may say: **« Moi, je n'achète que des produits bio »** or **« Je mange bio depuis plusieurs années déjà ».**

artificial fertilizer	**les fertilisants artificiels**
nitrate	**le nitrate**
pesticide	**le pesticide**
poison	**le poison**
weedkiller	**le désherbant**

Pollution *la pollution*

environmental pollution	**la pollution de l'environnement**
acid rain	**la pluie acide**
air pollution	**la pollution de l'air**
car exhaust	**les gaz d'échappement**
detergent	**le détergent**
biodegradable detergent	**le détergent bio-dégradable**
disinfectant gas emissions	**les émissions de gaz désinfectants**
global warming	**le réchauffement de la planète**
greenhouse effect	**l'effet de serre**
nuclear testing	**les essais nucléaires**
ozone layer	**la couche d'ozone**
radiation	**la radiation**
radioactive waste	**les déchets radioactifs**
radioactive waste recycling	**le retraitement des déchets radioactifs**
water pollution	**la pollution de l'eau**
ground water pollution	**la pollution de la nappe phréatique**

Power *l'électricité*

energy	**l'énergie**
nuclear power	**l'énergie nucléaire**
hydro-electric power	**l'énergie hydro-électrique**
tidal energy	**l'énergie marémotrice**
wave energy	**l'énergie houlomotrice**
solar power	**l'énergie solaire**
wind power	**l'énergie éolienne**
power station	**une centrale nucléaire**

Recycling *le recyclage*

glass, aluminium cans, paper, plastic	**le verre, l'aluminium, le papier, le plastique**
compost	**le compost**

Resources *les ressources*

natural resources	**les ressources naturelles**
sustainable resources	**les ressources durables**

renewable	**les ressources renouvelables**
the protection of the environment	**la protection de l'environnement**
of animals	**de la faune**
of plants	**de la flore**
national park/reserve	**un parc national/une reserve nationale**
protected area	**une zone protégée**
conservation area	**une zone de protection du patrimoine**
listed building	**un bâtiment classé**
ancient/historic monument	**un monument historique**
archeological site	**un site de fouilles archéologiques**

Useful verbs

to protect	**protéger**
to conserve	**préserver**
to destroy	**détruire**
to dispose of	**se débarrasser de**
to throw away	**jeter**

15.6 Religion

Core vocabulary

religion	**la religion**
faith	**la foi**
belief	**la croyance**
Buddhism	**le bouddhisme**
Christianity	**le christianisme**
Hinduism	**l'hindouisme**
Islam	**l'islam**
Judaism	**le judaïsme**
I believe/I don't believe in God.	**Je crois/je ne crois pas en Dieu.**
atheist	**athée**
Buddhist	**bouddhiste**

Catholic	**catholique**
Orthodox Catholic	**catholique orthodoxe**
Protestant	**protestant**
Christian	**chrétien(ne)**
Hindu	**hindou(e)**
Jew	**juif/juive**
Moslem	**musulman(e)**
Quaker	**quaker**
Jehovah's witness	**témoin(e) de Jéhovah**
God	**Dieu**
Buddha	**Bouddha**
Christ	**le Christ**
Mohammed	**Mohammed**
prophet	**le prophète**
Jehovah	**Jéhovah**
place of worship	**le lieu de culte** *or* **le lieu de prière**
prayer room	**la salle de prière**
cathedral	**une cathédrale**
chapel	**une chapelle**
church	**une église**
mosque	**une mosquée**
temple	**un temple**
synagogue	**la synagogue**

Religious leaders ***les leaders religieux***

bishop	**l'évêque**
imam	**l'imam**
monk	**le moine** *or* **le religieux** *or* **le frère**
nun	**la religieuse** *or* **la sœur**
priest	**le prêtre**
rabbi	**le rabin**
minister	**le ministre** *or* **le pasteur**
prayer	**la prière**
hymn	**le cantique**

Religious services ***les services religieux***

mass	**la messe**
baptism	**le baptême**

christening	**le baptême chrétien**
communion	**la communion**
wedding	**le mariage**
funeral	**l'enterrement** *or* **l'inhumation**

Useful verbs

to attend church	**aller à l'église**
to attend the service	**aller au service**
to believe	**croire**
to pray	**prier**
to preach	**prêcher**
to kneel	**s'agenouiller**
to sing	**chanter**
to chant	**entonner**
to worship	**louer**

15.7 Social issues

Core vocabulary

community	**la communauté**
charity	**une association** *or* **une organisation bénévole**
volunteer	**un(e) bénévole**
social services	**les services sociaux**
social work	**le travail social**
quality of life	**la qualité de la vie**
financial problems	**des problèmes financiers**
poverty	**la pauvreté**
misery	**la misère**
debt	**la dette**
psychological problems	**les problèmes d'ordre psychologique**
depression	**la dépression**
emotional deprivation	**le sevrage affectif**
insecurity	**l'insécurité**

loneliness	**la solitude**
mental health	**la santé mentale**
neglect	**la négligence**
racial tension	**les tensions raciales**
stress	**le stress**
unemployment	**le chômage**
environmental problems	**les problèmes d'environnement**
sub-standard housing	**un habitat insalubre**
family problems	**des problèmes familiaux**
inner city	**des quartiers défavorisés**
lack of food/clean water/sewage	**un manque de nourriture/d'eau potable/d'égouts**
overcrowding	**la surpopulation**
unhealthy/sub-standard living conditions	**des conditions de vie insalubres**
help/assistance	**aide/assistance**
social worker	**le travaillleur social** *or* **le travailleur de rue**

Useful verbs

to do charity work, to volunteer	**être bénévole/travailler comme bénévole/faire du bénévolat**
to counsel	**conseiller**
to assist	**aider**

TEST YOURSELF

À vous !

A mini stock-taking exercise on the unit you have just worked on

1 Un **député** in French means…

- **a** a deputy mayor
- **b** a Member of Parliament
- **c** a sheriff deputy

2 'To make a speech' in French is…

- **a** discourir
- **b** faire un speech
- **c** faire un discours

3 **Le fisc** in French means…

- **a** financial services
- **b** Customs and Excise
- **c** Inland Revenue

4 Give three possible ways in which you can say that your account is overdrawn.

- **a**
- **b**
- **c**

5 On 1 May in France, you might buy and give to a friend or a loved one…

- **a** une rose blanche
- **b** une couronne de nénuphars
- **c** un brin de muguet
- **d** un brin de bruyère
- **e** un bouquet de violettes

6 'Paperwork' in French is...

- **a** le travail sur papier
- **b** la paperasserie
- **c** les papiers officiels

7 'Driving licence' in French is...

- **a** la licence pour conduire
- **b** la licence de conducteur
- **c** le permis de conduire
- **d** le permis de conducteur

8 **Réveillonner** in French means...

- **a** to wake up to loud music
- **b** to wake up just before going out
- **c** to organize a festive dinner on Christmas Eve and/or New Year's Eve

9 'To dispose of' in French is...
[*note: more than one answer possible*]

- **a** disposer de
- **b** se débarrasser de
- **c** jeter

10 'A conservation area' in French is...

- **a** l'aire de conservation
- **b** l'aire de préservation
- **c** la zone de conservation
- **d** la zone de protection
- **e** la zone de protection du patrimoine

Answers: 1 b; 2 c; 3 c; 4 Je suis à découvert/Mon compte est débiteur/Je suis dans le rouge; 5 c; 6 b; 7 c; 8 c; 9 a b c; 10 e

16

The media

16.1 The press

Core vocabulary

the press	**la presse**
newspaper	**le journal**
magazine	**le magazine**
review	**la revue**
journal	**la revue**

Insight

The English *review* and *journal* correspond to the French **revue**. In particular, specialist reviews/journals: e.g. *Comparative Law Review* is **Revue de droit comparatif**; *Quarterly Journal of Astronomy* is **Revue trimestrielle d'astronomie.**

daily	**un quotidien**
weekly	**un hebdomadaire**
monthly	**un mensuel**
bi-monthly	**un bi-mensuel**
quarterly	**une revue trimestrielle**
yearly	**une revue/publication annuelle**
publisher	**un éditeur** *or* **une maison d'édition**

editor	**un éditeur**
journalist	**un(e) journaliste**
journalism	**le journalisme**
reporter	**le/la reporter**
correspondent	**le/la correspondant(e)**
special correspondent	**un/une envoyé(e) spécial(e)**
war correspondent	**le/la correspondant(e) de guerre**
critic	**un critique**
press agency	**une agence de presse**
front page	**la première page/en première page**
back page	**la dernière page/en dernière page**
headline	**le gros titre**
column	**un éditorial**
article	**un article**
brief report	**une dépêche**
press release	**un communiqué de presse**
advertisement	**une publicité**
notices	**le carnet**
obituaries	**les décès**
small ads	**les petites annonces**

News items *les nouvelles*

natural disaster	**une catastrophe naturelle**
flood	**une inondation**
earthquake	**un tremblement de terre**
tsunami	**un tsunami**
eruption of a volcano	**un volcan en éruption**
storm	**une tempête**
hurricane	**un ouragan**
tornado	**une tornade**
torrential rain	**des pluies diluviennes**

Insight

The adjective **diluviennes** (**diluvien/diluvienne**) is linked with the noun **déluge** and Noah's flood – **Le Déluge** – when **'il plut pendant quarante jours'**.

road accidents	**les accidents de la route**
car crash	**un accident de voiture**
collision	**une collision**
plane crash	**un accident d'avion**
terrorist attack	**un attentat**
demonstration	**une manifestation**
strike	**une grève**
strikes	**les grèves** *or* **des grèves** *or* **des mouvements de grève**
fire	**un incendie**

16.2 Books

Core vocabulary

title	**un titre**
author	**un auteur**
writer	**un écrivain**
illustrator	**un illustrateur**
cartoonist	**un dessinateur/une dessinatrice de bandes dessinées**

Insight

La bande dessinée is difficult to translate; the term *cartoon* does not do justice to the genre, which, in France, is a true art. **Une bande dessinée** usually refers to a book, on a variety of subjects, from science-fiction to love. The text and the drawings are of equal importance. If you want to know more, look up the **Festival de la bande dessinée** which takes place every year in Angoulême.

paperback	**un livre de poche**
biography	**une biographie**
autobiography	**une autobiographie**

novel	**un roman**
short story	**une nouvelle**
dictionary	**un dictionnaire**
encyclopedia	**une encyclopédie**
atlas	**un atlas**
guide book	**un guide**
fiction	**la fiction**
non-fiction	**une histoire vécue**

Useful verbs

to write	**écrire**
to edit	**éditer**
to print	**imprimer**
to publish	**publier**
to sign	**signer**

Useful phrases

What sort of books do you like to read?	**Quel genre de livres aimez-vous lire ?**
Who is your favourite author?	**Qui est votre auteur préféré ?**
I like reading books about...	**J'aime lire des livres qui parlent de .../qui traitent de.../sur ...**
I like reading books where...	**J'aime lire des livres où ...**
I like reading books that ...	**J'aime lire des livres qui ... que ...**

Literary genres *les genres littéraires*

mysteries	**les romans policiers**
novels	**les romans**
short stories	**les nouvelles**
epics	**les épopées**
saga	**la saga**
science-fiction	**l'anticipation** *or* **la science-fiction**
essays	**les essais**
foreign literature	**la littérature étrangère**
poetry	**la poésie**

16.3 Cinema and television

Core vocabulary

The cinema *le cinéma*

auditorium	**un auditorium**
screen	**un écran**
seat	**une place**
foyer	**le hall**
ticket	**le ticket**
booking office	**la caisse**
big screen	**le grand écran**

Films *les films*

thriller	**un film de suspense**
romance	**une comédie romantique**
love story	**une histoire d'amour**
historical film	**une fresque historique**
science fiction	**un film de science-fiction**
horror film	**un film d'horreur**
war film	**un film de guerre**
comedy	**une comédie**
detective	**un policier**
drama	**un drame psychologique**
adverts	**la pub**
the cast	**les acteurs**
film star	**une vedette** *or* **une star**
actor/actress	**un acteur/une actrice**
leading role	**le premier rôle**
supporting role	**le second rôle**
singer	**un chanteur/une chanteuse**
dancer	**un danseur/une danseuse**
director	**le metteur en scène/la metteuse en scène**
producer	**le producteur/la productrice**
cameraman	**le/la caméraman**
sound recordist	**le technicien/la technicienne du son**
crew	**l'équipe plateau**

video	**la cassette vidéo**
DVD	**le DVD**
video/DVD rental	**la location de cassettes vidéo/de DVD** *or* **le magasin de location de cassettes vidéo/de DVD**
dubbed/subtitled	**doublé/version originale sous-titrée**
televison	**la télévision**
TV guide	**le programme télé**
cable	**le câble**
satellite	**le satellite**
dish	**une parabole** *or* **une antenne parabolique**
video recorder	**un magnétoscope**
DVD player	**un lecteur DVD**
remote control	**la commande (à distance)**
channel	**la chaîne**
credits	**les crédits** *or* **le générique**

Insight

Typically, **les crédits** will be used by professionals, whereas **le générique** will be used by film-goers and the general public.

commercials	**la pub**
cartoons	**les dessins animés**
children's programmes	**les émissions pour les enfants**
chat show	**une émission de divertissement, avec des invités**
documentary	**le documentaire**
feature film	**un long métrage**
animation film	**un film d'animation**
game show	**un jeu**
news programme	**une émission d'information**
debate	**une émission-débat**
quiz	**un jeu**
soap	**un feuilleton**
weather forecast	**le bulletin météo**
news reporter	**le reporter**
news reader	**le reporter**
presenter	**le présentateur/la présentatrice**

interviewer	**l'interviewer**
commentator	**le commentateur/la commentatrice**
game show host	**l'hôte/l'hôtesse**
viewer	**le téléspectateur**
radio	**la radio**
station	**la station de radio**
programme	**le programme** *or* **l'émission**
broadcast	**la retransmission**
live broadcast	**une retransmission en direct**
frequency	**la fréquence**
on FM	**sur la FM (en modulation de fréquences)**
on LW	**sur les grandes ondes**
on MW	**sur les ondes moyennes**
disc jockey	**le DJ** *(pronounced: 'dee-jay')*

Useful verbs

to change channels	**changer de chaîne**
to channel-hop	**zapper**
to turn on/off the telly	**allumer/éteindre la télé**
to turn the sound up/down	**monter/baisser le son**
to broadcast	**retransmettre**
to record	**enregistrer**

Useful phrases

What is your favourite programme?	**Quelle est votre émission préférée ?**
Do you like documentaries?	**Vous aimez les documentaires ?**
Who is your favourite presenter?	**Qui est votre présentateur/présentatrice préféré(e) ?**
He/She is partial/impartial.	**Il/Elle est partial/impartial.**
Could you please turn up the volume?	**Est-ce que vous pourriez monter le son ?**
Could you please turn down the volume?	**Est-ce que vous pourriez baisser le son ?**

TEST YOURSELF

À vous !

A mini stock-taking exercise on the unit you have just worked on

1 In a book context, 'a mystery' in French is...

a un mystère
b un roman d'aventure
c un roman policier

2 'TV commercials' in French are...

a les commerciaux télévisés
b la pub
c la promotion commerciale à la télé(vision)

3 'A quarterly journal' is...

a un journal de quartier
b une revue de quartier
c une revue de quart
d une revue de trimestre
e une revue trimestrielle

4 'Demonstrations' in an industrial dispute context in French are...

a les démonstrations
b les manifestations
c les revendications

5 **La commande à distance** is...

a remote order
b remote command
c remote control

6 How would you say in French 'I like reading books about current affairs?' [*note: more than one answer possible*]

a J'aime lire des livres sur des sujets d'actualité
b J'aime lire des livres qui parlent de sujets d'actualité

- **c** J'aime lire des livres qui traitent de sujets d'actualité
- **d** J'aime lire des livres qui parlent d'affaires courantes
- **e** J'aime lire des livres sur les affaires en cours

7 'To record' in French is...
- **a** rencorder
- **b** raccorder
- **c** enregistrer
- **d** enrouler

8 'A radio programme' in French is...
[*note: more than one answer possible*]
- **a** une émission de radio
- **b** un programme radiophonique
- **c** une émission radiophonique
- **d** un programme radio

9 **Un long métrage** is...
- **a** long tape-measure
- **b** long recording
- **c** a feature film

10 How would you say in French 'Could you turn the volume down?'
- **a** Pourriez-vous retourner le volume?
- **b** Est-ce que vous pourriez tourner le bouton vers le bas ?
- **c** Pourriez-vous baisser le volume ?
- **d** Pourriez-vous baisser le son ?

Answers: 1 c; 2 b; 3 e; 4 b; 5 c; 6 a b c; 7 c; 8 a b c d; 9 c; 10 d

Taking it further

Writing in French

When you type in French using a PC with a numberpad, you can obtain accented letters in the following simple manner:

Ensure that the Num Lock green light is on. Press and hold the ALT key, and at the same time, key in the three-digit number that will give you the letter you require.

ALT + 130 = é
ALT + 133 = à
ALT + 136 = ê
ALT + 135 = ç
ALT + 128 = Ç
ALT + 138 = è

ALT + 131 = â
ALT + 140 = î
ALT + 147 = ô
ALT + 150 = û
ALT + 151 = ù

Or you may change the keyboard – if you have that option – and type using the French keyboard.

Reading in French

The press on the Web *la press en ligne*

Most newspapers and magazines are online and their addresses are easy to guess – usually 'nameofthepaper.fr' or 'name-ofthepaper.com', or 'nameofthepaper.be' for Belgian publications, or 'nameofthepaper.ch' for Swiss publications, and 'nameofthepaper.ca' for Canadian French publications. Or Google it! In French: **faire une recherche sur Google.**

Here is a selection of French language papers available online:

Le Monde is a very serious, independent French daily newspaper. It is a production of the Le Monde group, a non-profit making association. To get into the thick of French culture and thinking, you may want to look at the group's monthly publications, including *Le Monde Diplomatique*, *Les Dossiers & Documents du Monde*, *Le Monde de l'Education*, *Le Monde des Religions*...

www.lemonde.fr

A great weekly, ***Courrier international*** collects and selects a number of articles published throughout the world in various newspapers and magazines and translates them into French. A precious tool if one wishes to read and hear about different perspectives on the same matter!

www.courrierinternational.com

A good quality daily newspaper, ***Ouest-France***, published in the whole of the West of France, i.e. Normandy, Brittany, Vendée, Charentes, Pays nantais, has recently gone online. It covers international, national, regional and local news (in that order, according to the French convention of journalism) and a number of great webcams for a taste of France live!

www.ouest-france.fr

La Croix – The quality of a broadsheet in a tabloid format – exhaustive, rigorous, very balanced in views and subjects, this catholic publication is a non-complacent, visionary and modern product where religion and faiths – in the plural – is just one among the numerous regular features – including science and ethics, technology, international diplomacy, European news, etc.

www.la-croix.com

Listening to French

If you have satellite television, look for **TV5**, which is an international channel with a compilation of programmes, news, talk-shows and films from around the *Francophonie*, i.e. the French-speaking world.

On LW, to the left of Radio Four you will find **France Inter** (162 kHz), a major public radio station; to the right, **Europe 1** (183 kHz), not a public station, but the same kind of mix of news, politics, songs, hosts, phone-in programmes, etc.

I hope you've enjoyed using this book. I am always keen to receive feedback from people who have used the book, so why not write to me and let me know your reactions? I'll be pleased to receive your positive comments, but I should also like to know if things could be improved.

You can contact me through the publishers at:
Teach Yourself, Hodder Headline Ltd,
338 Euston Road, London NW1 3BH, UK

I hope that you will want to build on your French and practise using your new vocabulary on your next trip to France.

Au plaisir de vous lire, et en vous souhaitant un apprentissage fructueux,

Noël Saint-Thomas